Jules Verne:
Journeys in Writing

Jules Verne:
Journeys in Writing

Timothy Unwin

LIVERPOOL UNIVERSITY PRESS

First published 2005 by
Liverpool University Press
4 Cambridge Street
Liverpool L69 7ZU

British Library Cataloguing-in-Publication data
A British Library CIP record is available

ISBN 0-85323-468-X cased
0-85323-458-2 limp

Typeset by Northern Phototypesetting Ltd, Bolton
Printed and bound in the European Union by Bell and Bain Ltd, Glasgow

Contents

Acknowledgments

My first and most important debt of gratitude here is to the Leverhulme Trust, which made the writing of this book possible through the award of a Research Fellowship from September 2002 to June 2004. During the period of the Leverhulme award, I was able to conduct initial library work in Paris, and thereafter to continue and complete work on the project that resulted in the present volume.

I am also grateful to the University of Bristol, which supported this project both through replacement teaching and through the purchase of books for the library. Specific help in increasing the library's Jules Verne holdings was provided by Michael Howarth, formerly Arts Librarian at Bristol, to whom special thanks are due. I should also like to express my thanks to colleagues in the French Department for their co-operation and help, which has been essential throughout this project.

Some parts of this book have either appeared in a first version or were delivered as conference papers prior to their inclusion here. Sections on Jules Verne and the nineteenth century (Chapter 1) were sketched out in a paper given at the Nineteenth-Century French Studies annual colloquium in Tucson, Arizona in October 2003, then reworked as an article in *Science Fiction Studies*. The section on the history of the universe (in Chapter 2) was delivered as a conference paper at Royal Holloway, University of London, in September 2003, and is being published in a somewhat different version in *Ebauches: Projects and Pre-Texts in Nineteenth-Century French Culture*, edited by Sonya Stephens. An earlier draft of the section on the future of the text (in Chapter 2) was published in *AUMLA (Journal of the Australasian Universities Language and Literature Association)*. Sections on the conquest of nature (in Chapter 2) and on Verne's rewriting of Edgar Allan Poe (in Chapter 6) were initially delivered as part of a plenary lecture given at the Society for French Studies annual conference in Sheffield in July 2003, and appeared in a revised form in *Essays in French Literature*. A section from chapter six on the question of writing and rewriting, and part of the conclusion of this study, were included in an article in the *Australian Journal of French Studies*. I am grateful to colleagues for their comments and suggestions, and to the editors who have given me their permission to adapt published material for the purposes of the present study.

A number of individuals have also played a significant role and have provided important help as this study has progressed. Many scholarly questions were answered by members of the online Jules Verne Forum, and in particular I owe a debt of gratitude to Volker Dehs, Arthur Evans and Jean-Michel Margot.

Last but by no means least, I wish to record particular thanks to Kay Chadwick, whose help and support at all stages of this project have been crucial.

Timothy Unwin
24 March 2005

References, Translations, Abbreviations

References in this study to the *Voyages extraordinaires* [*Extraordinary Journeys*] are wherever possible to the fifty-volume *Les Œuvres de Jules Verne* (Lausanne: Rencontre, 1966–71). Primary Jules Verne texts not in the Rencontre edition are referred to in the editions listed in the main bibliography. In all cases references are given parenthetically in the text using title abbreviations from the list below, followed by the volume number in cases where a text covers more than a single volume, and the page. References to critical studies and secondary material are given in endnotes, with full bibliographical details of each item at the first mention.

All quoted material in French is followed by my own translation into English. Titles of Verne's works and of scholarly publications are given only in French in this study. However, the following reference list provides translations of all Jules Verne titles that are not identical in French and English, and also gives the year(s) of publication in volume form of the original French texts. Asterisks indicate posthumous texts or texts that have been re-edited and reissued in their original form. In the latter case, the dates both of the first publication and of the reissue are given here, together with the new title where applicable. Short stories which figure in volumes by another title are not listed separately.

Autour de la lune [Around the Moon]	AL	1870
Aventures de trois Russes et de trois Anglais [Adventures of Three Russians and Three Englishmen]	A3	1872
Bourses de voyage [Travel Scholarships]	BV	1903
César Cascabel	CC	1890
Cinq semaines en ballon [Five Weeks in a Balloon]	5S	1863
Claudius Bombarnac	CB	1892
Clovis Dardentor	CD	1896
De la terre à la lune [From the Earth to the Moon]	TL	1865
Deux ans de vacances [Two Years' Holiday]	2A	1888
Face au drapeau [Before the Flag]	FD	1896

Famille-sans-nom [Family Without a Name]	FSN	1889
Hector Servadac	HS	1877
Hier et demain (collected stories) [Yesterday and Tomorrow]	HD	1910
Kéraban-le-têtu [Keraban the Headstrong]	K	1883
L'Agence Thompson and Co. [The Thompson Travel Agency]	AT	1907
L'Archipel en feu [The Archipelago on Fire]	AF	1884
L'Ecole des Robinsons [The Robinson School]	ER	1882
L'Etoile du sud [The Southern Star]	ES	1884
L'Etonnante Aventure de la mission Barsac [The Astonishing Adventure of the Barsac Mission]	MB	1919
L'Ile à hélice [Propellor Island]	IH	1895
L'Ile mystérieuse [The Mysterious Island]	IM	1874–75
L'Invasion de la mer [The Invasion of the Sea]	IMer	1905
*La Chasse au météore [The Hunt for the Meteor]	CM	1908/1998
La Jangada [The Jangada]	J	1881
La Maison à vapeur [The Steam House]	MV	1880
Le Chancellor [The Chancellor]	C	1875
Le Château des Carpathes [The Carpathian Castle]	ChC	1892
Le Chemin de France [The Road to France]	CF	1887
Le Docteur Ox (collected stories) [Doctor Ox]	DO	1874
Le Pays des fourrures [The Fur Country]	PF	1873
Le Phare du bout du monde [The Lighthouse at the End of the World]	PBM	1905
*Le Pilote du Danube/Le Beau Danube jaune [The Danube Pilot/The Beautiful Yellow Danube]	PD/BDJ	1908/1997
Le Rayon vert [The Green Ray]	RV	1882
*Le Secret de Wilhem Storitz [The Secret of Wilhelm Storitz]	WS	1910/1985
Le Sphinx des glaces [The Sphinx of the Ice Floes]	SG	1897
Le Superbe Orénoque [The Superb Orenoco]	SO	1898
Le Testament d'un excentrique [The Testament of an Eccentric]	TE	1899
Le Tour du monde en quatre-vingts jours [Around the World in Eighty Days]	TM	1872
Le Village aérien [The Aerial Village]	VA	1901
*Le Volcan d'or [The Golden Volcano]	VO	1906/1985
Les Cinq Cents Millions de la Bégum [The Begum's Fortune]	500	1879

Les Enfants du capitaine Grant [The Children of Captain Grant]	CG	1866–68
Les Forceurs de blocus [The Blockade Runners]	FB	1865
Les Frères Kip [The Kip Brothers]	FK	1902
Les Histoires de Jean-Marie Cabidoulin [The Tales of Jean-Marie Cabidoulin]	JMC	1901
Les Indes noires [The Black Indies]	IN	1877
Les Naufragés du Jonathan/En Magellanie [The Survivors of the Jonathan/In Magellania]	NJ/M	1909/1987
Les Tribulations d'un Chinois en Chine [The Tribulations of a Chinaman in China]	TCC	1879
Maître du monde [Master of the World]	MM	1904
Mathias Sandorf	MS	1885
Michel Strogoff	MSt	1876
Mirifiques aventures de Maître Antifer [The Fabulous Adventures of Master Antifer]	MA	1894
Mistress Branican [Mrs Branican]	B	1891
Nord contre sud [North against South]	NS	1887
Paris au XXe siècle [Paris in the Twentieth Century]	P20	1994
P'tit bonhomme [Little Fellow]	PB	1893
Robur-le-conquérant [Robur the Conqueror]	RC	1886
San Carlos, et autres récits inédits [San Carlos and Other Tales]	SC	1993
Sans dessus dessous [Topsy-Turvy]	SDD	1889
Seconde patrie [Second Homeland]	SP	1900
Un billet de loterie [A Lottery Ticket]	BL	1886
Un capitaine de quinze ans [A Captain at Fifteen]	C15	1878
Un drame en Livonie [A Drama in Livonia]	DL	1904
Un prêtre en 1839 [A Priest in 1839]	P39	1992
Une ville flottante [A Floating City]	VF	1871
Vingt mille lieues sous les mers [Twenty Thousand Leagues under the Seas]	VML	1869–70
Voyage à reculons en Angleterre et en Ecosse [Journey Backwards to England and Scotland]	VR	1989
Voyage au centre de la terre [Journey to the Centre of the Earth]	VCT	1864
Voyages et aventures du capitaine Hatteras [The Voyages and Adventures of Captain Hatteras]	CH	1866

A writer of pot-boilers, adventure stories, cheap melodramas, children's literature. An author of educational textbooks dressed up as fiction. A copycat who plagiarised from the popular scientific and geographical publications of his day. A literary thief who took the ideas and sometimes the entire plots of his novels from the works of his contemporaries. A marginal figure in French literary history, a compulsive scribbler who wrote badly, carelessly, and far too swiftly for his own good. A novelist without any sense of style, whose rambling prose was driven by the desire for commercial success and the need to keep the pages rolling off the press. A storyteller whose inspiration was so defective that he ended up re-using his own texts.

The man who foretold the future of the world, who predicted an era of space exploration, electronic communications and global travel, and who understood the real impact that science would have on humankind and society. The novelist-engineer who assembled submarines, aircraft and other vehicles by looking ahead and understanding how technology would develop. The prophet who, through the combined power of imagination and intuition, 'invented' gadgets, devices and machines, and who accurately predicted the uses to which they would be put. The writer who stepped outside of his own century and visualised the world as it would be in our own time. The great Jules Verne, honorary world citizen and dreamer of scientific tomorrows, the writer translated into dozens of languages and adapted into every existing medium, still astonishing us with his 'uncanny' insights into the future.

There are endless clichés and generalisations about Jules Verne, many of them offering a simplified version of the truth, others misguided or just plain false. They come as much from his admirers as from his detractors. What nearly all of them have in common is that they overlook the self-conscious literary skills and compositional practices which went into the writing of the eighty or so titles in the *Voyages extraordinaires*, produced over a four-decade period between 1863 and 1905.[1] Part of the reason for the frequency of these clichés is undoubtedly the fact that, as one of the most translated authors of all time, Verne has been subjected to all manner of distortions and inaccuracies (only in recent years have accurate scholarly translations and editions of his works started to become more widely available in English).[2] As one of the figures of world literature most often adapted to other media, Jules Verne the writer is easily left behind as his legacy — fittingly, in a sense — is extended to new horizons, new visions, new forms. But, as any committed reader of Verne knows, there is often an uncritical blurring of the boundaries between the actual texts of the *Voyages extraordinaires* and Jules Verne the iconic figure who, in the modern cultural consciousness, has come to symbolise travel, technology, invention and 'the future'. Many so-called admirers of Verne are surprised even to discover that he was a Frenchman, so easily does his name lend itself to an Anglicised pronunciation that confers transnational status upon him. For others, it simply does not matter that he was a French novelist in the age of Realism, since they see his real 'home' as being in the era of cinema, television, information systems and space technology.

It is true that Verne has been plundered, pilloried and appropriated in such rich and inventive ways that his massive cultural legacy can quite simply overshadow the real literary output. A significant part of the purpose of the present study, then, is to step back from the myths, indeed to challenge the clichés about Verne, and to re-examine his writing from a more strictly literary perspective. What actually constitutes a 'literary' perspective is, of course, one of those questions that are repeatedly raised by the reading of Verne. However, I shall be focusing closely on questions of narrative technique, intertextuality, intergeneric borrowing, self-consciousness, encylopaedism, authorship and discourse construction, by way of showing the complexity and the sophistication of Verne's approach to the writing of novels. I shall also argue that we need to return to the literary and cultural context in which the *Voyages extraordinaires* were composed, and I shall maintain that Verne is neither the technological prophet

---

1 The number of titles in the *Voyages extraordinaires* is variously given by critics and biographers, and ranges from 62 upwards. But this depends on how the collection is counted: whether texts prior to 1863 are included; whether short stories and novellas are listed as separate titles; whether posthumous texts are included; whether separate or reissued versions of the same texts are counted twice; or whether the count is done by volumes rather than titles. The present figure of 80 is therefore given only as a rough count, and is based on the list to be found at the beginning of this study.

2 On translations and mistranslations of Jules Verne, see Arthur B. Evans, 'Jules Verne's English Translations', *Science Fiction Studies*, 32 (2005), pp. 80–104.

he is so often made out to be, nor the second-rate or paraliterary writer that he is sometimes seen as – but rather, that by combining scientific, literary and other discourses, he achieves his own uniqueness and originality as a novelist.

As a writer of realist fiction in the second half of the nineteenth century, Verne undertakes the vast enterprise of the *Voyages extraordinaires* at a time when the novel has come to assume huge importance in France. Like so many of his contemporaries, he writes in the ample shadow of Balzac. But it is a time when experiment, reflection about fiction, consideration of its uses and abuses, theorisations of its relationship to the so-called 'real' world, and problematisation of the ways in which narrative relays knowledge, are particularly intense. Verne, whose writing raises these key issues every bit as much as, say, Flaubert's, thus finds his natural starting-point in the French realist tradition, and unless he is seen and read in – and crucially, *against* – that context he will surely be misunderstood. It is beyond all doubt that he took his mission as a writer as seriously as did the other great canonical novelists of nineteenth-century France. The questions asked in this study focus, then, on his contribution to the genre. In what ways is his writing subversive, innovative or experimental? What are its ideological or philosophical undercurrents? How does he adapt the conventions of the realist novel to his own particular enterprise? To what extent does he, literally and literarily, push back the frontiers of fiction? What is the significance of the metaphorical relation between his own fictional and experimental journey – the 'journey of writing' that he undertakes time and again – and the actual physical 'journeys' that are so often the subject of his novels?

Questions about Verne's literary qualities and credentials have always been asked by French critics, and more especially since Michel Butor spearheaded the revival of Jules Verne studies in France with a groundbreaking article in 1949.[3] Yet what is noticeable to any Anglo-Saxon critic

---

3 Michel Butor, 'Le Point suprême et l'âge d'or à travers quelques œuvres de Jules Verne', in *Répertoire I* (Paris: Minuit, 1960 [1949]), pp. 130–62. Butor's work was followed by a host of studies (by no means always complimentary, but always showing the deep interest and relevance of what Verne did) by high-profile critics, philosophers and academics, including Roland Barthes ('Nautilus et bateau ivre', in *Mythologies* (Paris: Seuil, 1957), pp. 90–92, and 'Par où commencer?', in *Poétique*, I (1970), pp. 3–9), Michel Foucault ('L'Arrière-fable', in *L'Arc*, 29 (1966), pp. 5–12), Pierre Macherey ('Jules Verne, ou le récit en défaut', in *Pour une théorie de la production littéraire* (Paris: Maspero, 1966), pp. 183–275), and Michel Serres (*Jouvences sur Jules Verne* (Paris: Editions de Minuit, 1974)). The renewal and revival of Jules Verne studies in France has involved a rich variety of approaches ranging from the

who approaches Verne in the original is the relatively small quantity of scholarship in English devoted to close textual analysis and to critical readings of him as a writer and a stylist. Important and imaginative work has, it is true, appeared and its impact should not be underestimated. The first biography of Verne in English, still one of the best and most perceptive introductions to the writer despite the emergence in recent decades of much new information, was written by Kenneth Allott as long ago as 1941. The 1990s saw the publication of a major new English-language biography by Herbert Lottman, although this one was much less favourably reviewed.[4] And the end of the 1980s, a rich period for Vernian scholarship in English, saw the appearance of several serious and sustained book-length analyses, notably by Arthur Evans, William Butcher, and Andrew Martin.[5] However, readers of the latest Jules Verne volume in the Minard 'Lettres Modernes' series,[6] which provides a bibliographical update since 1991, will be struck by the fact that during a period of intense activity, involving editions or re-editions of manuscript material and the correspondence, only three books apart from the Lottman biogra-

---

psychocritical (e.g. Marcel Moré, *Le Très Curieux Jules Verne: Le Problème du père dans les Voyages extraordinaires* (Paris: Gallimard, 1960)) to the mythical (Simone Vierne in publications from 1971 onwards, e.g. *Jules Verne: Mythe et modernité* (Paris: Presses Universitaires de France, 1989)), to the study of literary and compositional techniques (notably Daniel Compère, *Jules Verne écrivain* (Geneva: Droz, 1991)).

4 Kenneth Allott, *Jules Verne* (London: The Cresset Press, and New York: Macmillan, 1941); Herbert R. Lottman, *Jules Verne: An Exploratory Biography* (New York: St Martin's Press, 1996). Lottman's biography was dismissively reviewed by Julian Barnes in an article entitled 'Back to the Future', *New York Times*, 26 January 1997, p. 4.

5 Arthur B. Evans, in *Jules Verne Rediscovered: Didacticism and the Scientific Novel* (Westport, Connecticut: Greenwood Press, 1988), addresses the crucial question of the impact of science and the pedagogical remit on the style of Verne's novels. William Butcher, in *Verne's Journey to the Centre of the Self: Space and Time in the 'Voyages extraordinaires'* (New York: St Martin's Press, 1990) looks at space and time, and their conjunction, in the *Voyages extraordinaires*, and provides insights into the construction of the Vernian text. Andrew Martin, in two studies (*The Knowledge of Ignorance: From Genesis to Jules Verne* (Cambridge: Cambridge University Press, 1985) and *The Mask of the Prophet: The Extraordinary Fictions of Jules Verne* (Oxford: Clarendon Press, 1990)) uses the critical work undertaken in France from the 1960s onwards to focus on the philosophical and epistemological problems raised by Jules Verne's writing.

6 Christian Chelebourg (ed.), *Jules Verne 8: Humour, ironie, fantaisie* (Paris: Minard, 2003). See the main bibliography (section on 'Conferences' etc.) for the list of items to date in this series.

phy have appeared in English.[7] Of these, two can properly be termed critical analyses of the work (one being a short study of a single text, the other a collective volume of essays on Verne). The third, Taves's and Michaluk's *Jules Verne Encyclopedia*, while containing one fascinating introductory chapter of criticism (Brian Taves's 'Jules Verne: An Interpretation'), is devoted very largely to Verne's reception in the broader cultural sphere. While this is an extremely important scholarly pursuit in its own right – especially in the area of film studies, covered comprehensively in the final chapter – there is a familiar danger about the enterprise, namely that the author's actual writings become marginalised. Elsewhere in the same volume Jules Verne is seen through the lens of his American readership, giving the unmistakable message that the writer cannot be dissociated from the activities of a nationally identifiable group of admirers. At moments there is a sense that Jules Verne the nineteenth-century French novelist is being transferred wholesale to an alien cultural context, and we might well be surprised by an almost total disregard of scholarship in French or of the texts in their original language.

In such circumstances, it is easy to see how Verne so often gets characterised as a non-literary, even non-French author, and how a second-hand, Anglicised or Americanised image of the writer can – for all the excellence of the scholarly works devoted to him – filter through to the popular consciousness.[8] The fact that so many Verne enthusiasts come from areas outside literature is, however, far from being inherently disadvantageous or damaging to Verne's claim to be a literary author. It tells us not that the literary is absent from his work, but rather that he expanded the very concept of what literature is or might be. How he achieved this

---

7   Timothy Unwin, *Verne: 'Le Tour du monde en quatre-vingts jours'* (University of Glasgow: Glasgow Introductory Guides to French Literature, 23, 1992); E. J. Smyth (ed.), *Jules Verne: Narratives of Modernity* (Liverpool: Liverpool University Press, 2000); Brian Taves and Stephen Michaluk (eds.), *The Jules Verne Encyclopedia* (Lanham: The Scarecrow Press, 1996). It should be added that during this period a number of important translations and critical editions in English have also appeared (notably three OUP World's Classics volumes, one volume under the Wordsworth Classics imprint, and the ongoing Wesleyan University Press series: see the main bibliography for further details).

8   Encouragingly, and somewhat against the grain of the popular view of Verne in the USA and elsewhere in the Anglo-Saxon world, a recent press item stressed his credentials as a nineteenth-century French writer highly attuned to the issues of his day. It also noted that a re-evaluation of Verne's work, based on the original texts and authentic translations of them, has for some time been gathering momentum. See Doug Stewart, 'Prescient and Accounted For', *The Smithsonian Magazine* (March 2005), pp. 103–107.

is one of the crucial questions that the present study addresses, and it starts with the axiomatic assumption that Verne's difference as an author requires close awareness of the tradition in which he wrote. For, if we are to gauge the originality of the *Voyages extraordinaires* as writing, we need to look at Verne's uses of the conventions of nineteenth-century realist literature, to measure the extent of his adaptations and innovations, and to examine the precise nature of his contribution to an evolving genre. Only by viewing his huge novelistic enterprise in its national, cultural, historical and literary context will we be in a position to judge the quality of his narrative techniques, to assess his exploitation of the theme of travel, or to appreciate his extraordinarily self-conscious manipulations of that theme.

That Verne was first and foremost a writer, working within a culturally defined tradition, is self-evident. Equally self-evident is that the basis of the 'Jules Verne phenomenon' will be found only by refocusing on the writer and wordsmith. The extraordinary journey of Jules Verne begins with the complex itinerary of his own writing. The present study concentrates, therefore, on his style and his uses of text, on his exceptional awareness not only of language, but also of broader literary and theatrical conventions, and on his unparalleled sensitivity to the problematic link between narrative and knowledge. It seeks to reassess Jules Verne as an author alongside his contemporaries, as a novelist who renews and revitalises the genre, and as a writer who situates himself clearly in a literary tradition. By returning to close analysis of the texts and context of the *Voyages extraordinaires*, the aim here will be to appreciate more fully the extent and the range of Verne's journeys in writing.

Chapter 1

Science, Literature and the Nineteenth Century

Of all the generalisations about Jules Verne, one of the most tenacious and potentially restrictive is the assertion that he is the 'father of science fiction'.[1] Now, while it is legitimate and proper to see Verne's scientific narratives as having initiated a new type of literature, the term 'science fiction' usually connotes a futuristic, anticipatory style of writing, speculative in scope and content, which extends reality into imaginary worlds that might or might not be possible. Moreover, science fiction is often considered to be an American genre, and Verne's association with it risks making it easier to forget that he was in reality a French author. The received wisdom about Jules Verne is that, since he foresaw the innovations of modern technology and was in some sense 'ahead of his time' (whatever such a phrase might be construed to mean), he naturally finds his niche alongside the great science fiction writers of the twentieth century. However, this is a case of Verne being damaged by those very readers who admire him, for this well-intentioned process of repackaging all too easily overlooks his very significant formal, stylistic and narrative innovations, his experiments with multiple ironic voices, his wit, his ludic self-consciousness, and his sophisticated uses and manipulations of nineteenth-century scientific and positivist discourses. In fact, as I shall stress in the course of this study, Jules Verne's novels are based extensively on documented fact rather than on speculation about the future, and his deeply complex use of sources is a major part of his interest as a writer. Moreover, it has often been observed by critics that Verne seems more preoccupied with the past than he is with the future, and that many of his stories are allegorical quests for lost origins.[2] This is nowhere more explicit than, for example, in *Voyage au centre de la terre*, which turns out not to be a departure to a brave new future at all, but rather a return to

---

1 This tendency is typically summed up in the title of Peter Costello's *Jules Verne: Inventor of Science Fiction* (London: Hodder and Stoughton, 1978).
2 See, for example, Vierne, *Jules Verne: Mythe et modernité*, 'L'aventure initiatique', pp. 111–67.

prehistory, as the travellers go downwards through the earth's crust and backwards in time to the evidence of ever earlier stages of the evolutionary process. No science fiction here, it seems – though there is science, and there is fiction.

Crucial to the 'science fiction' debate is the difference between Anglo-Saxon and Francophone critical responses to Verne. While in the English-speaking world Jules Verne is quite likely to be read and studied in the context of science fiction and/or film and cultural studies courses, in France he has for some decades been perceived as a 'mainstream' literary author (with all the potentially negative connotations that such an expression, in its turn, carries). Although the popular French press may still tend to talk of Verne as a 'visionary',[3] French critics and academics – who have sometimes been accused of sanctifying the notion of Literature – usually dismiss out of hand the claim that Verne is a science fiction author, which in their eyes would be to relegate him to a sub-genre. By and large, they hold axiomatically that prediction of the future and anticipation of technological or scientific development is simply not what Jules Verne is about. The remarks of Michel Serres are typically incisive on this subject:

> La fiction des *Voyages* est, dit-on, une science-fiction. Cela est faux, tout bonnement. Jamais une règle mécanique n'y est outrepassée, nulle loi naturelle, de physique, de résistance des matériaux, de biologie, n'y est extrapolée. Le contenu de science, en général, est même fort en retard sur son âge: Bouvard et Pécuchet sont des encyclopédistes d'une autre lignée, mieux avertis, moins enfantins dans le romanesque. Loin d'être d'anticipation, ces romans, sur ce point, ne sont pas à la page. Songez qu'on y célèbre la vapeur et l'électricité. Pour les performances techniques, elles sont des reprises ou des rétrospectives, quand elles paraissent des projets.[4]

> [The fiction of the *Journeys* is, it is said, a form of science fiction. That is, quite simply, false. No mechanical law is ever bypassed, and no natural law of physics, material resistance or biology is ever extended. The scientific content is by and large very much behind the times. Flaubert's Bouvard and

---

3 An example can be found in the special Jules Verne issue in November 2003 of the magazine *Géo*. In an article entitled 'Jules Verne: père de la science-fiction?' (*Géo* (Hors série Jules Verne, 2003), pp. 50–53), Yves-Marie Lucot starts out promisingly by suggesting that 'ses inventions ne relèvent pas de la pure fantaisie. Elles s'appuient toujours sur les connaissances de l'époque' (p. 50) ['His inventions are not pure fantasy. They are always based on contemporary knowledge']. However, the cliché reasserts itself only two pages later where Verne is described as 'un visionnaire dont les machines préfigurent celles d'aujourd'hui' (p. 52) ['a visionary whose machines anticipate those of our own time'].

4 Serres, *Jouvences sur Jules Verne*, p. 82.

Pécuchet are encyclopaedists with a quite different pedigree, because they are more alert and less childish in their fictional world. Far from being futuristic, these novels are not even up to date. After all, steam and electricity are still being celebrated in them, and as for technical inventions, they are rehearsals or throwbacks, though having the appearance of projects.]

While some might say that Serres exaggerates his point – contrary to his claim, electricity was still being hailed in the later decades of the nineteenth century as a novel form of energy[5] – he is right to insist that in the *Voyages extraordinaires* there is a fundamental respect for, and observance of, the laws of the natural world. This is generally what places Jules Verne apart from the writers of science fiction, and it is a point that the writer himself made in two interviews published in English towards the end of his life (1903 and 1904), when he was asked about the similarities between himself and H. G. Wells.[6] In the first interview, Verne affirms that there is absolutely no comparison between his and Wells's work. In his own novels, he says, there is no invention because he makes use of the known laws of physics. Wells, on the other hand, goes to Mars in an airship constructed of a metal which defies the laws of gravity. Verne adds, as if issuing a challenge to Wells: 'But show me this metal. Let him produce it.' In the second interview, Verne explains their differences at greater length:

> Our methods are entirely different. I have always made a point in my romances of basing my so-called inventions upon a groundwork of actual fact, and of using in their construction methods and materials which are not entirely without the pale of contemporary engineering skill and knowledge. […] The creations of Mr Wells, on the other hand, belong unreservedly to an age and degree of scientific knowledge far removed from the present, though I will not say entirely beyond the limits of the possible.

There may, it is true, be a degree of disingenuousness in these remarks, since comparison of the works of Verne and Wells had by then become commonplace, and it was important for Verne to stress the differences between them. Interestingly, however, the distinction made by Jules Verne in 1903–1904 was to be taken up later – and a little more edgily –

5   The rise of electricity was recorded in the *Exposition internationale de l'électricité* held in Paris in 1881, and further celebrated two years later in Albert Robida's influential *Le Vingtième Siècle* (Paris: Decaux, 1883).

6   R.H. Sherard, 'Jules Verne Revisited', *T.P.'s Weekly* (9 October 1903), and Gordon Jones, 'Jules Verne at Home', *Temple Bar*, 129 (June 1904), pp. 664–71. Both interviews are reproduced on the Jules Verne website at the following URLs: http://jv.gilead.org.il/sherard2.html; http://jv.gilead.org.il/evans/Gordon_Jones_interview_of_JV.html.

by Wells himself, who, in a short introduction to his own stories published in 1934, insisted that there was 'no literary resemblance whatever' between his work and Verne's. Whereas Verne 'dealt almost always with actual possibilities of invention and discovery', said Wells, his own intention was to 'hold the reader to the end by art and illusion, and not by proof and argument'.[7] Implicitly Wells is suggesting that, because he invents rather than bases his novels on scientific fact, his is the more difficult and the more exacting art. We shall let him score his point here, for the basic distinction he makes is nonetheless correct. Astonishingly, though, what he appears to overlook is that the process of holding the reader's attention by 'art and illusion' – creating that willing suspension of disbelief – is precisely one of the conventions that Verne's fiction most consistently subverts and flouts. That, indeed, is one of the many attractions of the *Voyages extraordinaires*. One sustained example of this process is to be found in *Claudius Bombarnac*, an intensely ludic novel representing the narrator's attempts to write a dramatic story that will hold his readers in thrall. By stepping outside of the diegetic process and showing it up for the artifice it is, Verne deliberately draws attention to the literary framework that Wells would like his own readers to forget. Verne rarely allows us to overlook for too long that his is an imaginary world, even where it carries a heavy dose of scientific and objective fact, and that is one of the reasons why his approach is both complex and original.

However, it is also – and paradoxically – because Verne's novels engage so closely with what is real, verifiable and attested that they blur the traditional boundaries between 'fiction' and 'reality'. The nineteenth-century world that Verne most often represents is itself constituted of all manner of documents and textual accounts. Text often becomes the object represented, rather than merely a framework. This is realism in a new guise. Where Balzac famously stated in the opening pages of *Le Père Goriot* that 'all is true', Verne creates the sense not so much that his own imaginary world is in some sense 'real' or 'believable', but that the world beyond the text is itself a vast narrative mediated through many different discourses, and that it remains to be explored, retold, rewritten, re-read, remapped. Text, fiction and narrative are everywhere. Writing is itself a process of colonisation, partly because there are so many texts out there, so much written 'territory' that must be appropriated and reigned in. So Verne's writing of journeys is also quite obviously an engagement in the journey of writing – not only in his own writing, but more generally the

7   H. G. Wells, 'Jules Verne and I', reproduced in Peter Haining (ed.), *The Jules Verne Companion* (London: Souvenir Press, 1978), pp. 62–63.

great mass of textual materials (narratives, witness accounts, scientific and geographical reports, technical exposés, guidebooks, travel diaries, *récits* of all kinds) that mediate the world for us and that constitute so much of our reality. In this respect, Verne is very much a man of his own century, and a major part of his interest lies there. To remove him from this nineteenth-century textual context would be to deny a crucial dimension of his work.

While it seems wrong to pigeonhole Verne categorically as the 'father of science fiction' (and the patriarchal undertone of that phrase suggests that there are other consequences of the way he has been represented), the argument about how to classify him is itself a pointer to the innovative and problematic nature of his writing. If French criticism has by and large attempted to 're-canonise' Verne in its literary hall of fame, while Anglo-Saxon criticism has sometimes tended to exploit him in science fiction, cultural studies and film studies programmes, this must surely tell us at the very least that he is a writer with a difference, that the concept of 'literature' mediated by the *Voyages extraordinaires* falls somewhat outside the traditional or the currently available generic boundaries. Mixing scientific discourses with narrative self-consciousness, serious pedagogical intentions with playful humour, social and political analysis with plots that come straight from the vaudeville, fairytale and children's scenarios with sombre tales of war and destruction, narratives of exploration with a sophisticated debunking of narrative conventions, Verne's style is in every sense a hybrid. Just how different his fictional world was from that of so many of his contemporaries (despite its many obvious anchor points within the same conventions) can and most certainly should be judged by the measure of its scientific and technological content. In 1863, when Verne claimed his first major success under Hetzel with the publication of *Cinq semaines en ballon*, the combination of technology and literature was still almost unthinkable. For nearly thirty years, since Gautier's celebrated affirmation in the preface to *Mademoiselle de Maupin* (1836) that 'rien de ce qui est beau n'est indispensable à la vie' ['nothing beautiful is indispensable to life'], there had been the sense of a fundamental division between the practical concerns of life and the gratuitous quality of art, whose function was above all to capture and express beauty. This division was relayed and echoed by countless writers and poets, for whom the world of technology, science, industry, commerce and progress was categorically opposed to the concerns of art, and vice versa. True, with Baudelaire a major reorientation had begun, as the trappings of modernity and the scenes of urban life were increasingly held to be compatible with the quest for an aesthetic ideal. However, while many writers develop a complex poetic concept of travel and exploration, Verne focuses above all on its practicalities, showing an interest in the technical details of locomotion, communication and what we nowadays call 'lifestyle'. This represents a seismic shift in relation to what was seen as a fitting subject for the novel.[8] All at once, science, travel, geography and technology loom massively in the frame. Significantly, too, there is a broadening of the settings. Where Balzac and Flaubert concentrated on Paris and the provinces, with Stendhal alone occasionally pushing the settings of his novels beyond French borders, Jules Verne now offers stories which are set in all the regions of the globe. This difference cannot be over-stressed, for Verne puts the colonial (soon postcolonial) world firmly within the purview of literature, at last giving the novel a truly international scope.

Much to his credit, Verne's editor Pierre-Jules Hetzel saw this novelty when he accepted the manuscript of *Cinq semaines en ballon* and, on 26 October 1862, issued the first of six publishing contracts that the novelist would sign with him. Hetzel himself would memorably define the originality of his protégé's approach in the famous preface to the 1866 reissue of *Voyages et aventures du capitaine Hatteras*, a flagship publication for his new 'Bibliothèque d'Education et de Récréation' series. Here is how he put it:

> Les Romans de M. Jules Verne sont [...] arrivés à leur point. Quand on voit le public empressé courir aux conférences qui se sont ouvertes sur mille points de la France, quand on voit qu'à côté des critiques d'art et de théâtre, il a fallu faire place dans nos journaux aux comptes-rendus de l'Académie des Sciences, il faut bien se dire que l'art pour l'art ne suffit plus à notre époque, et que l'heure est venue où la science a sa place faite dans le domaine de la littérature. Le mérite de M. Jules Verne, c'est d'avoir le premier et en maître, mis le pied sur cette terre nouvelle.[9]

> [The novels of Mr Jules Verne have come at the right moment. When we see the eager public hurrying to lectures taking place all over France, and when we see that, in our newspapers, space has had to be found alongside art and theatre reviews for the proceedings of the Academy of Sciences, it becomes apparent that art for art's sake is no longer enough in our time, and that the moment has now come at which science has its place in the literary sphere. Mr Jules Verne's merit is in having been the first, and the most masterful, to set foot in this new area.]

8 The question of the 'opening up of a literary text into a non-literary one' is interestingly explored by Daniel Compère in 'Jules Verne and the Limitations of Literature', in Smyth (ed.), *Jules Verne: Narratives of Modernity*, pp. 40–45 (p. 41).

9 'Avertissement de l'éditeur', in *Voyages et aventures du capitaine Hatteras* (Paris: Hetzel, 1866), pp. 1–2.

Science, then, is henceforth to be considered a legitimate new territory for the novelist. Jules Verne, according to Hetzel, has perceived and exploited a change in the attitudes of the reading public and in artistic taste, out of which he has fashioned an entirely new style. In this preface that doubles as a manifesto, the moment of a major transition is thus captured, perhaps more clearly than at any other stage of the nineteenth century. The concerns of modern industrial society, the idea of progress itself, become central to the artistic quest. The explorations of art and the explorations of technology go hand in hand, while knowledge is mediated through imagined worlds as much as through real discovery. The novelist and the scientist now join forces in a common quest. It is small wonder that so many of Verne's heroes are engineers and scientists endowed with the imagination and the talent of creative artists. Often, indeed, they take over from the novelist or the narrator himself and 'retell' the story of progress, underlining that new symbiosis of art and technology. And so, in 1866, with the publication of Hetzel's preface, artistic 'capital' – which as Pierre Bourdieu has shown was at one stage a reverse image of the mechanisms of economic and industrial capital[10] – begins to establish itself in concert with such mechanisms. This is all the more true in Verne's case, since under Hetzel's influence and guidance the novel itself becomes a mass-marketed commodity. In such a context of change, it is understandable that Hetzel refused the manuscript of *Paris au XXe siècle* in 1863, for despite its technological content Verne's manuscript relays what was by then a dated concept of the artist figure rejected and marginalised by society. We shall, however, have more to say about this curious but failed text in the next chapter.

The major shift towards new horizons brought about with the writing of the *Voyages extraordinaires* is not without its problems. As a result of Verne's massive reliance on scientific and technological discourses, and because his style is such a mixture of apparently different elements, questions have always been asked about his literary credentials. And, since his promotion of the idea of progress is so closely attuned to the production and marketing of his own novels, it was perhaps inevitable too that his artistic good faith would be doubted. Does his work belong, in a proper sense, to the 'literary field' that Bourdieu has described? Given its obvious difference from so much literary output of the century, can it be considered literature at all? While from a twenty-first-century perspective it does not seem unreasonable to conclude that Verne was extending and

---

10   The concept is fully developed in Bourdieu's *Les Règles de l'art: genèse et structure du champ littéraire* (Paris: Seuil, 1992).

redefining the very concept of literature, by no means all of his contemporaries saw it in this way. Zola among others dismissed the *Voyages extraordinaires* as commercial art that had no literary relevance. He wrote: 'Si les *Voyages extraordinaires* se vendent bien, les alphabets et les paroissiens se vendent bien aussi à des chiffres considérables... [Ils sont] sans aucune importance dans le mouvement littéraire contemporain.'[11] ['If the *Extraordinary Journeys* sell well, then so too do ABC books and prayer books, in considerable numbers. They have absolutely no significance for the contemporary literary movement.'] The dismissive attitude has persisted right through to modern times and, despite the revival of Jules Verne studies in France and his reinstatement alongside the great figures of French literature, a current of scepticism surfaces regularly on both sides of the Channel about whether such fiction is genuinely artistic, or whether it was simply a canny money-making venture. George Orwell, in a 1941 review of Kenneth Allott's biography, acknowledged the literary context in which Verne wrote, but found it difficult to relate him to it. 'It seems strange,' he observed, 'that so unliterary a writer as Verne should have behind him the familiar history of a nineteenth-century Frenchman of letters. But it is all there – the early tragedies in imitation of Racine, the encouragement of Victor Hugo, the romantic starvation in a garret.'[12] For William Golding, though Verne's novels had the saving grace of gusto, the endless lists lose their thrill and Verne's 'verbal surface lacks the slickness of the professional; it is turgid and slack by turns'.[13] Back on the other side of the Channel, for the Barthes of *Mythologies* Jules Verne was a peddler of trite myths and unstated bourgeois assumptions, and for all his 'openness', ultimately traded in a very confined and limited view of the world. For Michel Picard thirty years later,[14] Verne was guilty of both ideological and psychological imposture in his novels, and *L'Ile mystérieuse*, that supposedly educational text, was in fact nothing of the sort since it merely restated what was already known.

The accusation that Verne is facile and/or naïve, or simply not 'literary', is one that recurs so frequently that it indicates how uneasy the literate reading public feel about an author who targets the young and

11 Emile Zola, 'Jules Verne', in *Le Figaro Littéraire*, 22 December 1878, reprinted in *Les Romanciers naturalistes* (Paris: 1881), pp. 356–57.
12 George Orwell, 'Two Glimpses of the Moon', *The New Statesman* (18 January 1941), reprinted in *The Jules Verne Companion*, pp. 17–19.
13 William Golding, 'Astronaut by Gaslight', *The Spectator* (9 June 1961), reprinted in *The Jules Verne Companion*, pp. 79–87 (p. 83).
14 Michel Picard, 'Le Trésor de Némo: la double face des tricheries', in *La Lecture comme jeu* (Paris: Editions de Minuit, 1986), pp. 171–89.

recycles contemporary textbook material with pedagogical intentions. How can such an approach be deemed compatible with literature? In answer to this, let it first be said that novelists have traditionally experienced difficulty in having their writing accepted as high art (a problem that Madame de Lafayette recognised – and avoided – by refusing to have the first editions of *La Princesse de Clèves* published under her own name). In the nineteenth century, when literary realism bought with it a massive shift towards the common or the banal, the debate about what constituted acceptable literature was particularly intense. However, were it not for a certain restrictive or normative notion of literature which censures its trespassing into other forms of writing, such a debate would simply not have taken place. Even in the climate of experimentation and of expansion of the literary that occurred in the nineteenth century, it is clear that for some Verne's style strayed too far into foreign, non-literary territory. But Verne's sin is perhaps to have made it obvious throughout his works that he did also have literary pretensions, alongside pedagogical and commercial ones. That the utilitarian should rub shoulders with the artistic in this way has never been fully accepted by the literary establishment. The worst failing of the *écrivain* ['writer'] is to become, in Barthes's famous nomenclature, an *écrivant* ['producer of texts'].[15] In Verne's defence, however, it needs to be stressed that while he held an exalted view of his literary task, the notion of literature itself was something that he wished to subvert and re-examine, somewhat as Flaubert did in *Bouvard et Pécuchet*, by using material and techniques that had traditionally been considered anti-literary. So what Verne does is open up the frontiers of literature in every sense, using a range of styles, voices, materials and narrative modes in the making of the text, thus giving it an intensely modern, 'unfinished' feel. Measured passages of description and recorded fact lead on to episodes put together with what Golding called 'the trowel of farce';[16] dramatic sequences are suspended by the inclusion of detailed lists and inventories; character analyses feature alongside encyclopaedic digressions. There is a sense of the fragmented and of the hybrid, precisely because of the range of Verne's styles and the scope of his fiction. Text is a process, a patchwork of different materials that stands as a reminder of its own arbitrariness, rather than as a finished product which closes off all insights into its creation.

15 Roland Barthes, 'Ecrivains et écrivants' (1960), reprinted in *Essais critiques* (Paris: Seuil, 1964), pp. 147–54.
16 'Astronaut by Gaslight', p. 83.

And if Verne is so often misread as a marginal or a non-literary figure, this is partly too because he directed his writing at the young and quite deliberately encouraged his readers not to place the notion of Literature in some idealised and sanitised environment which tolerates nothing other than High Culture. Rather, the reader is invited to view the literary text as entirely compatible and continuous with a whole range of other pursuits and disciplines. If the Russian Formalists later attempted, in one of the most fascinating experiments ever undertaken in literary theory, to section both literature and literary criticism into autonomous, self-contained arenas, Verne's writing provides a sustained demonstration of the opposite view: that literature is by its very nature interdisciplinary and polyphonic. It will of necessity overrun any boundaries that are artificially imposed upon it, since one of the definitions of so-called 'literary' language is precisely that it is self-denying and self-transcending, always crossing the lines into the territory of what is considered 'non-literary'.[17] Though not marginal in the sense that his detractors would have it, Verne's work most certainly does explore – with a momentum and an intensity that are no accident – the margins of what 'acceptable' literature is. Of course, it flouts the standards of 'good taste' on occasions, but then so too does the writing of Balzac, Stendhal, Zola and even Proust. And not the least of its fascinations is that this concerted exploration of literature and its boundaries is mirrored by, and mirrors, the central theme of the *Voyages extraordinaires*, namely, the exploration of the geographical 'margins' of nineteenth-century civilisation. Verne is working at the frontiers in every sense. His very notion of literature is of a journey into foreign territory. The subject of exploration and travel is a vast metaphor of what the writer himself undertakes.

That Verne saw his own work as an attempt to make a literary impact becomes abundantly clear both from the extensive network of literary references throughout the *Voyages extraordinaires*, and from the remarks about style that he makes in his correspondence with Hetzel. We shall look much more closely in due course at Verne's uses of literary references and his reworking of sources. Suffice it to say at this point that these create a network of associations which has the far from naïve function of positioning Verne's own work within a specifically literary context and tradition. Whether it be in mentions of Poe or Hoffmann, in echoes of Rabelais, Molière, La Fontaine, Diderot, Hugo, in resonances of Homer

---

17 For a very useful discussion of this issue see Jonathan Culler, 'At the Boundaries: Barthes and Derrida', in Herbert L. Sussman (ed.), *At the Boundaries* (Boston: North-eastern University Press, 1984), pp. 23–41.

and Shakespeare, in homages to Sterne, James Fenimore Cooper, Alexandre Dumas *père*, Melville and a host of others, Verne gives the consistent impression not only that he is knowingly circulating with the great writers of history and modernity, but also that he is quite consciously weaving his own individual path through the intertexts of literary tradition. His rewritings of the Robinson Crusoe legend and his *reprises* of the stories of Poe are just two indications of his extensive literary culture and his highly alert and sophisticated manipulations of it. Like his contemporary Flaubert, Verne seems to make a very modernistic statement about the collapsing relationship between writing and rewriting. There is no such thing as an 'original' text, for the modern writer is dealing at all times with the already written, which he must re-use and recycle. Of course, it is in this act of reappropriation and renewal that a more modern and a more anxious novelty is achieved, in and against the murmur of a million texts that went before.

Yet for all this – and again, like Flaubert – Verne holds to a traditional concept of stylistic elegance. His descriptive passages, with their accumulation of exotic and scientific terminology, sometimes have an intensely poetic and incantatory force about them in which, as William Butcher puts it, 'literal mindedness topples over into poetic ecstasy'.[18] Apocryphally, Apollinaire is reported to have exclaimed, not without a sense of the Vernian paradox: 'Quel style! Rien que des substantifs!'[19] ['What a style! Nothing but nouns!'] Perec goes even further when he writes: 'Quand, dans *Vingt mille lieues sous les mers*, Jules Verne énumère sur quatre pages tous les noms de poissons, j'ai le sentiment de lire un poème'[20] ['When Jules Verne lists all the names of fish over four pages in *Twenty Thousand Leagues under the Seas*, I feel as though I am reading a poem']. Many scholars have focused their attention on Verne's extraordinarily daring and innovative descriptive powers,[21] and the recent edition of the Verne–Hetzel correspondence has enabled us to see more clearly

18 *Verne's Journey to the Centre of the Self*, p. 167.
19 The remark is now regularly quoted without a reference, and its precise attribution remains uncertain. See, for example, Peter Costello, *Jules Verne: Inventor of Science Fiction*, p. 53, and Andrew Martin, *The Knowledge of Ignorance: From Genesis to Jules Verne*, p. 151. Although Apollinaire is known to have been a great admirer of Verne, there is no specific record of this revealing judgment.
20 Georges Perec, 'J'ai fait imploser le roman', *Galerie des arts*, 184 (1978), p. 73.
21 Notably Alain Buisine, 'Un cas limite de la description: l'énumération. L'exemple de *Vingt mille lieues sous les mers*', in *La Description. Nodier, Sue, Flaubert, Hugo, Verne, Zola, Alexis, Fénéon*, textes réunis par Philippe Bonnefis et Pierre Reboul (Lille: Presses Universitaires de Lille, 1981), pp. 81–102.

than ever before that Verne was concerned to secure his own place in literature as a 'stylist'.[22] His remarks, let it be said, also harbour an ironic awareness of the fact that his literary ambition *needs* to be expressed, that it is not self-evident given the radically different type of writing he is engaged in. As early as 1864, as he is writing *Voyages et aventures du capitaine Hatteras*, Verne affirms: 'Ce que je voudrais devenir avant tout, c'est un *écrivain*, louable ambition que vous approuverez pleinement' ['What I aspire to become above all else is a *writer*, a praiseworthy ambition of which you will fully approve']. And later in the same letter: 'Tout ceci, c'est pour vous dire combien je cherche à devenir un *styliste*, mais sérieux; c'est l'idée de toute ma vie'[23] ['All this is to stress how much I am trying to be a *stylist*, but a serious one; that is the central idea of my life']. It is an ambition he retains throughout his writing career, and in later years it becomes the source of a regret as he senses that proper recognition of his stylistic achievements has yet to come about. Though the *Voyages extraordinaires* had received the recognition, stated on the title page of the Hetzel editions, of being 'couronnés par l'*Académie Française*' ['crowned by the French Academy'], Verne's own wish to be elected a member of the Académie was not to be fulfilled, and in an 1894 interview with the journalist Robert Sherard, he claimed regretfully: 'Je ne compte pas dans la littérature française'[24] ['I do not count in French literature']. Yet by the late twentieth century Verne's literary interest, in France at least, was no longer in question. Though he continues in our own day to have his detractors, as does any writer, he figures prominently on university courses, has been the subject of many dissertations and theses, and is regularly the subject of high-powered academic conferences which have repeatedly brought out the complexity, the depth, the subtlety and the striking originality of his style. He is firmly established as a 'respectable' literary figure.

But then Verne has always had a strong literary following in France, notwithstanding the efforts of Zola and others to debunk him. The long line of admirers stretches from his own contemporaries through to writers such as Albert Camus, Michel Butor, Michel Tournier, Julien Gracq,

---

22 Olivier Dumas, Piero Gondolo della Riva and Volker Dehs (eds.), *Correspondance inédite de Jules Verne et de Pierre-Jules Hetzel (1863–1886)*, vol. I (1863–1874), vol. II (1875–1878), vol. III (1879–1886) (Geneva: Slatkine, 1999, 2001 and 2002).

23 Letter of 25 April 1864, in Dumas, Gondolo della Riva and Dehs (eds.), *Correspondance inédite*, vol. I, p. 28.

24 R. H. Sherard, 'Jules Verne at Home: His Own Account of his Life and Work', in *McClure's Magazine* (January 1894). The interview is reproduced on the Jules Verne website at http://jv.gilead.org.il/sherard.html.

and J. M. G. Le Clézio.[25] The ringing endorsement of Verne by two writers who met him in Amiens towards the end of his life is typically revealing. The first, Pierre Louÿs, made the pilgrimage to the elderly writer's home on 7 July 1894 in order, as he writes, to tell Verne 'qu'il est le seul romancier actuellement en exercice, du génie duquel il convient de se préoccuper'[26] ['that he is the only practising novelist today whose genius should be of interest to us']. Another of Verne's visitors in Amiens, who was to pay extravagant homage to him in *Comment j'ai écrit certains de mes livres* and elsewhere, was Raymond Roussel. Roussel once wrote in a letter about Verne: 'C'est Lui, et de beaucoup, le plus grand génie littéraire de tous les siècles; il "restera" quand tous les autres auteurs de notre époque seront oubliés depuis longtemps'[27] ['It is He, and by a long way, who is the greatest literary genius of all time; he will remain when all the other authors of our time have faded into oblivion']. That practising writers have consistently placed Jules Verne so high in the pantheon of literary greats is not only a sign that he should be seriously considered alongside them, it also suggests that they sense something fundamental in his work about the deeper function and the reality of literature. In some of Roussel's remarks we have the sense that writing itself takes on an almost magical dimension, and that with Verne we are ultimately confronted with the tangible reality of words as they open up the Pandora's box of imaginary realms. It may also be that, when such writers read Verne, they are taken back to a sense of the mythical truth of text. Word is the beginning, and the beginning is the word. The naming ceremony that so often takes place in his stories – typically in *L'Ile mystérieuse* when the castaways map out Lincoln Island in language that gives it identity and familiarity – is a reminder of Verne's central concern with language and its bewitching power, and his constant assertion that in the end everything flows from, and returns to, text. In that sense, as Roussel so clearly understood, he is the most literary of writers.

25 Le Clézio's admiration for Verne is documented in his *témoignage* for the special issue of the magazine *Géo*. See J. M. G. Le Clézio, 'J'ai grandi avec ses livres', *Géo*, hors série, Jules Verne (2003), pp. 6–11.

26 Pierre Louÿs, letter to Louis-Ferdinand Herold, quoted in Jean-Paul Goujon, *Pierre Louÿs: une vie secrète (1870–1925)* (Paris: Fayard, 2000), p. 261.

27 See Michel Leiris, 'Une lettre de Raymond Roussel', *Arts et Lettres*, 15 (1949), pp. 100–101.

Chapter 2

Textual Environments

The conquest of nature

In *Cinq semaines en ballon*, the novel that launches the *Voyages extraordinaires* in 1863, Jules Verne narrates the westward flight across Africa of his scientist-hero Dr Samuel Fergusson in search of the sources of the Nile. Fergusson is accompanied by a manservant called Joe, and by his friend Dick Kennedy. As is the case in so many of Verne's novels, we are confronted with two characters who are exact but inseparable opposites, for as the narrator tells us, 'l'amitié ne saurait exister entre deux êtres parfaitement identiques' (5S, p. 14) ['friendship cannot exist between two perfectly identical beings']. Where Fergusson is calm, measured and objective, Kennedy is volatile, eccentric and excitable. Fergusson is a man of the air, Kennedy a man of the earth. But the biggest difference between the two is in their attitude towards the environment. While Fergusson has an encyclopaedic knowledge that is the constant mark of his respect for the natural world, Kennedy is a plunderer who wilfully vandalises the terrain he passes through. Shooting almost everything in sight, he eats what he can and happily abandons what is not needed. The concepts of conservation and recycling have no place in his ideological arsenal. As for his arsenal of weapons, detailed early in the novel, we are assured that it is sufficient to cause destruction and havoc among whatever species of animals he will come across. When they fly low over Lake Chad, Kennedy sees the chance of adding a hippopotamus to his already substantial list of trophies. Fergusson attempts to call him to order: 'il me semble que, sans parler du menu gibier, tu as déjà une antilope, un éléphant et deux lions sur la conscience' ['it seems to me that, without mentioning the small game, you already have an antelope, an elephant and two lions on your conscience']. To this reasoned intervention – not without its echoes of Rabelais's famous 'sans compter les femmes et petits enfants'[1] ['without

---

1 See Rabelais, *Gargantua*, chapter 16 ('Comment Gargantua paya la bien venue es Parisiens: & comment il print les grosses cloches de l'eglise nostre dame'), available

mentioning the women and little children'] – Kennedy retorts, showing that conscience is the least of his concerns: 'Qu'est-ce que cela pour un chasseur africain qui voit passer tous les animaux de la création au bout de son fusil?' (5S, p. 261) ['What does that matter to an African hunter who sees all the animals of creation at the end of his gun-barrel?'] An argument develops between the two of them about the uses and abuses of hunting, and it is the manservant Joe who, at the end of the chapter, finally arbitrates: 'Il n'est vraiment pas naturel de pénétrer jusqu'au centre de l'Afrique pour y vivre de bécassines et de perdrix comme en Angleterre!' (5S, p. 264) ['It really is not natural to reach the heart of Africa, only to live off snipes and partridges as we do in England!'] The colonising instinct is, it seems, too strong at this point for Fergusson's more objective arguments.

The figure of the ecological vandal is one that we come across repeatedly in the *Voyages extraordinaires*, most obviously and memorably a few years later with the harpoonist Ned Land of *Vingt mille lieues sous les mers*. What is striking in the example of *Cinq semaines* is that Jules Verne appears to offer us two possible ways of 'reading' this figure. On the one hand, the hunter is an obvious product of the colonialist enterprise, which appears to give him an absolute prerogative to treat the environment in whatever way he deems fit. It is another way of appropriating untamed territories, asserting mastery over the natural order, and emphasising the technical magnificence of modern weaponry. It is the incursion of the so-called civilised world into one which was until this moment untouched and unspoiled, the meeting place of modern society and a virgin wilderness, the bringing together of the 'known' and the 'unknown' worlds whose coexistence is so strikingly affirmed in the series title that appears on the cover of the Hetzel editions: *Voyages extraordinaires dans les mondes connus et inconnus* [Extraordinary Journeys into the Known and Unknown Worlds]. Hunting underpins that quintessential notion of conquest which runs throughout the corpus and which, for

---

online at the Athena site: http://un2sg4.unige.ch/athena/rabelais/rab_garg.html. Verne's 'Rabelaisian' phrase, together with a typically Rabelaisian enumeration, will return in a remark about Pharamond Barthès in *L'Etoile du sud*: 'Il avait déjà tué trois lions, seize éléphants, sept tigres, plus un nombre incalculable de girafes, d'antilopes sans compter le menu gibier' (ES, p. 79) ['He had already killed three lions, sixteen elephants, seven tigers, and an incalculable number of giraffes and antelopes, without mentioning the small game']. The important link between Rabelais and Jules Verne, most notably in the delight both authors take in enumeration, is pointed out by Daniel Compère in *Jules Verne écrivain*, p. 21.

Pierre Macherey among others, is at the centre of the writer's ideological programme.[2]

Although the figure of the hunter, in *Cinq semaines* as elsewhere, becomes something of a caricature, he is even in his Rabelaisian excess the embodiment of a simple, not to say simplistic, nineteenth-century imperialism that seeks to conquer by destruction. Closely allied to the notion of hunting is that of eating, a point that will later be reinforced in the character of Ned Land whose appetite knows no bounds, and almost no boundaries. On the other hand, though, there is clearly a sense of unease about such acts of demolition and destruction, expressed most obviously in the reaction of Fergusson in *Cinq semaines*, and embodied in almost all of Verne's 'responsible' scientist-explorers. Fergusson's voice of reason continues to provide a reference point in the text, offering the valid alternative to ecological delinquency. The environment is a potential utopia that will yield inestimable riches to those who respect it and husband its resources wisely – a message that will be underlined almost throughout the *Voyages extraordinaires*, and will be quintessential to novels such as *L'Île mystérieuse*. Man tampers with the natural world at his peril, and nature herself, always subject to explosive outbursts in the Vernian universe, is liable to wreak revenge for his irresponsible acts.

It is clear, then, that for Verne the shooting of a hippopotamus, an antelope, a lion – or an elephant, as George Orwell in his turn will point out in a memorable essay of 1936[3] – is an act loaded with ideological significance. Such action is seen in all its ambivalence, for the urge to demonstrate mastery over nature by destructive behaviour is accompanied by the contrary sense of nature's miraculous wonders, her magical munificence, her immaculate Edenic order. Sometimes the awareness of nature's magic is experienced by even the most wasteful and irresponsible of Verne's characters, the implication being that human interference, in such circumstances, is an act of frivolous sabotage, both ideologically bankrupt and morally stupid. Verne's own 'shooting an elephant' scenes confront the reader (if not always the hunter himself) with the inhumane consequences of his society's arrogant and destructive colonising actions. *Aventures de trois Russes et de trois Anglais dans l'Afrique australe* (1872) offers one typically poignant and powerful elephant-shooting passage, comparable in its intensity with George Orwell's later description of a similar episode:

2 *Pour une théorie de la production littéraire*, pp. 183–89.
3 George Orwell, 'Shooting an Elephant', in *Collected Essays* (London: Secker and Warburg, 1961), pp. 15–23.

[L'éléphant] tomba sur les genoux, près d'un petit étang à demi-caché sous les herbes. Là, pompant l'eau avec sa trompe, il commença à arroser ses blessures, en poussant des cris plaintifs. [...] En effet, l'énorme animal était mortellement blessé. Il poussait des gémissements plaintifs; sa respiration sifflait; sa queue ne s'agitait plus que faiblement, et sa trompe, puisant à la mare de sang formée par lui, déversait une pluie rouge sur les taillis voisins. Puis, la force lui manquant, il tomba sur les genoux, et mourut ainsi. (A3, p. 86)

[The elephant fell onto his knees, near a small pond half-hidden in the grass. Sucking the water through his trunk, he began to wash his wounds, uttering plaintive cries. [...] Indeed, the animal was fatally wounded. He uttered pitiful groans, his breathing sounded increasingly strained, his tail moved weakly, and his trunk, drawing up the blood which he himself had shed, sprayed a red rain on the surrounding thickets. Then, as his strength deserted him, he fell on his knees and died.]

In *Cinq semaines*, however, Kennedy is not only a wasteful vandal (though he certainly is that), he is also on occasions a genuine admirer of nature's abundance and generosity. It is true that his reaction is closely linked to the less than humane satisfaction of finding sitting targets, especially when he is overwhelmed by the quantity of animals he finds. However, there is also a paradox in the fact that the hunter's very enthusiasm for destruction is dependent on nature's ability to continue as provider. Kennedy's amazement is basically that of all Verne's hero-explorers, who worship nature as a provider of infinite quantities of flora and fauna, and as a store of new, uncultivated territories into which they may venture. Man's conquest of nature is accompanied by the sense that there is always more to discover and appropriate, always something else out there beyond the realm of the already known. Where man invades, orders and destroys (destruction being his imprint), nature springs up anew, offering him over and over again the opportunity to despoil her infinite treasures and, consequently, to demonstrate his futile superiority. Man's instinct for sabotage is matched by nature's fabulous energy, but the balance is always a delicate one. In the 1881 novel *La Jangada*, an entire rainforest is cut down to create a huge raft that will carry a group of travellers down the Amazon and then be abandoned. Man's interference in nature, while providing him with the wherewithal to marvel at her wonders, can also turn into a dangerous and a wanton indulgence. As a writer, Verne appears both to condone and to censure this attitude.

But the confrontation between notions of destruction and abundance, of waste and productivity, of vandalism and creativity, is an intensely expressive one in Verne's writing. While in so many of his stories nature's vast expanses are curtailed by a harmful human order, there remains the sense that the urge to destroy must never be fulfilled if colonising man is to retain new territories at his disposal. And so too it is with the writing process itself, for the depiction of nature is the sign of a tension at the very heart of Verne's literary approach. Text imposes order and coherence, yet in its energetic diffuseness it simultaneously mimics the abundance of those untamed expanses. On the one hand we find an attempt to cover and appropriate the globe in words, to make the vast unknown, undifferentiated expanses 'readable' by processing everything into language. Text, like the colonising civilisation itself, spreads into every unknown corner of the globe, gets everywhere. Yet, on the other hand, in doing this, text proliferates wildly, and in its huge, encyclopaedic attempt to write the history of the universe itself, it runs amok. As it does so, it loses its civilised familiarity, becomes alien and other, itself turning into a kind of 'second nature'. So text, the instrument of colonisation, soon also proves to be the problem, the thing that has in its turn to be colonised and reigned in. Like nature, words run riot. They spring up with all the vigour of new species of flora and fauna. For every phenomenon and every creature, the lexicon in its fantastic generosity provides a new term, until text becomes as widespread and as seemingly infinite as the universe itself.

Narrative form and textual order are, then, constantly threatened both by the self-perpetuating munificence of the natural world and by the cornucopian richness of the dictionary or encyclopaedia. As words multiply (almost endlessly, it might seem) in Jules Verne's novels, the descriptive function that is so powerfully implied by the presence of technical, botanical, zoological or geographical terminology is undermined by excess of detail and precision. The external world that the writer aims to represent and to classify for his readers seems thereby to become so remote, so utterly 'verbal', that his words can only point to their own strangeness and otherness. Language takes on its own momentum, reversing the scientific and linguistic confidence upon which it was premised. Whereas at the outset Verne seems to express a very nineteenth-century confidence in the precision, range and signifying potential of technical and scientific vocabulary, his texts also suggest the impossibility of any reductive or synthesising representations of the world, ultimately the impossibility of coherence itself. If language is as widespread as nature, it is implied, then like nature itself it abhors a vacuum. Multiplying endlessly, it almost ceases to have any intrinsic signifying function or descriptive power. And words, like the swarm of locusts in this passage from the 1872 novel *Aventures de trois Russes et de trois Anglais*, are the sign of

the abundant and chaotic fare that nature serves up – swallowed indiscriminately by every creature in sight, to the point where they end up
even devouring themselves in a final cannibalistic act:

> Les oiseaux se jetaient sur [ces insectes] en poussant des cris rauques et ils les
> dévoraient avidement. Au-dessous de la masse, des serpents attirés par cette
> friande curée, en absorbaient des quantités énormes. [...] Le gibier de la
> plaine, les bêtes sauvages, lions ou hyènes, éléphants ou rhinocéros,
> engloutissaient dans leurs vastes estomacs des boisseaux de ces insectes.
> Enfin, les Bochjesmen eux-mêmes, très-amateurs de ces 'crevettes de l'air',
> s'en nourrisaient comme d'une manne céleste! Mais leur nombre défiait
> toutes ces causes de destruction, et même leur propre voracité, car ces
> insectes se dévorent entre eux. (A3, pp. 184–85)[4]

> [The birds threw themselves at these insects, uttering loud squawks, and
> devoured them greedily. Beneath the throng, snakes drawn by the scramble
> for food swallowed enormous quantities of them. The beasts in the plain –
> wild animals, lions, hyenas, elephants or rhinceros – gobbled up great
> amounts of the insects, which disappeared into their vast stomachs. The
> Bushmen themselves, very keen on these 'shrimps of the air', fed on them as
> though they were manna from heaven! But their sheer number defied all
> attempts to destroy them, and even defied their own greed – for these insects
> also devoured one another.]

The view of language and writing in the *Voyages extraordinaires* is,
then, one both of a miraculously accurate instrument and of a self-canni-
balising system. The quest for total knowledge goes hand in hand with
the ever-present sense of potential chaos and destruction. Indeed, coherence and disintegration cohabit both in the subjects of Verne's novels –
where so often a natural disaster puts paid to all the order that the characters have brought to their environment – and in the very conception of
the writing which, as an attempt at a total classification and résumé of
knowledge, appears to end up as disordered accumulation. The language
of nature and the nature of language mirror each other: articulating the
quest for totality, they also express the danger of fragmentation.

---

4 See the interesting discussion of this text by Michel Serres in *Jouvences sur Jules
   Verne*, pp. 63–78. Serres suggests that this novel repeatedly echoes the Book of
   Exodus. In a conflation of two episodes of the biblical text, Verne's plague of locusts
   here is, he says, also a reminder of manna falling from heaven.

The history of the universe

The view of language and nature just described extends to Verne's entire fictional project, and it is replicated in his totalising but apparently self-defeating attitude to knowledge. It was Hetzel who, in the 1866 preface I have already discussed, first formulated that gigantic, synthetic ambition which was to remain at the heart of the *Voyages extraordinaires*: 'Son but est, en effet, de résumer toutes les connaissances *géographiques, géologiques, physiques, astronomiques*, amassées par la science moderne, et de refaire, sous la forme attrayante et pittoresque qui lui est propre, l'histoire de l'univers'[5] ['His goal, indeed, is to summarise all the knowledge of geography, geology, physics and astronomy that modern science has amassed, and to retell, in the attractive and picturesque way that is his hallmark, the history of the universe']. More than simply grappling with virgin nature, Verne's enterprise is to write the history of the universe itself. The aim is to colonise the whole of reality in the written word, to cover not just the globe, but creation in its entirety, with words that rein it in and make sense of it.

It is, let it be said, a mad, colossal, monstrous literary ambition, and one that makes the enterprises of other nineteenth-century novelists such as Balzac, Sue, Dumas or Zola seem utterly modest and reasonable by comparison. If Jules Verne is to be judged in terms of such a programme, then he will always be found wanting, his textual universe a feeble and forlorn simulacrum of the gigantic immensity that it attempts to seize in language. But then, the history of the universe, like the history of colonisation and exploration, like nature itself, can only ever be a metaphorical representation of the nature of Verne's own writing. The encyclopaedic enterprise is riven with contradiction and paradox from the outset. For all that, the attempt to achieve some chimerical completion, total coverage of the globe and of our knowledge about it, remains as one of the defining characteristics of the *Voyages extraordinaires*, the guiding impulse that shapes the author's vision and our reading of his work. As Michel Serres so convincingly points out, Verne's work represents a cartography of knowledge comparable with Comte's *Cours de philosophie positive*, a modern epic of Homeric proportions, indeed a manual of manuals.[6] Hetzel's early statement sets the agenda, defining the scope and the ambition of Verne's project, and that ambition is re-echoed in various ways throughout Verne's

---

5 'Avertissement de l'éditeur', in *Voyages et aventures du capitaine Hatteras* (Paris: Hetzel, 1866), pp. 1–2.
6 *Jouvences sur Jules Verne*, pp. 11–17.

career. In an 1891 autobiographical text entitled *Souvenirs d'enfance et de jeunesse*, Verne formulates it once more, but recognises the finite nature of his means in the face of the infinite task before him when he writes: 'Cette tâche, c'est de peindre la terre entière, le monde entier, sous la forme du roman, en imaginant des aventures spéciales à chaque pays, en créant des personnages spéciaux aux milieux où ils agissent. Oui! Mais le monde est bien grand, et la vie est bien courte! Pour laisser une œuvre complète, il faudrait vivre cent ans!'[7] ['This task is to depict the whole earth, the entire world in the shape of the novel, imagining adventures particular to each country and creating characters particular to the surroundings in which they live. Ah yes! But the world is very large, and life is so short! To complete my work, I would need to live a hundred years!']

Like Kennedy in his natural domain marvelling at the abundance of animals and wishing he could bag them all, the writer himself is amazed at the generosity and immensity of his textual domain. And, like the hunter, he seems to be reduced to shooting almost indiscriminately, ever aware of the arbitrariness of his act of conquest. Yet what also seems to emerge from Verne's statements about his act of artistic conquest is less the abstract sense of the novelist's fundamental textual condition, than the awareness of the practical nature of his task and of the limits imposed by lack of time. In one sense he has a precise notion of what completion represents, since his aim is to place the setting of his works, at some stage, in all the main parts of the globe. It might seem, then, that this is less some Romantic quest for possession of the infinite than a straightforward desire to map out the globe schematically in his writing. Although there are obvious gaps in Jules Verne's charting of the oceans and continents, there is a credible attempt at systematic geographical coverage. As the geographical kaleidoscope turns, story after story is situated in a different region until a substantial part of the globe is accounted for. Geography, rather than history or even science, was in fact the discipline that seems to have most interested Verne, the one that underpins his quest for total coverage. It is through geography that history finds its way into the overall representation (as is the case, for example, when the geographer Paganel recounts the history of the exploration of Australia in *Les Enfants du capitaine Grant*). Nor should it be forgotten that, for the nineteenth century with its great explorers, geography is essentially a scientific discipline around which a cluster of other disciplines gather: archaeology, zoology, geology, palaeontology, botany, oceanography, astronomy, to

7 Jules Verne, *Souvenirs d'enfance et de jeunesse* in *Monna Lisa* suivi de *Souvenirs d'enfance et de jeunesse* (Paris: L'Herne, 1995), pp. 109–10.

name only the most obvious. Again and again, Verne will comment on the geographical features and characteristics of the various regions that his characters pass through, until in the course of the *Voyages extraordinaires* an astonishing amount of material has been amassed. Geography and the knowledge it brings is central to the colonising instinct. It is, for Verne the writer, the ultimate instrument of conquest.

Many readers of Verne have commented on the sheer geographical range of his work and noted the ways in which he systematically and patiently marks out the globe into its different regions. Interviewed for the *Revue Jules Verne* in 2000, Julien Gracq gives an especially good account of the manner of Verne's coverage. He notes that there is, in the *Voyages extraordinaires*, a hierarchical approach. At the heart of the corpus we find what he calls the 'grands romans cosmiques' ['great cosmic novels']. These are based on one of the fundamental elements – the sea (*Vingt mille lieues sous les mers*), the air (*Cinq semaines en ballon*), the earth (*Voyage au centre de la terre*) – or on one of the key points of the globe such as the North Pole (*Voyages et aventures du capitaine Hatteras*), or the Antarctic (*Le Sphinx des glaces*). Then there is a whole series of novels that are set in major regions of the planet: South America, the United States and Canada, Africa, Russia, the Mediterranean, China, Oceania and so on. And finally, says Gracq, there are the intercontinental novels, linking the different regions and binding the Vernian corpus into a coherent entity, such as *Le Tour du monde en quatre-vingts jours*, or *Les Enfants du capitaine Grant*.[8] To this we might add the novels dealing with journeys into space (*Autour de la lune*, *Hector Servadac*), which seem to complete the programme by exceeding and therefore delimiting that area of the universe that is our human habitat. The four elements – earth, air, fire and water (or its solid equivalent, ice) – mark out the geographical parameters of the *Voyages extraordinaires*, and give them a mythical scope that has certainly not gone unnoticed by commentators. Systematic coverage does not mean that every country or every region of the globe gets a mention in Jules Verne's work. Nor does it mean that each region is covered only once before the author moves on. Verne has his favoured settings – Scotland, Oceania, the polar regions, South America, southern Africa – to which he returns in two or more novels. However, the overall representation of the globe is astonishingly detailed and widespread, as well as being interconnected through linked series of texts, and in itself suggests a determination on the part of the author to reach out and 'claim' huge regions of the planet through his writing. The writer too is a hunter-coloniser, very

8 'Entretien inédit: Julien Gracq', *Revue Jules Verne*, 10 (2000), pp. 60–61.

much in tune with the ideologies of his day,[9] writing in an era of expansion which is mirrored in his approach. Like Kennedy in *Cinq semaines*, he marvels at the richness and variety of nature's provision, and seeks therefore to leave his imprint. But unlike his hunter, he is also engaged on a quest for an overarching sense of coherence, totality, unity. As the corpus of novels grows, numerous texts pick up and integrate elements of previous texts, so that the whole system becomes a vast but precariously unified, often self-referring network. His textual environment thus depends on the contrasting sense of multiplicity and variety on the one hand, synthesis and control on the other hand.

I have suggested that Jules Verne is driven first and foremost by a practical ambition to cover or to 'conquer' the globe. Nonetheless, there is also in his work a vaguer, and less easily identifiable, yearning for totality – total knowledge, total coverage, total possession: a metaphysical, Faustian ambition to possess the infinite, to lay hold of all areas of human endeavour and insight, to bring knowledge together into some vast alchemical synthesis that will magically exceed the sum total of its parts. This deeper, more mysterious philosophical ambition is nourished in part by his reading during the 1840s of epic works such as *The Divine Comedy*, *Paradise Lost, Faust*, and the novels of Hugo, Eugène Sue and Alexandre Dumas.[10] It is about developing a grand vision of society and of the human condition, putting together a comprehensive archaeology of knowledge, painting the broader canvas and linking the separate elements in cohesive structures. It is also about the relationship of knowledge and experience, for knowledge, in Jules Verne's typically nineteenth-century view, is the key to our mastery of the environment. That vision of knowledge is apparent even in some of Verne's earliest writings in the 1850s. In a story entitled 'Un voyage en ballon' published in the *Musée des Familles* in 1851, a balloonist finds himself accompanied by a madman who rehearses the entire history of lighter-than-air navigation, revelling in this knowledge which for him is almost a means of mythical transcendence: 'Je possède toute la science possible dans ce monde' ['I possess all learning possible in this world'], he exclaims. 'Depuis Phaéton, depuis Icare, depuis Architas, j'ai tout recherché, tout compulsé, tout compris! Par moi, l'art aérostatique rendrait d'immenses services au monde, si Dieu me prêtait vie!'[11]

---

9 On this subject, see for example Andrew Martin, *The Mask of the Prophet*, pp. 19–25.
10 On Verne's reading during this period, see the useful 'postface' by Christian Robin to Jules Verne, *Un prêtre en 1839* (Paris: Le Cherche Midi, 1992), pp. 213–21 (p. 214).
11 'Un voyage en ballon', in Marc Soriano, *Portrait de l'artiste jeune, suivi des quatre premiers textes publiés de Jules Verne* (Paris: Gallimard, 1978), pp. 89–90.

['From the age of Phaeton, Icarus and Architas onwards, I have researched everything, read everything, understood everything! Through me, aerostatic art would render immense services to the world, if God were to grant me a long enough life!'] Not only is there an implicit belief here that knowledge is both the key to and the very image of reality – that, in this case, to know the history of balloon travel is in some sense a guarantee of being able to control and influence its entire destiny – there is also an attempt to be the rival of God. That mythical temptation will recur everywhere in the writing of Jules Verne, and the figures of Vulcan, Prometheus, Icarus, Neptune and others reappear in modern guise, as engineers and scientists become godlike creatures in their turn, reaching out and almost touching the infinite.[12] But the presence of some metaphysical hubris is never far away, and the wish to equal God is also fraught with danger. The pilot Robur, in his second incarnation in the novel *Maître du monde* (1904), will be struck down in flight, Icarus-like, when he encounters a thunderstorm. In a much earlier story, *Maître Zacharius, ou l'horloger qui avait perdu son âme* (1854), the godlike aspirations of the hero are written explicitly into the plot, and the ancient myth acquires a more modern, Faustian ring. The story is about a Swiss clockmaker who believes that the timepieces he creates are so perfect that they contain the secret of life itself. On one of his timepieces are inscribed mottoes such as 'Il faut manger les fruits de l'arbre de science' ['We must eat the fruit of the tree of knowledge'] and 'L'homme peut devenir l'égal de Dieu' ['Man can become the equal of God']. Yet Zacharius, believing too much in himself, is punished by the failure of his timepieces, indeed the failure of time itself. The desire to possess the infinite, to touch the essence of creation, leads to his undoing. It is a tragic pattern that will remain and recur in the writings of Jules Verne, notwithstanding the exuberant levity of so many of his stories. His heroes are always potential outcasts or monomaniacs who have rejected or are rejected by society. In the case of Nemo, in *Vingt mille lieues sous les mers*, or Le Kaw-djer, hero of *En Magellanie*, they create a parallel world in which they are miniature gods and enjoy almost supreme power.

So the infinite, though it may be yearned for and almost grasped by some Vernian characters, is never reached. They return – in some cases tragically – to their human condition and their destructive quest for knowledge is exposed as an interference in nature's or God's procedures, comparable with the depredations of the hunter in *Cinq semaines* and else-

---

12 This aspect of Jules Verne is comprehensively reviewed by Simone Vierne in *Jules Verne: Mythe et modernité*.

where. Contrary to what is sometimes maintained about Verne,[13] the religious sense of God's presence is everywhere, and not only in the obvious cases such as *Le Chancellor* where Miss Herbey's Christian faith is central in the unfolding of the plot. The sense of the sanctity of creation is almost always tangible, and this is much more than some vague sense of religious awe. It is often implied in the *Voyages extraordinaires* that since man cannot challenge God, his claim to control society or nature is a wanton disruption of an order that is not his own. The invisible and all-powerful Nemo, a demi-god in his underwater realm, is ultimately weakened and undermined by his hatred and desire for revenge on his fellow-mortals. Or, as the narrator points out in the concluding sentence to *L'Ile à hélice*, the story about an artificial island inhabited by two warring communities who finally destroy it: 'créer une île artificielle, une île qui se déplace à la surface des mers, n'est-ce pas dépasser les limites assignées au génie humain, et n'est-il pas défendu à l'homme, qui ne dispose ni des vents ni des flots, d'usurper si témérairement sur le Créateur?' (IH, p. 363) ['is not creating an artificial island, an island which moves around the surface of the seas, going beyond the limits prescribed to human genius? And is it not forbidden to man, who controls neither the wind nor the waves, to usurp with such temerity the Creator's role?']

Just as Verne's characters fail in their quest to transcend the limits of the human condition and create a new order of reality through the power of technology and learning, so too there is an implicit acknowledgment throughout the *Voyages extraordinaires* that the original project of achieving a vast, groundbreaking synthesis of human learning leads inevitably

---

13   See, for example, Ghislain de Diesbach, *Le Tour de Jules Verne en quatre-vingts livres* (Paris: Perrin, 2000 [1969]), p. 200: 'Il n'y a point [...] de dialogue entre le Créateur et sa créature, point d'effusion mystique et surtout peu de prêtres. On y trouve seulement, à l'égard de Dieu, une sorte de déférence qui s'adresse au grand horloger de l'univers plutôt qu'au rédempteur du genre humain.' ['There is no dialogue between the Creator and his creature, no mystical effusion, and especially, very few priests. All that one finds is a kind of deference towards God, but addressed more to the cosmic clockmaker than to the redeemer of mankind.'] Diesbach also cites the famous letter by Louis Veuillot who, second-hand, talks of the absence of God in the *Voyages extraordinaires*: 'Je n'ai pas encore lu les *Voyages extraordinaires* de M. Verne. Notre ami Aubineau me dit qu'ils sont charmants, sauf une absence [...] qui désembellit tout et qui laisse les merveilles du monde à l'état d'énigme. C'est beau mais c'est inanimé. Il manque quelqu'un.' (*Le Tour de Jules Verne en quatre-vingts livres*, p. 199) ['I have not yet read Mr Verne's *Extraordinary Journeys*. Our friend Aubineau tells me that they are charming, except for an absence which tarnishes everything and leaves the marvels of the world in a state of enigma. It is beautiful, but inanimate. Someone is missing.']

to its own failure. Knowledge is only ever a borrowing from known sources, and any unveiling of the unknown has been accomplished prior to the relaying process. And like knowledge, travel too, so clearly the means of progressing to new places and new realities, often seamlessly mutates in Jules Verne's work into a return journey – as is the case in novels such as *Autour de la lune* or *Le Tour du monde*, where the straight line of the outward trajectory turns out to be an ellipse or a circle leading the travellers back home. On many different levels, Verne's writing returns us to the already known, the already seen, the already written, rather than straightforwardly pushing the frontiers of knowledge into new, unexplored territories. The attempt to totalise knowledge is premised, paradoxically, upon the suggestion of total indebtedness, for the text itself is an intertext made up of, and leading back to, infinitely many other texts. Or, to replace the image of the ellipse with that of a constellation, any particular text is an infinitesimal point in the giddying firmament of knowledge, always potentially lost in the infinite spaces of words. The greater the coverage, the more numerous the gaps that are revealed, so the totalising ambition can be expressed only through a process of fragmentation. Like a constellation, the corpus of novels can represent only a schematic series of points in the immense emptiness, acknowledging their own inability to cover the ever-widening gaps between those infinite spaces. Verne discovers, as did Balzac before him through the portrayal of Restoration and post-Restoration France, that the process of expanding his fictional universe leads to an ever-increasing sense of its incompleteness, as the open spaces widen.

The tension in Verne's writing between the totalising, universalising project and its fragmentation at the point of execution has repeatedly drawn the attention of commentators who see in it the source of a creative disjunction. Pierre Macherey shows in his rich and influential study that the master plan is proved radically impossible in the course of its execution, and indeed that this deviation from, or subversion of, the original intention is precisely the point of interest of the *Voyages extraordinaires*. Marie-Hélène Huet, who sees a certain sense of abdication in the final novels of the corpus, interprets this as a confirmation that the planned résumé of human knowledge is now seen as impossible, but she stresses the paradox that its very impossibility confirms its chimerical existence: 'C'est ainsi que le projet ambitieux qu'Hetzel avait assigné au jeune écrivain se trouve réalisé par son échec même'[14] ['Thus it is that the

---

14   Marie-Hélène Huet, *L'Histoire des Voyages extraordinaires. Essai sur l'œuvre de Jules Verne* (Paris: Minard, 1973), p. 167.

ambitious project assigned to the young writer by Hetzel is brought to completion precisely through its failure']. And Andrew Martin, drawing attention to the Vernian dream of completing the circle of knowledge and closing it off, similarly emphasises that the closing of the gap entails only further fragmentation. Jules Verne stands, he says, as an ironic commentator on the processes of totalisation of knowledge, for knowledge is no more than the discovery of ignorance and emptiness, or at best the return to the already known. Verne's primary ambition, that of having nothing more to say, would in any case destroy itself in its fulfilment.[15]

The fictional quest to reach out and claim vast unknown territories of land or of learning is clearly accompanied in Jules Verne's work by the sense of a return – a return to the physical point of departure, a return to the already said, a return to the already known. The search for new knowledge goes hand in hand with the awareness that any attempt to relay it is an act of repetition and recycling. In this literary journey into *les mondes connus et inconnus* [the known and unknown worlds], the 'unknown' thus remains in some senses as an unreal, unreachable domain, for as soon as it is claimed and articulated, it is by definition shuttled into the territory of the known. The 'known' belongs to the past (for it is a land that has already been conquered and claimed), the 'unknown' to the future. Nonetheless if the unknown, when claimed, becomes the known and shifts into the past tense, then the already known, when revisited, still contains the thrilling promise of new futures. The known and the unknown, the past and the future, stand in a profoundly ambivalent and problematic relationship. We shall now look more closely at some examples of this temporal paradox and at the ways in which it enriches the overall textual environment of the *Voyages extraordinaires*.

The future of the text

In 1994 the long-lost manuscript of *Paris au XXe siècle* re-emerged almost miraculously after an absence of over a century and a half, discovered in an old safe believed to be empty.[16] Its publication was an immediate *cause célèbre*, both in the world of literary scholarship and among the wider reading public. Excited articles appeared in newspapers, and periodicals around the world proclaimed the importance of this

---

15 Martin, *The Knowledge of Ignorance*, pp. 178–79.
16 See Jules Verne, *Paris au XXe siècle*, préface et établissement du texte par Piero Gondolo della Riva (Paris: Le Cherche Midi, 1994).

trouvaille.[17] The novel would, announced some reviewers, throw new light on the entire corpus of the *Voyages extraordinaires*, notwithstanding the fact that Verne's editor Hetzel had summarily rejected the manuscript and that Verne himself had subsequently lost interest in it. Most probably penned in 1862-63, *Paris au XXe siècle* was hailed by its late-twentieth-century readers as a futuristic fiction predicting many of the technological innovations of modern times. In fact, as we shall see, it did nothing of the sort, but its publication fuelled many of the familiar myths and clichés about Verne as a visionary and a writer of science fiction *avant la lettre* – thus putting the clock firmly back in relation to so much of the careful scholarly work that had been carried out over the previous decades.[18]

Despite its title, which is surely a stroke of genius, Jules Verne's work has neither the apocalyptic frisson of Huxley's *Brave New World* nor the political punch of Orwell's *1984*. To discuss it alongside such works, as so many of its press reviewers understandably felt inclined to do, is to decontextualise it and to convey an entirely wrong impression. *Paris au XXe siècle* is a sketchily written novel with a flimsy plot and often reactionary

17 The huge and instantaneous press interest in *Paris au XXe siècle* was exemplified in the front-page article of *Le Monde des livres* on 23 September 1994 ('Jules Verne inédit'). Special articles also appeared in English-language publications, for example in the *Chicago Tribune* (23 September 1994) and a few days later in *The New York Times* (27 September 1994). An English version of the novel was then published as *Paris in the Twentieth Century*, translated by Richard Howard, with an introduction by Eugen Weber (New York: Random House, 1996). This spawned a further series of articles, often hailing Verne as a techno-prophet. The following is a selection: Herbert Lottman, 'Back to the Future', *Los Angeles Times*, 15 December 1996, p. 10; Richard Bernstein, 'New Jules Verne. A Sketchy Predecessor to *1984*', *The New York Times*, 27 December 1996, p. B22; Edward Rothstein, 'All Hail Jules Verne, Patron Saint of Cyberspace', *The New York Times*, 3 February 1997, p. D5. Julian Barnes ('Back to the Future', *The New York Times*, 26 January 1997, p. 4) also reviews the English-language version of Verne's novel.

18 A perceptive critical account of Verne's novel is offered by David Platten, 'A Hitch-hiker's Guide to Paris: *Paris au XXe siècle*', in Smyth (ed.), *Jules Verne: Narratives of Modernity*, pp. 78–93. Platten takes issue with the facile assessments of the novel in press reviews, but argues nonetheless that this text reveals new complexities in Verne's work. For Platten, the real interest of Verne's novel is not the so-called 'prediction' of the twentieth century, but its representation of the city and of the relationship between human and machine. Given the novel's similarity of tone with some of Verne's later texts, Platten also suggests that the manuscript may have been wrongly dated. Attractive as it is, this hypothesis is extremely unlikely, not least because Hetzel's letter of refusal explicitly refers to the recent publication of *Cinq semaines en ballon*. For a reliable account of the discovery and the dating of the manuscript see the preface by Piero Gondolo della Riva (P20, pp. 11–24).

or superficial ideas.[19] It evokes a dystopia which is much more a projection of nineteenth-century disillusionment than the mark of a futuristic visionary. Ironically, to readers familiar with the nineteenth-century context and who pick up on the obvious clues in the text, this novel in fact undermines the myth of Verne as prophet. This is first and foremost the case because it very explicitly addresses a nineteenth-century readership, whose cultural or artistic values provide a framework within which evocation of the 'future' can take place. The future it adumbrates is not a real future at all, but a vision above all of the nineteenth century itself. As Julian Barnes observed in his review of Richard Howard's translation for Random House publications in 1996, predictions about the future – most famously, Orwell's *1984* – invariably say more about the period in which they are made rather than the period to which they look ahead. And Barnes adds with an appropriate touch of acidity, given the difference between the truth of the text itself and the commercial imperatives that go with its re-editing: 'Naturally, someone at Random House believes that Jules Verne's *Paris in the Twentieth Century* […] is "an astonishingly prescient view into the future". We could hardly expect them to bill it as a "fairly interesting view into the past".' [20] But this is, in the event, exactly what Verne's novel does offer, and it does so quite explicitly. Its opening two pages, typically, contain anchoring references to mid-nineteenth-century values and issues (we should remember, of course, that its narrative present is in the 1960s, a vantage point from which it looks back): 'ce qui s'appelait le Progrès, il y a cent ans, avait pris d'immenses développements' ['what was called Progress, a hundred years ago, had now accelerated immensely']; 'ne soyons pas surpris de ce qui eût étonné un Parisien au dix-neuvième siècle' ['let us not be surprised by what would have astonished a Parisian in the nineteenth century']; 'Au dix-neuvième siècle, n'avait-on pas inventé les sociétés immobilières, les comptoirs des entrepreneurs, le Crédit Foncier, quand on voulut refaire une nouvelle France et un nouveau Paris?' (P20, pp. 29–30) ['In the nineteenth century, had they not already invented investment companies, managers' branches, and the Crédit Foncier when they wanted to create a new France and a new Paris?'] In so far as the twentieth century is visualised at all, it is seen

---

19 See for example chapter XII, 'Des opinions de Quinsonnas sur les femmes', pp. 139–50, a lament on the perfidy of woman. To the general lament with its obligatory reference to Eve, Verne adds a more specific localisation of woman's fall from grace in the nineteenth century, seen as a catastrophic period of transition in social values (p. 143). This is one instance among many of the way in which the text remains firmly anchored in representations of the nineteenth century.
20 Barnes, 'Back to the Future'.

as fundamentally dependent on the nineteenth century as its originating moment, and able only to look backwards to its beginnings there. The 'future' locates itself firmly in the past, and certainly has no future of its own towards which it looks.

Hetzel, who had already published *Cinq semaines en ballon* and was now steering Verne towards a new form of scientific and educational fiction, immediately felt that *Paris au XXe siècle* was an inferior work and said so in emphatic terms to his new protégé. 'Il n'y a pas là une seule question d'avenir sérieux [sic] résolue, pas une critique qui ne ressemble à une charge déjà faite et refaite', he wrote in his letter of rejection (P20, pp. 15-16) ['You have not answered a single serious question about the future, nor made a single criticism that does not look like a charge already made time and again']. He saw Verne's style here as anything but visionary, and very much more as a rehashing of standard clichés about the future. Certainly, if we are tempted to find anything of our own world in Verne's vision of a soulless and materialistic society, we should remember that his story of a young poet living in a world in which literature is dead was one of the great clichés of his own age.[21] Even where Verne does appear to offer an authentic vision of technological progress, he is not inventing, but using a method that serves him throughout his writing career: he simply rewrites what is already known and documented. What may sometimes look like a daring imaginative leap into the future is nothing more than the fruit of Verne's copious and compulsive note-taking from popular contemporary sources. It is wrong to claim, as Barnes does in his review, that Verne is essentially a 'techno-nerd' whose literary skills go into describing the clever simplicities of mechanical systems. On the contrary, there is virtually no descriptive skill involved here at all, since so much of what he writes is based on his pillaging of contemporary texts. However, far from covering this up and pretending to be the visionary he is not, he quite openly reveals it. His depiction of a metro system with driverless trains (pp. 43–46), of automobiles propelled silently by gas (pp. 46–47), and more curiously of a kind of fax technology (pp. 69–70) is a reworking of topical issues which he had read about in the press. The metro of *Paris au XXe siècle* is based on a system proposed by the geographer Adolphe Joanne: mentioned by name in the text, Joanne was the founder of the *Guides Joanne*, prototype of the later *Guides bleus*. Verne here describes an elevated railway in the American style rather than the

---

21 Chapter XIII, 'Où il est traité de la facilité avec laquelle un artiste peut mourir de faim au XXe siècle', pp. 151–66, is clearly Verne's own variation on the nineteenth-century theme of the poet starving in his garret.

underground one of the London system – where, by an interesting coincidence, the first underground trains had run in 1862 (Glaswegians claim that their own system was running before that). As for the so-called 'gazcabs', they are based on a gas motor invented in 1859 by Etienne Lenoir – also acknowledged in Verne's text – which became the blueprint for the modern internal combustion engine. By 1865, there would be some five hundred gas-powered carriages on the streets of Paris, a sign that the world was on the verge of huge technological change. Meanwhile the fax technology, which at first sight might seem like a futuristic bull's-eye on Verne's part, is in its turn a reference, as we are explicitly told, to a machine that had been devised by the Italian inventor Giovanni Caselli in the late 1850s. Caselli's pantelegraph, based on a system of signals transmitted through the electric telegraph which were then decoded by a receiver, can today be viewed in the *Musée des arts et métiers* in Paris. It attracted very considerable attention and was the subject of numerous newspaper articles. Napoleon III even visited Caselli's workshop and allocated funds to the development of his system, which ultimately failed for commercial, not technical reasons.[22] If Verne is able to evoke the existence of a sophisticated telecommunications system, it is not that he himself invents, but rather that he relies on his usual technique and refers through available sources to current knowledge and speculation.

As has often been said, Verne rarely if ever goes beyond what is actually known and documented.[23] Where there is uncertainty he opts deliberately for imprecision and vagueness, as will be the case in the description of the implausible electricity source which powers the *Nautilus* in *Vingt mille lieues sous les mers*. What is unknown is only glimpsed briefly in Verne's novels, and his world is largely one of unwieldy nineteenth-century contraptions put together with the textual means at the writer's disposal. In *Paris au XXe siècle* the vision of the future may include suggestions of electronic technology, but on the other hand it does not extend to the invention of steel-nibbed pens, and Verne has his hero Michel write with quaintly old-fashioned nineteenth-century quills. No suggestion here, either, of the advent of the typewriter which, patented in the US in 1868, was on the point of transforming commercial life as Verne was writing his text. The calculating machines are, we are told, like 'de vastes pianos' (pp. 68–69) ['huge pianos'], improbable instruments when compared with our modern laptops or credit card calculators,

---

22 For a full account of Caselli's pantelegraph see Julien Feydy, 'Le Pantélégraphe de Caselli', *Musée des arts et métiers. La Revue*, 11 (1995), pp. 50–57.
23 See for example Martin, *The Knowledge of Ignorance*, pp. 152–59.

though perhaps not so far from the computers of 1960 when Verne's story takes place.[24] But it is an uneven world that Verne presents, based on a collage of documents to which he had access, and the real interest of his technique is the placing of fiction within a framework of contemporary scientific debate and discourse. Fascinatingly, Verne provides an echo of his own time as he recycles and re-uses the texts available to him. This may be disappointing to the believers in a 'futuristic' Verne, but any assessment of his real quality as a writer must emphatically discard the false premise that he was the Nostradamus of the nineteenth century.

It is sometimes easy for the modern reader to forget that so much of the technology in Verne's novels was already in existence. Yet the apparent novelty of his world to the twenty-first-century reader is attributable not to the fact that it is uncomfortably close to our own – what could be further from modern space travel than those astronauts in *Autour de la lune* wearing top-hats and pouring a Côtes de Nuits to celebrate their release from the earth's atmosphere?[25] – but precisely because he draws attention to the phenomenal pace of change, and to the debate about the uses of technology in his own time. Vernian scholars have often pointed out, in a refutation which is by now standard, that the *Voyages extraordinaires* are far from being the work of a technological prophet.[26] And certainly, when we look at the corpus of Verne's work, it is clear that only a small number of his texts are, like *Paris au XXe siècle*, actually set in the future – the most notable being two which may not even have been penned by Verne himself, but by his son Michel: *La Journée d'un*

24 Verne's calculating machine also has a number of well-known models, the inventors of which (Perrault, Stanhope, Colmar, Mauret and Jayet) are cited in the text. The model to which it appears to bear the closest resemblance is the *arithmomètre* ['arithmometer'] devised by Thomas de Colmar (1785–1870), who has a well-established position in histories of computing as the inventor of the first commercially successful calculating machine. Colmar's machine, two metres long and capable of calculations of up to thirty digits, had been on display at the 1851 and 1855 Universal Exhibitions in London and Paris respectively.

25 'Enfin, pour couronner ce repas, Ardan dénicha une fine bouteille de Nuits, qui se trouvait "par hasard" dans le compartiment des provisions' (AL, p. 293) ['And finally, to crown the occasion of this meal, Ardan brought out a fine bottle of Côtes de Nuits which "by chance" happened to be in among the provisions']. On another occasion, Ardan brings out a bottle of 1863 Chambertin from his 'cave secrète' (AL, p. 475) ['secret cellar'].

26 Two examples among many of the now standard refutation in scholarly works of the popular view of Verne as prophet are Evans, *Jules Verne Rediscovered*, pp. 1–5, and Daniel Compère, *Jules Verne, parcours d'une œuvre* (Amiens: Encrage, 1996), pp. 82–83.

journaliste américain en 2889 and 'L'Eternel Adam'. We shall be returning shortly to these interesting and intensely problematic texts.

Since the myth that Verne's work is 'futuristic' is so tenacious despite the almost ubiquitous focus of the *Voyages extraordinaires* on the nineteenth century itself, we should ask why this is so. As Julian Barnes points out in his review of *Paris in the Twentieth Century*, we are all essentially indulgent of prophets and prognosticators. We want them to exist, and we want to believe them right. It is true that many readers simply *want* to see Verne as a soothsayer, and will not face the disappointment of having to revise their view of him. But another, perhaps more serious reason for this view of him is that in the nineteenth century the interest in technological or scientific change was itself suggestive of a spectacular new dawn. Science and technology were still considered innovative and magical, for they indicated the emergence of a new lifestyle which excited and fascinated people. The popularity of the *Expositions universelles* in the second half of the century, accompanied at various stages by those *Salons* which celebrated commercial or industrial achievements, is itself an indication that this century believed it was reaching out to new technological futures through its inventiveness and its industrial power. Verne's fascination with the machine is apparent throughout the *Voyages extraordinaires*, and almost unfailingly the machine is the symbol of the miracle of human progress.[27] As steam replaces sail for long ocean voyages, ships become particular objects of admiration for Verne – be they new and powerful warships, as in *Les Forceurs de blocus* (1865), or majestic oceanliners, such as the *Great Eastern* on which Verne himself travelled and which he describes fulsomely in *Une ville flottante* (1870). The future in Verne's work is rarely anything other than a concentration on the

---

27 On this point, see Vierne (*Jules Verne: Mythe et modernité*, pp. 77–88), who points out that Verne's attitude towards science is imbued with a sense of its miraculousness, and that in this he is very much a representative of his time. The point is made on more than one occasion by Verne himself. An interview published in the *Chicago Evening Post* on 25 March 1905, the day after his death, quotes him as saying: 'Ecrire une histoire du XIXe siècle serait un travail gigantesque pour un jeune lettré. J'entends par là que tout ce progrès, de la chandelle à la lumière électrique, de la diligence au train express qui roule à cent kilomètres-heure environ, est simplement si extraordinaire que la majorité des gens n'arrive pas à le comprendre.' ['Writing a history of the nineteenth century would be a huge task for a young scholar. What I mean by that is that all the progress made, from the candle to electric light, from the stagecoach to the express train which moves at around sixty miles an hour, is quite simply so extraordinary that the majority of people cannot grasp it.'] See Daniel Compère and Jean-Michel Margot (eds.), *Entretiens avec Jules Verne 1873–1905* (Geneva: Slatkine, 1998), p. 231.

magnificent, cornucopian present which promises so many possibilities. His particular originality as a writer, as we have seen, is to have introduced the mechanical or technological dimension into the literary text at a time when literature and science were still held to be puzzlingly incompatible. Whatever image of the future there is in Verne's work, it almost always remains fixed in nineteenth-century realities and beliefs.

As for the practical and ideological constituents of technological change in Verne's work, these are firmly grounded in the documents and discourses of his own era. Nemo's fantastic submarine is a textual construct based largely on records of developments that had already taken place. Peter Costello claims that by the year of publication (1869) of *Vingt mille lieues sous les mers* some twenty-five submersible craft had successfully taken to the water, and that the name *Nautilus* itself comes from a craft built by one Robert Fulton in 1800.[28] William Butcher points to the considerable number of titles of works in the late 1860s dealing with underwater vessels, and claims that craft named *Nautilus* were commonplace, including a vessel that Verne himself saw during his visit to the Paris *Exposition universelle* of 1867.[29] It is symbolically appropriate – for this underlines the essential bookishness and textuality of Verne's world – that the submarine's most important room is the fabulous and (as anyone who has visited a modern submarine will know at once) quite impossible library, containing no less than 12,000 volumes among which Aronnax finds all the canonical scientific works of his age. The *Nautilus* is less a feat of engineering than a collage of documents assembled by the author, who thus proceeds exactly as does the narrator of his tale, in a revealingly specular relationship. That modern Vernian enthusiasts should make drawings or models of the *Nautilus* in an apparently well-intentioned attempt to demonstrate its seaworthiness or the modernity of its design seems charmingly beside the point. Although it might in its unrealistic spaciousness be a good deal more comfortable than any modern submarine, the *Nautilus* would in reality be an impossible, implausible, impractical machine, even supposing it were capable of travelling an inch. To gain some perspective on the futility of electricity as a source of motor power, we need look no further in our own era than at the humble British milk float – in which phenomenally low speeds are matched by extremely limited running time – or perhaps at Sir Clive Sinclair's C5 single-person

28 Costello, *Jules Verne: Inventor of Science Fiction*, p. 102.
29 See the Introduction to *Twenty Thousand Leagues Under the Seas*, translated by William Butcher (Oxford: Oxford University Press, World's Classics, 1998), pp. ix–xxxi (p. xiv).

vehicle, that spectacular technological flop of the 1980s. As for Verne's
rocket in the lunar novels, its source of power is even less plausible, for it
is in fact a bullet that would have killed its inhabitants on take-off. Even
if they had survived that cataclysm, they would have died of cold or of
lack of oxygen in space, especially when they unthinkingly opened the
spacecraft's hatch. Later, in *La Maison à vapeur* (1880), the travellers cross
the Indian subcontinent in the most ungainly of contraptions – an
amphibious steam-powered vehicle in the shape of an elephant, which
draws carriages behind it like a train. And in *Robur-le-conquérant* (1886),
the flying machine which Robur constructs is a hybrid device, part-aero-
plane, part-helicopter, based on contemporary debate about the possibility of heavier-than-air flight. But like so many of Verne's vehicles, it is
'futuristic' only in so far as it proclaims a triumphant belief in the progress
of nineteenth-century technology, as evidenced in available texts. As
Verne realised, the easiest, cleanest, cheapest and most convenient way to
travel is in word, thought and text.

That Verne should have envisaged a form of literature which achieves
a fusion between contemporary journalistic or scientific documents and
the requirements of fiction is itself of far more interest than the quality of
the scientific vision he proposes. Yet that form of writing further anchors
him as a man who captured the mood of his century – a true nineteenth-
century believer in the role that science and technology must henceforth
play in every aspect of life, and a firm advocate of the very ideology of
progress. As a framework, then, nineteenth-century ideology wholly
determines the construction of Verne's so-called futuristic visions – not
only because his own century is held up as the birthplace of scientific and
technological innovation, but also because his belief in that originating
moment is itself such a powerful illustration of the nineteenth-century
positivistic beliefs on which the *Voyages extraordinaires* rest.

So in the very same gesture by which they suggest a vision of
progress, appearing to point to the future, Verne's texts also return us
firmly to the nineteenth century itself, with its cranky but often spectacular technologies and its grandiose but sometimes downright rickety
ideas. The vision of the future goes full circle and returns to an earlier era,
even as that earlier era presupposes a future which will remain fixated on
it. The outward journey – as so often in Verne's stories – is nothing other
than the journey home, and this appears to be true both of time and of
space. We have two temporal continents, and the only journey that can be
made between them is that of words and texts which shuttle back and
forth, with literature the vehicle that transports us from one place to
another. And since the journey into an unknown future is accomplished

in writing, Verne's subject is less the discovery of new worlds than the business of writing itself, in which the 'fiction' of the future enables him to revisit and make sense of the present, perhaps indeed to question its underlying ideologies. While the *Voyages extraordinaires* suggest progress towards the future, progress is also a turning back or, to use the expression which figures in the title of another Verne manuscript published in the latter stages of the twentieth century, a 'voyage à reculons' ['journey in reverse'].[30]

One striking instance in the Vernian corpus of a work which confronts two temporal zones in this way is the short story 'La Journée d'un journaliste américain en 2889', included in the posthumous 1910 collection *Hier et demain*. It seems appropriate to use the words 'the Vernian corpus' here, because it is certain that Verne's son Michel had more than a hand in this story, the first published version of which appeared in English in the American review *The Forum* in February 1889, under the title 'In the Year 2889'. Much has been written about Michel Verne's involvement in the later and the posthumously published writings of his father, and this is not the place to reopen that discussion.[31] However, critical debate about Michel's interventions, while conceding that their precise nature and extent is still a matter of uncertainty, acknowledges that many of his reworkings are well attuned to the corpus and must be treated as integral to it.[32] 'La Journée d'un journaliste américain en 2889' is, indeed,

---

30 *Voyage à reculons en Angleterre et en Ecosse*, édition établie par Christian Robin (Paris: Le Cherche Midi, 1989). The metaphor of moving backwards is central to this fictionalised account of the journey to Britain which Verne and his friend Aristide Hignard made in 1859. In 1862, Hetzel refused to publish the manuscript, which subsequently found its way into the extensive holdings of the Bibliothèque de la Ville de Nantes.

31 For a reliable account of Michel's role in his father's work, and a discussion of the various voices which resonate in the Vernian corpus, see Compère, *Jules Verne, parcours d'une œuvre*, pp. 58–62. The case of 'La Journée d'un journaliste américain en 2889' is complicated by its publication in both English and French. For comments on the role played by Michel in the writing of the first version, then in the rewriting of Jules Verne's own version of the story, see Piero Gondolo della Riva, 'A propos d'une nouvelle', in *L'Herne: Jules Verne*, 25 (1974), pp. 284–88.

32 As Compère puts it: 'Quelle que soit l'importance des interventions de Michel Verne sur les textes posthumes, il faut constater que ceux-ci prennent parfaitement leur place dans la série des *Voyages extraordinaires*' (*Jules Verne, parcours d'une œuvre*, pp. 60–61) ['Whatever the importance of Michel Verne's interventions in the posthumous texts, it has to be said that they fit perfectly into the series of *Extraordinary Journeys*']. The extent of Michel Verne's alterations to some of the unfinished texts of the *Voyages extraordinaires* has become clearer in the last twenty years, with the re-editing of a number of novels from the original manuscripts. Olivier Dumas, who has

a paradigmatic illustration of the Vernian future-in-the-past, or past-in-the-future. Like *Paris au XXe siècle*, it is actually set at a future date but addresses itself clearly to its present-day readership. The chosen year of its setting, 2889, is purely a function of the year of its initial composition and publication, 1889, and this story ostensibly depicting the twenty-ninth century is an examination of contemporary dystopian nightmares. It portrays a world in which the United States has become the universal political and commercial power, and – in a very nineteenth-century vision – the dominant colonising nation. Francis Benett, owner of the New York-based *Earth Herald* (formerly the *New York Herald*), spends his day visiting his offices in various locations, video-conferencing with his wife who has gone shopping in Paris, and totting up the profits made by his highly successful newspaper which is printed world-wide from electronic copy. It is a perfectly coherent vision of a capitalist and technological utopia (though perhaps Verne did not need to fast-forward by ten centuries to find it), a global village of which New York is the communications epicentre. Yet as in *Paris au XXe siècle* this representation is held up as a mirror of the nineteenth century with its colonising and positivistic ideologies, and it is here that the reader is constantly beckoned to find the seeds of any future world. In a vision which itself exemplifies the positivism of its age, the story positions the nineteenth century as the starting-point, that vital first moment of technological innovation. If new inventions are to be admired because they surpass earlier ones, then, by the same logic, earlier progress has also to be admired for what it made possible. As in the Parisian novel, there is a constant looking back to the time at which the text was written. In the early stages of the story, we come across phrases such as: 'A la fin du XIXe siècle, les savants n'affirmaient-ils pas déjà que...?' (HD, p. 188) ['At the end of the nineteenth century, were scientists not already claiming that...?']. From its remote location in time, the story envisions a nineteenth century that is astonishing and extraordinary. If it looks ahead to a new world, it nonetheless looks through it and back to the time of its writing and its initial readership. The journey in time is like the journeys in space described in *Autour de la lune* and *Hector Servadac* – an elliptical trajectory that returns the narrative to its own starting point.

The virtual world in which Francis Benett lives in 'La Journée d'un journaliste américain en 2889', conducting his online, on-screen

---

written prefaces to *En Magellanie*, *Le Beau Danube jaune*, *Le Secret de Wilhelm Storitz* and *Le Volcan d'or* (see the main bibliography), is considerably more severe regarding Michel's interventions.

relationship with his absent wife, may seem tantalisingly 'futuristic' to a twenty-first-century reader who is eager to see Verne as a man ahead of his time. But there is nothing new or original in Verne's speculations. Albert Robida's *Le Vingtième Siècle*, published in 1883, had already described an apparatus called the telephonoscope in some detail, and in a tone not dissimilar to Verne's own when he discusses such technologies. Here is what Robida writes:

> Parmi les sublimes inventions dont le vingtième siècle s'honore, parmi les mille et une merveilles d'un siècle si fécond en magnifiques découvertes, le téléphonoscope peut compter pour une des plus merveilleuses, pour une de celles qui porteront le plus haut la gloire de nos savants. L'ancien télégraphe électrique, cette enfantine application de l'électricité, a été détrôné par le téléphone et ensuite par le téléphonoscope, qui est le perfectionnement suprême du téléphone. L'ancien télégraphe permettait de comprendre à distance un correspondant ou un interlocuteur, le téléphone permettait de l'entendre, le téléphonoscope permet en même temps de le voir. Que désirer de plus?[33]

> [Among the sublime inventions that have brought honour to the twentieth century, among the thousand and one marvels of an era so rich in magnificent discoveries, the telephonoscope must be considered one of the most marvellous, one that will bring the greatest glory to our scientists. The old electric telegraph, that application of electricity in its early years, was ousted first by the telephone, then by the telephonoscope, which is the perfect final development of the telephone. The telegraph made it possible to understand a remote interlocutor or correspondent, the telephone to hear him, the telephonoscope to see him at the same time. What more could we wish for?]

What Robida calls 'l'ancien télégraphe' will in Verne's story be called 'cet appareil antédiluvien' (HD, p. 188) ['that antediluvian device']. The sense of amazing progress beyond what had existed even a few years earlier is very much of the late nineteenth century, and one of the ways in which such progress was measured by authors such as Robida and Verne was precisely their use of the 'flash-forward' technique. But in both cases, the evocation of the future is a means of returning to the present (which, in the stories' proleptic framework, becomes the past). Both authors were men of their century, recording the inventions and discoveries that had been taking place from the mid-1870s. Electrical communications apparatuses, in particular, had taken a huge leap forward in recent years under the impetus of inventors such as Alexander Graham Bell, whose telephone was patented in 1876, or Clément Ader, who, at the Exposition

33 Albert Robida, *Le Vingtième siècle* (Paris: Decaux, 1883), p. 53.

internationale de l'électricité in Paris in 1881, presented an apparatus called the *théâthrophone* ['theatrephone'], enabling remote listening to concerts taking place at the Opéra (an invention which would be used by Jules Verne for his descriptions of virtual concerts in *L'Ile à hélice*, published in 1895). With progress from the telegraph to the telephone, much experimentation was now also taking place in relation to the capture of images, some by Thomas Edison, and some by Bell himself, who in the late 1870s was working on an apparatus which Louis Figuier called the *télectroscope*. It was by no means unthinkable in such a climate to conclude that real-time sound-and-image communication was not far off, and there was feverish speculation about the possibilities it opened up. Somewhat later in Verne's *Le Château des Carpathes* (1892) the beautiful diva, La Stilla, is captured after her death on phonograph recordings that are combined with a crude projection using mirrors and her portrait. This is hardly cutting-edge, futuristic science (Edison and Cros had patented the phonograph as early as 1877). The visions of writers such as Robida and Verne are echoes of contemporary speculation – and sometimes, as in *Le Château des Carpathes*, even a little behind the times – rather than being the products of daringly original thinking.

The vision of the future itself in 'La Journée d'un journaliste américain' is therefore a sketchy one, and is held in check throughout by a preoccupation with that future's own past. So the journey to an unknown future, just like the journey to unknown spaces and places in so many of Verne's novels, leads back to what is known. If a new temporal dimension opens up, it returns us inexorably to the old, and the idea of forward movement is itself a constant journey in reverse. The text is merely a fiction of the future that displays its own fictional quality and returns us to the nineteenth century. There is, as I have suggested, an obsession throughout Verne's work with his own century as both a culminating and an originating moment. Many of his stories lead up to, and end in, a narrative present which is usually also the moment of their real-life composition. The present is the pinnacle of human achievement. Yet if the present is so alluring, it is partly also because it has the ability to appeal to the future as the guarantor of its own spectacular quality. The American train in which Phileas Fogg travels in *Le Tour du monde en quatre-vingts jours* epitomises the magic of modern engineering – magic indeed, for the train actually leaps across an open gulf at Medicine Creek where a bridge has collapsed, defying all the laws of physics and mechanics in the process. The train here represents the triumph of civilisation over nature, the future over the past. It symbolises the taming of wild expanses through the willpower of the engineer, that most revered of figures in the *Voyages extraordinaires*. This apotheosis of human ingenuity suggests that the present is itself a kind of future, for the train is a place where everything can now be considered possible. Ordinary 'wagons' are no longer mere 'wagons' in this dawning technological utopia. Notice the tenses in the following sequence: 'Les voyageurs *pouvaient* circuler d'une extrémité à l'autre du convoi, qui *mettait* à leur disposition des wagons-salons, des wagons-terrasses, des wagons-restaurants et des wagons à cafés. Il n'y *manquait* que des wagons-théâtres. Mais il y en *aura* un jour.' (TDM, p. 225, my italics) ['Passengers were able to move from one end to the other of the train, which provided them with saloon carriages, terrace areas, restaurant cars, and café compartments. All that was missing were theatre carriages. But they will come, one day.'] Here is the predictive moment, the future tense surrounded by imperfects, and thus firmly located within the admiration of a magical previous era. So too, for Michel Ardan in *De la terre à la lune*, present and future are united, cohabiting simply in the tenses of his speech at Tampa Town: 'On *va* aller à la Lune, on *ira* aux planètes, on *ira* aux étoiles, comme on *va* aujourd'hui de Liverpool à New York, facilement, rapidement, sûrement' (TL, p. 166, my italics) ['We shall go to the moon, we shall go to the planets, we shall go to the stars, just as today we go from Liverpool to New York, easily, quickly, safely']. The future is already with us, and it is nothing other than the present.

Yet, in the confrontation between two temporal zones in the *Voyages extraordinaires*, there is also a dark hint at absurdity, and herein lies much of the richness and the complexity of Verne's narrative mode. Just as the quest for conquest of new territories leads back to its starting point, and just as the search for new knowledge ends up in a repetition of the old, so too the vision of the future leads back to the past even as the past looks out to its own future. In this journey of departure and return, past and future stand face to face, reflecting and referring to each other in a potentially infinite vacuum. As we have seen in 'La Journée d'un journaliste américain en 2889', the future is an extrapolation from the past and constantly looks backwards to it. Meanwhile, the past looks out to the future. That self-referring relationship between two tenses will be exacerbated – very nearly to the point of absurdity – in one of the most curious works in the entire Vernian corpus, 'L'Eternel Adam'.

Like 'La Journée d'un journaliste américain', 'L'Eternel Adam' was included in the posthumous collection *Hier et demain*, though it had not benefited from prior publication during the author's lifetime. Commentators are aware that Michel Verne's role in this story was considerable. Yet its interest is precisely in the fact that it pushes the Vernian structure of a future-in-the-past to its absolute limit, and to that extent it has been seen as continuous with, and deeply revealing of, one of the underlying prob-lems of the *Voyages extraordinaires*.[34] In a footnote on the first page, Michel Verne as 'editor' of his father's text states that the story was writ-ten by Jules Verne in his final years, and that 'cette nouvelle offre la par-ticularité de tendre à des conclusions plutôt assez pessimistes, contraires au fier optimisme qui anime les *Voyages extraordinaires*' (HD, p. 213) ['this story has the particular characteristic of leading to somewhat pessimistic conclusions, contrary to the proud optimism which characterises the *Extraordinary Journeys*']. Yet it could be said that the story does no more than lay bare the pessimism which is implicit in so many of Verne's novels, *Paris au XXe siècle* included. There is always the possibility, or the danger, of an infinitely recurring journey between the two temporal points, a meaningless shuttling back and forth, finding the justification for the present in the future and the meaning of the future in the past. The title of 'L'Eternel Adam' is itself an ironic and quite specific echo of the Niet-zschean idea of eternal recurrence. The story projects us twenty thousand years into the future, where a scientist-philosopher, the 'zartog' Sofr-Aï-Sr, reflects on his own period of history as the apotheosis of civilisation. In his view, human knowledge – in very positivistic fashion – strides for-ward on the strength of previous discoveries and, as its insights accumu-late, it is able to delve ever more deeply into the past where it finds the cause and the explanation of its own superiority. Although mysteries remain, the 'zartog' believes in the possibility, one day, of total knowledge and revelation through the power of the human mind. He feels sure that such knowledge will justify his view of history as an ascending move-ment.

Yet the 'zartog' knows too that documents of previous civilisations have been destroyed, and that total knowledge will ultimately come only from delving back into the archive of earlier civilisations. Only out of the past does the future (now the present) emerge – yet another illustration of the centrality in Verne's writing of the quest for the past and of the search

---

34 Two Anglo-Saxon critics who make much of the place of 'L'Eternel Adam' in the *Voy-ages extraordinaires* are William Butcher (see *Verne's Journey to the Centre of the Self*, especially pp. 75–93, where it is suggested that the structures of return and recom-mencement are pushed to the limit), and Andrew Martin (in *The Knowledge of Igno-rance*). As Martin points out, 'L'Eternel Adam' gives the lie to the Vernian idea of progress towards the future, since far from 'ascending a ladder into a cornucopian future, [humankind] is trapped in a futile iterative loop' (p. 148). A complete exami-nation of the place of 'L'Eternel Adam' within the thematic structure of the *Voyages extraordinaires* as a whole has been carried out by Jean Roudaut, 'L'Eternel Adam et l'image des cycles', in *L'Herne: Jules Verne*, 25 (1974), pp. 180–212.

for lost origins, and another example of the way in which so many of the journeys of the *Voyages extraordinaires* are journeys backwards in time. One day in his investigations the 'zartog' discovers by chance a record of a previous civilisation, a civilisation which, as it turns out, had acquired all the knowledge and certainties of his own age. His belief in progress, his certainty that his own age is the culmination of man's struggle to dominate nature with knowledge and power, is completely shattered. He is now forced to recognise that, far from ascending progressively to perfection, history is cyclical. A major part of this text includes, in an appropriately specular fashion, an earlier text which documents the end of a previous civilisation. The real story is the 'story within the story', a *mise en abyme* of the very writing process itself which displays its own origins and methods. As in so many of Verne's works, the text of the future is based on the documents, the texts, and the materials of the past upon which it is entirely dependent. But in 'L'Eternel Adam', inner and outer texts – the past and the future – mirror each other in endless self-reference, for each leads up to and completes the other. This is the void of eternal recurrence, the admission of the potential absurdity of all writing and all progress, where text becomes the echo of all previous texts, the text-within-a-text, the unending repetition of a lost origin.

Verne's view of writing, indeed his very writing practice, is thus absolutely at one with his view of human progress. The journey into unknown regions is a journey in words and time that is also a journey back to the point of departure. All that writing can ever be is a palimpsest, each text a mere layer in the infinite accumulation of documents, unable to do anything more than acknowledge its enclosure within a proliferating system. In such an acknowledgment, text becomes deeply self-conscious, and Verne's writing heralds the anguish that would later be expressed by Jorge Luis Borges in a memorable 1941 story entitled 'The Library of Babel'. In Borges's story there is a library containing all the books ever written, but there is no infallible way of locating what you want, no hierarchy of knowledge, no progression through learning (not even Borges could predict a system as wonderfully efficient as Google). Various systems and superstitions are propounded; then, one day, someone proposes a regressive method. In order to locate book A, first consult book B which indicates A's position. But, to locate book B, you must first consult book C, then book D, and so on. This of course leads nowhere but backwards – but backwards is the only way forwards. The quest for knowledge itself is, in Borges's story, a regression into infinitely diminishing returns.

'L'Eternel Adam' foreshadows that epistemological wasteland expressed so powerfully by Borges and others. It underlines the lurking and expressive anxiety in so much of the *Voyages extraordinaires*, and suggests why Verne's writing is so modern. If the explicit ideological project is to stress the forward movement of history and the fabulous onward strides of human progress, then the method of asserting such an ideology ends up by reversing it. Writing needs to look backwards to its own sources if it is to measure the extent and the scope of the particular journey it undertakes. Like Axel and Lidenbrock who delve into the archive of the past in the depths of the earth whose centre they wish to reach, the Vernian explorer must return to his origins as a precondition to finding the future. As Macherey writes, in a striking insight into Vernian narrative structure: 'L'anticipation ne sera que la recherche des origines. Ainsi, la structure de la fable est toujours ramenée à un modèle très simple: la marche sur les pas de quelqu'un d'autre, et elle est en fait l'histoire d'un retour.'[35] ['Anticipation will be nothing other than the quest for origins. Thus, the structure of the story is always brought back to a very simple model – the process of following in someone else's footsteps – and it becomes the story of a return.'] Therefore the forms which the text takes on mirror those of the adventures it recounts. Every text becomes a journey into its own past and its own intertexts, and as it is poised on a knife-edge between the known and the unknown, the recycled and the new, it runs the constant risk of being overrun and invaded by its own antecedents. It is a problem with which Flaubert too will wrestle long and hard as he writes *Bouvard et Pécuchet* from the early 1870s through to his death in 1880. Verne's massive borrowings from the *Grand Larousse* and elsewhere for the lists of marine life in *Vingt mille lieues sous les mers* are one sign among many that the extraordinary fictions he creates are at permanent risk from all manner of predators – not least the words they wrest free from other texts and other places, and which threaten to come back and gobble them up. Like Flaubert, he discovers in this paradox the very essence of writing, with the fundamental questions this raises about ownership and originality. Since text is everywhere, everything has been said and there can be nothing new. The writer's journey into the unknown can only make use of what is known, and while it tries to be a creative remix, it faces the peril of its own repetitions. This is the hostile textual environment Verne deals with and attempts to appropriate.

Through its vision of technological and ideological progress, Verne's work does suggest a powerful belief in the future. But, as we have seen, the very logic of his system is at best paradoxical, at worst potentially self-destructive. It is precisely because the present is so magically

---

35 Macherey, *Pour une théorie de la production littéraire*, p. 215.

anticipatory, so quintessentially forward-looking, that any future it suggests leads inexorably back to it. But the logic of this position is that the present too has a past towards which it must turn, and that in the end there may nowhere be a locus of meaning or sense. All we have is perpetual displacement, the endless *différance* of the textual journey. Perhaps this is one reason why so many of Verne's journeys deviate from their quest. In *De la terre à la lune* the astronauts go round the moon and back to the earth. In *Voyage au centre de la terre*, Axel and Lidenbrock are spewed out of the earth's crust as they delve deeper into its volcanic past and its immeasurable secrets. If, in Verne's system, only the past can explain the present or the future, then the future – indeed, time itself – must always look backwards. But this also accounts for the richness and the fascination of his writing, and gives it a subtlety and a complexity that are so sadly missed by those who would see in his work a straightforward act of prediction. The journey forwards into new and unknown places is, by the same token, the anticipation of a return, a nostalgic revisiting via some speculative outside vantage-point of distant pasts which will explain the mysteries of humankind's engagement with our own environment. That journey is quintessentially a textual one, for it is built with words and out of words, and it refers constantly to its own verbal status.

Chapter 3

All the World's a Text

Jules Verne's writing is, as we have seen, firmly grounded in the ideologies and concerns of his own century. But, whether it focuses on hunting and the environment, or on the quest for total coverage of the globe, or on notions of progress and the future – those three key areas highlighted in the last chapter – his writing consistently unveils the complexities and the ambiguities of its own nineteenth-century framework and, crucially, re-enacts these in its textual practices. Writing mirrors the environment in its proliferation and profusion, yet mimics the attempt to contain and control it; writing re-stages the contradictions of the century's encyclopaedic ambitions, by aiming for totality yet recognising its fragmentedness; and, in its representation of the future, writing deconstructs the nineteenth century's notions of temporality and progress. While Verne ostensibly subscribes to the first principle of realism – that the world can be represented objectively through words – it rapidly becomes apparent that his writing is itself the symbolic locus of the struggles and conflicts that it purports to describe. Ostensibly a window on the world, writing also turns back on itself and problematises its procedures, even as it grapples with the great themes and subjects of its century.

Not least among the paradoxes facing the reader of Verne is the recognition that this writer, who uses so much scientific and factual information as the basis of his fiction, believes perhaps less than any other so-called realist novelist in the objective validity of his verbal representations. The novel, negotiating and recycling the 'text' of reality, is an extravagantly textual construct that puts its own verbality, sometimes its own verbosity, on display. Language itself may never be more than a representation or an image, a copy, a paltry fiction, even a distortion in the Vernian world. However, the existence of what lies beyond language, or is incapable of being linguistically defined, has no place either for the novelist or for his characters, as Michel Ardan makes clear when challenged about the difficulties of covering the distance between the earth and the moon. 'La distance est un vain mot, la distance n'existe pas!' he exclaims (TL, p. 169). ['Distance is a futile word. Distance does not exist!']

If distance itself – that most fundamental and real of obstacles – cannot be considered anything other than a word in the nineteenth-century space traveller's lexicon, then it is clear that there will never be any escape from language. The Vernian explorer may have to navigate round the physical obstacles of a material reality, but above all else he must chart a path through the language that lies in his way, and he must deal with the verbal representations of which he is both the recipient and the purveyor. The world is a text, both metaphorically in that it has to be 'read' and understood, and literally since it is so extensively constituted of written documents. Words are everywhere; text is ubiquitous. Nature herself is a vast dictionary full of wondrous and exotic terminologies.

Words are, then, both the object and the medium of Verne's representations. Fiction is the relaying and the recasting of multiple intertexts, the novel a dramatisation of language itself as much as the representation of a physical journey. Daniel Compère, who more than any other critic has emphasised the polyphonic, composite nature of the Vernian text, puts it thus: 'Assimilant une multitude de discours extérieurs, Verne fait texte de tout et intègre à la littérature les éléments les plus disparates qui doivent se couler dans un discours unique, mais plurivoque'[1] ['Assimilating a multitude of external discourses, Verne turns everything into text and integrates into literature the most disparate elements, which must meld together in a single, though multivocal discourse']. Vernian writing is about the assembling of different texts in the creation of fiction, and is truly a celebration of its own multiplicity. The task of the forthcoming pages will be to look more closely at this overtly textual quality of Verne's universe, and to focus on some of its components by way of bringing out more fully that unique resonance and 'texture' of the *Voyages extraordinaires*.

Textual sources and working methods

Crucial to this aspect of Verne's writing is the extensive use of written sources throughout his career as a novelist. Verne was a compulsive reader and note-taker, and his basic working method was to create novels out of the vast patchwork of data that he amassed patiently and elaborately on a daily basis.[2] His task was much like that of the scholar, digesting a range

1 Compère, *Jules Verne, parcours d'une œuvre*, p. 40.
2 Verne's working methods have been fully described by Compère in *Jules Verne écrivain*, pp. 42–46. What follows here is a recapitulation of the essentials, by way of emphasising the intensely textual nature of his medium.

of different texts, condensing his knowledge into note form, then working from those notes and re-ordering, rewording, recasting or re-using them as appropriate. As is the case with other realist novelists, the notes are part and parcel of the preparatory dossiers that go through numerous stages of refinement until the final work is wrested from them. But in Verne's case the sources often remain openly on display, either because he refers explicitly to them, or indeed because he conspicuously writes in different modes and assumes the voices associated with different forms of text (scientific, journalistic, pedagogical, and so on).[3] And what singles Verne out from his contemporaries is the extent of his reliance on written material in the construction of his novels, rather than the on-the-spot research that was carried out by, say, Flaubert when he travelled to Tunisia in order to revisit the site of Carthage as he was embarking on the writing of *Salammbô*. Verne works from text, through text, and back into text, in a circular process that rarely takes him far from his verbal medium. His preference for written material over practical research is, in the first instance, a matter of simple expediency, as explained in the well-known interview published in the *Chicago Evening Post* the day after his death: 'Je pense qu'une lecture attentive des ouvrages les plus documentés sur n'importe quel sujet nouveau vaut mieux que l'expérience concrète, du moins lorsqu'il s'agit d'écrire des romans. Un bon livre sur les coutumes et mœurs d'un pays ne peut être écrit qu'après des années de séjour, alors que moi, au mieux, je ne pourrais y effectuer qu'un rapide voyage.'[4] ['I consider that an attentive reading of the most carefully documented works on any new subject is better than concrete experience, at least when it comes to writing novels. A good book about the habits and customs of a country can be written only after many years there, and for my part, I would be able to make only a brief trip there at best.'] The admission that textual documents may provide only second-hand knowledge does nothing to detract from the inestimable advantages they have for the novelist researching the background of his stories, for it means that Verne's material is already in the target medium. Cynics might claim that this renders it easier to recycle, a major bonus for a prolific scribbler in a hurry to move on with his task. Yet anyone who looks closely at Verne's

---

3 Verne's use of different textual voices is discussed by Michel Foucault in 'L'Arrière-fable'. For Foucault, scientific discourse in particular appears in the Vernian text as a foreign element which breaks into the story and takes over. This is paralleled by the status of the scientist figure as an outsider who comments and provides knowledge to the others. I shall further discuss Foucault's view of scientific discourses in Chapter 6.

4 Compère and Margot (eds.), *Entretiens avec Jules Verne 1873–1905*, p. 232.

use of source material will see that it is in some way always reworked and recast, even where the novelist wishes to retain the tone and tenor of the original text. And where a text appears to have been indiscriminately 'lifted', it is almost always accompanied by an implicit metatextual comment about the use of sources, the compositional process, and the status of the fiction that results from it. The act of borrowing raises quite as many questions as it answers, and returns us repeatedly to the issue of the textual construction or reconstruction of reality. This is no doubt one of the many reasons why Verne's work has increasing fascination for a postmodern literary community.

But more than this, there is throughout Verne a sense of the magic of text, and this too might help to explain why the guidebook, the manual, the newspaper article or personal eye-witness account is given such high value in the writing process. It may be, as Barthes claimed in his famous chapter of *Mythologies* ('Nautilus et bateau ivre'), that Verne is the ultimate armchair traveller, but Verne more than once gives palpable expression to the excitement of verbal, bookish tourism. Text is the *open sesame* that unlocks the power of the imagination and enables the reader-writer to 'see' his world with greater acuity. Text becomes in some sense more 'real' than reality itself – one of the reasons, perhaps, why Rimbaud among others succumbed to the fascinations of Verne (a point that Barthes, of course, recalls in the title of his own chapter, echoing Rimbaud's most famous poem).[5] There is the sense that the incantatory or symbolic representations of text have an extraordinary and overwhelming intensity; and perhaps, too, a feeling of amazement that a few hieroglyphics and symbols, carefully arranged on the page, can in themselves conjure up such a vast range of human experience and knowledge. Text with its adjuncts (for example, illustrations or maps) produces that magical sense of plenitude so powerfully described by Baudelaire in the last poem of *Les Fleurs du Mal*, 'Le Voyage': 'Pour l'enfant, amoureux de cartes et d'estampes, / L'univers est égal à son vaste appétit' ['The child in love with maps and prints / Finds the world equal to his vast appetite']. Yet the power of text is also often suggested in very practical, straightforward terms by Verne. At the beginning of Chapter 6 of *Clovis Dardentor*, the narrator points out that tourism in the Balearics would be absolutely unnecessary for anyone who has seen a copy of the work on this region by Archduke Louis-Salvator of Austria: 'Il suffirait de s'enfermer dans

---

5 On Rimbaud's uses of Verne, see M. Lacroix, 'Présence et influence de *Vingt mille lieues sous les mers* dans l'œuvre poétique de Rimbaud', *Bulletin de la Société Jules Verne*, 148 (2003), pp. 2–51.

une bibliothèque [...], d'en lire le texte si complet et si précis, d'en regarder les gravures en couleurs, les vues, les dessins, les croquis, les plans, les cartes, qui font de cette publication une œuvre sans rivale' (CD, p. 68)[6] ['It would suffice to lock yourself up in a library, to read this full and accurate text, to look at its colour prints, its pictures, its drawings, sketches, plans and maps, which make of this volume a work without equal']. He thus suggests that text, complemented by maps and illustrations of various kinds, creates a more complete perception of the region than would be possible by travelling through it.

In the *Chicago Evening Post* interview cited above, Verne gives further insights into his bookish approach, explaining: 'Je lis tous les ouvrages scientifiques qu'on publie. En bref, tout ce qui peut m'intéresser sur le marché du livre. Je suis également abonné à tous les journaux scientifiques.'[7] ['I read all the scientific works that are published. In sum, any books on sale that might interest me. I also have a subscription to all the scientific newspapers.'] Writing starts with the act of reading and annotating, and this process provides above all the factual and scientific detail that will be included. One of the best-known descriptions of this process was provided by the American journalist Marie Belloc, who published an interview with Verne in the *Strand Magazine* in February 1895.[8] The journalist translates the novelist's remarks to her thus: 'As to the accuracy of my descriptions, I owe that in a great measure to the fact that, even before I began writing stories, I always took numerous notes out of every book, newspaper, magazine, or scientific report that I came across. These notes were, and are, all classified according to the subject with which they dealt.' And Belloc herself, in a description of Jules Verne's library, gives a graphic account of the reality of the processes which produced Verne's famous card-index system: 'The room is lined with bookcases,' she writes, 'and in the middle a large table groans under a carefully sorted mass of

---

6 Archduke Ludwig Salvator, 1847–1915 (Louis-Salvator in Verne's novel) was a nephew of Emperor Franz Joseph of Austria. He was the author of a number of important geographical studies, and the work on the Balearics to which Verne refers received a medal at the Exposition Universelle of 1889. In an interview published in *Le Gaulois* on 28 October 1895, Jules Verne gives an account of a meeting he had in July 1884 with the Archduke in Venice. See Volker Dehs, 'Une interview ignoré de Jules Verne', forthcoming in *Australian Journal of French Studies*, 42.3 (2005).

7 Compère and Margot (eds.), *Entretiens avec Jules Verne 1873–1905*, p. 232.

8 Marie A. Belloc, 'Jules Verne at Home', *Strand Magazine*, 9 (February 1895), online at http://www.math.technion.ac.il/~rl/JulesVerne/belloc/. The interview has been translated back into French and included in Compère and Margot (eds.), *Entretiens avec Jules Verne 1873–1905*, pp. 99–109.

newspapers, reviews, and scientific reports, to say nothing of a representative collection of French and English periodical literature. A number of cardboard pigeon-holes [...] contain the twenty-odd thousand notes garnered by the author during his long life.' Though essentially correct, this needs a little qualification. Apart from the fact that Verne did not read English fluently (though he did read German) his index cards were usually thrown away once used. This was for very obvious reasons, as he explained to Hetzel *fils* in 1896: 'Vous comprenez, par crainte de me répéter, je déchire ces notes quand elles m'ont servi'[9] ['You understand that, for fear of repeating myself, I tear these notes up once I have used them']. This means that Belloc's figure of 20,000 is more likely a guess at the number of index cards that Verne had in use just at the time of the interview (probably the autumn of 1894, according to the editors of *Entretiens avec Jules Verne*).[10] However, the huge number of notes that Verne must have used overall — for the index card was one of the basic tools of his craft throughout his long career — serves to underline the primacy of reading and documentation in his method.

As for the actual material that Verne read and annotated, the picture we have is a very clear one, for he himself declared to Belloc that he had subscriptions to all the mass-circulation scientific and geographical publications of his day such as *Le Magasin pittoresque, Le Musée des Familles, Le Tour du monde, La Science illustrée* and others. Many of these reviews were composite publications which included literature, reviews, scientific information and general knowledge. The subtitle of *Le Musée des Familles* gives an indication of the typical range of its contents: *Monde pittoresque. Religion. Morale. Sciences. Littérature. Beaux-Arts. Actualités, etc.* A number of Verne's own early stories appeared in this very review (notably 'Un voyage en ballon', 1851, and 'Martin Paz', 1852). Later, many of the major novels in the *Voyages extraordinaires* were serialised in Hetzel's own *Magasin d'Éducation et de Récréation*, a particularly successful example of the popular review, which Verne also received and annotated for his own purposes. This underlines not only that Verne had a huge appetite for reading, but also that it was fundamental to his compositional approach. The major difference between Verne and Flaubert or, perhaps, Zola was that he concentrated largely — though not exclusively — on the popular side of the publications market. By and large, this goes also for his reading of works by contemporary scientists, where he chose to focus on works by the likes of Louis Figuier, Jacques Arago and Camille

---

9   Quoted by Compère in *Jules Verne écrivain*, p. 43.
10 Compère and Margot (eds.), *Entretiens avec Jules Verne 1873–1905*, p. 99.

Flammarion, all of whom had massive reputations as scientific popularis-
ers.[11] Yet it is clear too that he read and was deeply influenced by, among
many others, Darwin, Cuvier, Fourier, Proudhon and Saint-Simon, and
that he had an immense literary culture as well. These diverse readings
reappear not only as references, but also as points of discussion or as trig-
gers for Verne's own plots, which themselves are so often constructed
around the reading of texts. Darwin is a major presence – for example, in
Voyage au centre de la terre where the question of evolution is central,
though there is also a kind of anti-Darwinism in *Le Village aérien*, where
the scientist Dr Johausen is integrated into a primitive tribe of ape-men –
while Saint-Simon, Fourier and Proudhon are all explicitly referred to and
criticised in *En Magellanie* (M, p. 141).

Crucially, then, the Vernian text is constructed through a process of
grafting, in which the author's readings are exploited and recycled. This
is a two-way process. Not only is Verne's own text conspicuously grafted
onto other texts, but these other texts in their turn are grafted onto it. The
overt borrowings and citations are a constant reminder that the representation of reality is above all textual. Every text that purports to be 'about'
reality has in its turn to negotiate and contend with a host of other texts,
as well as to contend reflexively with its own status as text. Rather than
hide this truth, Verne displays it, sometimes in a playful and overtly
experimental mode that is reminiscent of Barbey d'Aurevilly's deconstruction of 'plot' in *Les Diaboliques*.[12] But Verne's foremost tactic is to
quote known authoritative sources at length, and to situate his own narrative within a context of scholarly debate and discussion. He joins in the
erudite discussion, weaving a path through its known landmarks, frequently moving beyond the plot and onto an altogether different level of
discourse. A typical example of this is in the description of the Amazon
in *La Jangada*, Part I, Chapter 5. Here, two young men, Benito and
Manoel, are poetically enthusing about the river's qualities when, in a

---

11 Louis Figuier was the author of many works of scientific vulgarisation, ranging from
    La Terre avant le déluge (1863) – a major source for *Voyage au centre de la terre* – to *Les
    Merveilles de la technologie*. Jacques Arago was a traveller, scientist and geographer,
    whom Jules Verne met in Paris in 1851. Already blind, Arago continued to travel and
    write in the encyclopaedic tradition, and finally died in Brazil in 1885. Camille Flam-
    marion, best known as the founder of the Société Astronomique de France in 1887,
    was also the author of the massively successful *Astronomie populaire* (1879) which,
    coincidentally, helped to establish his brother Ernest's still famous publishing house.
12 For more on Barbey's experimental style, with comparisons to Verne, see Timothy
    Unwin, *Textes réfléchissants: réalisme et réflexivité au dix-neuvième siècle* (Oxford and
    Bern: Peter Lang, 2000), pp. 153–65.

characteristic move, the Vernian narrator steps in and takes over. Speaking, as it were, 'over the characters' heads', he describes the Amazon in scholarly and pedagogical fashion and comments on the texts about it. The discourses from within the diegesis give way to a heterodiegetic discourse, in a move that represents both a clash of opposing narrative modes, and a transition from one to the other. The narrative voice itself broadens into a more general 'voice of science' (this is the *arrière-fable* ['background fable'] of which Foucault speaks)[13] – the discourse of the scholarly expert conversant with the texts and authorities on the subject. In truth, there is not simply one scholarly discourse here, but a whole network of different ones, so that even as science takes over from the voice of the omniscient narrator, science itself fragments into multiple voices. But Verne always proceeds with texts in hand and citations at his fingertips. Notable among the authorities the narrator quotes directly – because he was a contemporary figure whose work was well known – is the Swiss scientist Louis Agassiz, who in his early years studied under Cuvier, and who published an account of his exploration of the Amazon in a work entitled *Voyage au Brésil* (1868).[14] But to the name of Agassiz he adds those of the earliest European explorers, dating back to the sixteenth century, and then gives details of expeditions by Humboldt and a host of more recent travellers to the region. The texts of travel and discovery are legion, but Verne's referencing of the best-known and most respected authorities is a typical strategy. The insertion of travellers' comments, either verbatim or paraphrased, gives 'scientific' discourses a constant presence within fiction and suggests continuity between its different levels, as well as reminding us that travel is above all a textual affair.

But at certain moments, the voices of science take over entirely from the narrative – or are entirely appropriated within it, which is perhaps the same thing. In *Hector Servadac*, Part II, Chapter 9, there is a lengthy wholesale quotation from Camille Flammarion's *Récits de l'infini* – which we are told the learned young lieutenant Procope reads in the Russian translation – on the subject of the relative ages of the planets (HS, pp. 392–94). Similarly, at the beginning of Part III of *Mathias Sandorf*, there is a long direct citation from Michelet about the Mediterranean: 'La Méditerranée est belle, surtout par deux caractères: son cadre si harmonique, et la vivacité, la transparence de l'air et de la lumière... Telle

13 See Foucault, 'L'Arrière-fable'.
14 Jean Louis Rodolphe Agassiz (1807–73) studied in Paris under Cuvier in 1831–32 and made his reputation with the publication of *Recherches sur les poissons fossiles* (1833–44) and his study of glacier formation, *Etude sur les glaciers* (1840). He emigrated to the United States in 1846 and took up a professorship at Harvard in 1848.

qu'elle est, elle trempe admirablement l'homme. Elle lui donne la force sèche, la plus résistante; elle fait les plus solides races.' ['The Mediterranean is beautiful, especially in two of its facets: its beautiful setting, and the vivacious, transparent quality of the air and light. Such as it is, it waters the human species perfectly. It gives that hard strength, the most resistant of all, and it creates the firmest of races.'] Such borrowings, far from being a sign of some narrative weakness, reinforce the central impression in the *Voyages extraordinaires* that wherever there is travel, and wherever there is writing, we shall find the imprint of previous journeys and previous texts. So the use of other texts reinforces a vision about travel and the text, because it suggests that every 'journey' (be it in words or in physical space) depends on many other journeys. By bringing in the murmur of many voices, Verne makes that murmur into a central component of his own unique voice as a novelist, and he underlines the essential truth that every text is, in some way, a palimpsest.

Reading, writing, and the circulation of texts

If reality has no apparent substance beyond words and language in the Vernian world, it follows that the most crucial of qualities are, first and most obviously, the ability to speak and to engage in dialogue, and second, the ability to read and write. The nineteenth century's discoveries and advances on all fronts remain, almost by definition, an absolutely closed book to the illiterate. In a century which witnesses the massive democratisation of reading and writing, Verne plays a central role in promoting the merits of literacy, and he does so with obvious pedagogical intentions, as Arthur Evans has demonstrated in his study of the *Voyages extraordinaires*.[15] Time and again in Verne's work we come across characters who save themselves and their companions by their ability to read, to write and to reconstitute the 'text' of their world. Indeed, the reader's value-judgment of a character often depends on that character's mastery of the skills of literacy. The point can sometimes be taken to absurd extremes, for example in the case of Dingo the writing dog in *Un capitaine de quinze ans*. Of all the intelligent animals we find in the *Voyages extraordinaires* (and there are many) Dingo must surely be the one who takes first prize. Found on the wrecked hull of a ship at the story's outset, he soon proves his intelligence by his continuous hostility towards a character named Negoro, whose scheming and skulduggery he is able to signal

---

15 Evans points out that book knowledge and writing, especially, are placed centre-stage as practical skills in Verne (*Jules Verne Rediscovered*, pp. 47–48).

to his human companions. The latter, in their turn, are able to 'read' what
Dingo tells them. But one day, Dingo does even better. From a set of
wooden play-bricks, he picks out those marked with the letters S and V,
and puts them in order. Prompted by this cue, the ship's captain then tells
the story of Samuel Vernon, a French explorer who had set out from West
Africa to cross that continent two years previously. Since it was in West
Africa that Dingo had been found, a search is now launched for a lost
explorer who will also turn out to be Dingo's first master. The plot will
thus turn on nothing less than the dog's literacy skills. This is Verne at his
most mawkish, no doubt. But every writer is allowed his lapses, and the
point is nonetheless proven: literally everything can depend on reading
and writing.

Not all of the principal actors in Verne's stories have quite such an
intuitive mastery of text as this clever canine, though almost unanimously
they recognise its merits and advantages. Such is the case of the first-
person narrator of *Le Chemin de France*, Natalis Delpierre, who, having
remained illiterate well into adulthood, recounts in the course of the story
how he learned to read and write. Apart from its interest as one of the rare
historical novels in the *Voyages extraordinaires* (the action here is set in
1792), this story is also exceptional in its recounting of a journey back to
France rather than, more typically, outwards to the remoter corners of the
world. Crucially, however, it chronicles the developing literacy of
Delpierre under the guidance of the Keller family whom he accompanies
on their perilous journey to the homeland. Without the ability to write,
Delpierre would not be able to tell the story or to achieve his goal of
explaining a two-month absence during a period of military leave. Since
different accounts of Delpierre's absence are in circulation, and since he
wishes to challenge them, his story is in every sense a textual negotiation.
Yet it is also – and significantly – the account of the emergence of the very
skill which enables that negotiation to take place. Thus, the 'real' story of
Delpierre's journey is accompanied by a metatextual commentary on its
own coming into being as text. It is a story that explores its own beginnings, and in this sense it is deeply self-reflexive.

Negotiation and interaction with the world is here a matter of writing, but in other instances, the process can just as easily be based on reading, since the two activities are so closely related. The young hero of *Un
capitaine de quinze ans*, Dick Sand, is ruefully aware that his education is
defective since he went to sea before he had a chance to complete his
schooling. However, as a good and worthy citizen of the world, he recognises that knowledge acquired through books is essential to survival, and
he has made strenuous efforts to instruct himself as fully as possible in his

own time. Conversant with a number of important texts, he uses this bookish knowledge at key moments of the narrative, and it turns out to be a vital tool in his survival kit as he finds himself in charge of a ship adrift on the high seas. When the group of castaways unexpectedly ends up on West African soil, 'Dick Sand se souvint alors, et fort à propos, de ce qu'il avait lu des voyages de Livingstone' (C15, p. 306) ['Dick Sand then remembered, and at just the right moment, what he had read of Livingstone's journeys']. Somewhat later, as they are about to be taken to a slave market at Kazonndé, we read: 'Dick Sand, au courant des faits de la géographie moderne, connaissait assez exactement ce que l'on savait de Kazonndé' (C15, p. 354) ['Dick Sand, aware of the facts of modern geography, had a fairly precise idea of what was known about Kazonndé']. Clearly this is a case of serendipitous reading and an ability to recall it at the right moment, but with other heroes in Verne, reading matter is chosen with a specific aim in mind. In *P'tit-Bonhomme*, Part II, Chapter 4, the young hero buys a tourist guide entitled *Guide du touriste aux lacs de Killarney* when sent out by his master, Count Ashton, to find something interesting that the count might read. Not unreasonably, since they are travelling to the Killarney region, P'tit-Bonhomme imagines that this should be the ideal book, perfectly attuned to the circumstances. Count Ashton, however, has already distinguished himself in the story as a self-ish, superficial and ignorant fool. For him, reading in order to interact more fully and more profitably with the world he sees is not on the agenda. The chapter digresses into a series of reflections about good and bad tourism, and we are informed that P'tit-Bonhomme does not understand that some people, like Count Ashton, 'ne voyagent que pour dire qu'ils ont voyagé' (PB, p. 237)[16] ['travel simply in order to be able to say that they have travelled']. For P'tit-Bonhomme, however, the book now affords an excellent opportunity to learn about this region, since Count Ashton himself angrily rejects the suggested reading matter. Already the model tourist, curious to instruct himself about the history and particularities of the area and open to the beauties of nature at all times, P'tit-Bonhomme is able to supplement his natural tourist's instinct with the knowledge that comes from a text, thus increasing exponentially his

16 The phrase carries interesting echoes of Baudelaire's lines in 'Le Voyage', the final poem in *Les Fleurs du Mal*: 'les vrais voyageurs sont ceux-là seuls qui partent/Pour partir' ['real travellers are those who set out for the sake of setting out']. However, there is a world of difference between Baudelaire's journeying for its own sake (because travel is the quest to capture a dream rather than to arrive at a destination) and Verne's criticism of those who travel merely in order to say that they have done so.

ability to 'see' the world. In its later stages, the chapter broadens out to an authoritative account of this region – some of it focalised through P'tit-Bonhomme himself, some of it given by an omniscient narrator. This shift of focus has been achieved precisely through P'tit-Bonhomme's own interest in a book. His reading thus has visible consequences for the narrator's manipulation of the story. Built explicitly on another text, this episode of the novel grafts both metafictional discourses and non-fictional, geographical discourses onto the ongoing narrative. It shows us once again how Jules Verne's style works in a composite manner, bringing together different levels and styles of discourse in a single sweep.

However, in the case of many of Verne's major characters, the reading process has been deeply ingrained since their earliest youth. They have acquired a vast range of references and resources – akin to Verne's own index-card system – into which they can delve and retrieve information almost at will, processing it accordingly in their travels and adventures. Samuel Fergusson, the first great Vernian polymath, is the ultimate reader-traveller, for whom knowledge and geographical discovery go hand in hand. Wherever they are, it seems, Fergusson is able to intersperse his conversation with disquisitions and anecdotes about the people, mores, climate, conditions and history of the region, or with historical accounts about the conflicts, struggles and expeditions that have taken place there. This astonishing power of recall, which will be a feature of so many of Verne's heroes, makes of the character both a reader and a narrator. And, often, the trigger can be something apparently trivial, as with the following 'text' that Fergusson spontaneously assembles when Joe points to a strange-looking group of trees that he is unable to recognise:

> Ce sont des baobabs, répondit le docteur Fergusson; tenez, en voici un dont le tronc peut avoir cent pieds de circonférence. C'est peut-être au pied de ce même arbre que périt le Français Maizan en 1845, car nous sommes au-dessus du village de Deje la Mhora, où il s'aventura seul; il fut saisi par le chef de cette contrée, attaché au pied d'un baobab, et ce Nègre féroce lui coupa lentement les articulations, pendant que retentissait le chant de guerre; puis il entama la gorge, s'arrêta pour aiguiser son couteau émoussé, et arracha la tête du malheureux avant qu'elle ne fut coupée! Ce pauvre Français avait vingt-six ans! (5S, pp. 86–87)

> ['They are baobabs,' replied Dr Fergusson. 'Look, there is one whose trunk could be a hundred feet in circumference. It may be that the Frenchman Maizan perished at the foot of that very tree in 1845, for we are above the village of Deje la Mhora where he ventured alone. He was seized by the local chief and tied up at the foot of a baobab. The ferocious Negro slowly cut his joints as the war chant rang out, then started on the throat, stopped in order

to sharpen his blunted knife, and ripped off the unfortunate man's head before it had been severed! That poor Frenchman was twenty-six years old!']

Fergusson's ability to recognise a baobab tree that he has never yet seen, and to tell its 'history' so comprehensively, is a conspicuous endorsement of the benefits that come from learning. The episode exemplifies that appropriation of the wilderness, down to its last details, by a European civilisation with its cherished belief in the need to record and pass on all knowledge. Fergusson himself is a man who appears to think in paragraphs and to reproduce ready-made 'chunks' of text, though often (as here) with a dose of drama that no doubt makes history more exciting and interesting to Verne's young readers. Fergusson's sources, if not explicitly quoted, are always implicitly there in the background, somewhere along his trajectory like those of the Nile in search of which his journey had started. The use of the past historic tense in this episode is one of several markers that point to its textual origins. A man of vast reading, he has updated himself fully before his departure on this voyage. Some of his sources are, interestingly, given in the text itself, and they include the *Bulletins de la Société de Géographie de Londres* (the title given interestingly in French); or the atlas published by Petermann entitled *Der Neuester Entdekungen* [sic] *in Afrika* (this volume containing the accounts of journeys by Burton and Speke, Barth, Guillaume Lejean, Baikie and others); or, finally, the improbably transcribed *The sources of the Nil* [sic], *being a general surwey* [sic] *of the basin of that river and of its heab* [sic] *stream with the history of the Nilotic discovery by Charles Beke, th. D* [sic] (5S, p. 88). But even where Fergusson's own sources are not revealed, it is clear that his knowledge and his remarks come from texts, and they are recycled in a form which itself often has the hallmarks of the learned text or lecture. He is a walking, talking manual, a text-man par excellence. Like Verne with his index-cards, he works from text and back into text, and at times it seems as if the actual journey in a balloon is a mere adjunct to the real adventure of reading and writing in which Fergusson is so deeply involved.

Throughout the *Voyages extraordinaires*, and from Verne's earliest stories onwards, we also find characters actively engaged in the business of writing – memoirs, scholarly or scientific reports, diaries and journals, logbooks and so on. In some cases, writing is simply a part of the character's normal activity: Aronnax and Lidenbrock, for example, are authors and teachers who produce texts as part of their professional duties, while Axel takes notes for another purpose, that of maintaining a logbook of events during the journey down the Snaeffels crater. In other cases, writing is a secret, possibly even a guilty activity that must be hidden, since it is indicated that the outcome of the story may depend on the textual revelations that the character produces. Throughout the corpus, however, the act of writing is represented as a *mise en abyme* of the storytelling process itself: it is often the 'story within a story' that is constructed in order to suggest an alternative to the official or accepted version of events. Such is the case in one of Verne's earliest novels, the unfinished *Un prêtre en 1839*, written between 1845 and 1849, in which the former bellringer Joseph is represented as engaged intensely in writing a secret text. What this text contains is, though, something that not even the reader finds out. The manuscript of the novel was abandoned by the young Verne at a point when his two heroes are about to reveal the contents of Joseph's text in their own rewritten version. However, what we do know is that the writing of this text is Joseph's lifeblood, the one activity to which he still attaches importance. He is represented as deeply involved in that act of writing: '[Joseph] écrivait. Sans cesse. Le soir, une lumière tremblotante vacillait à la lucarne de la logette: Joseph réfléchissait à sa table; le matin puis le soir le retrouvaient à la même place; [...] il ne semblait tenir à la vie que par un lien, une seule intimité le retenait à cette terre qu'il avait l'air de détester.' (P39, p. 61) ['Joseph wrote. And he did so without ceasing. In the evening, a flickering light swayed in the skylight of his garret. Joseph sat thinking at his table. Morning, then the next evening, found him at the same spot. He seemed to hold on to life by one link. Only one bond kept him on this earth that he seemed to detest.'] Much later, the image of a man writing a memoir which is to him a matter of life and death will return with the character of Joam Garral in *La Jangada*. Pursued for a murder that he did not commit, Garral had fled from Brazil to Peru and, under a new identity, had lived as a farmer and raised a family there. However, on his first return to Brazil since the events of his previous life, he is determined to clear his name. Aboard the 'jangada', a massive river-craft constructed to transport his family down the Amazon through Brazil, Garral shuts himself away in his cabin and writes for his life: 'De ce qu'il écrivait ainsi, il ne disait rien, [...] et cependant cela prenait déjà l'importance d'un véritable mémoire' (J, p. 120) ['Of what he was writing, he said nothing, and yet it had already assumed the proportions of a real memoir']. What we subsequently learn is that Garral is hoping to present this memoir to the judge who was in charge of the case, and to clear his name. The clash of different accounts of the same event, such as occurs in stories like this one or in *Les Frères Kip*, where the innocent are wrongly accused and convicted as a result of a false version of events having circulated, puts the whole question of text and storytelling centre-stage, since it makes it apparent that the same events can be worked into quite different stories. The act of writing in which figures such as Garral engage is crucial to their survival. Their lives and their well-being depend on a text, so in that sense text is their reality.

At regular intervals in the *Voyages extraordinaires* we are confronted with a problem of credibility, when narrators write in circumstances that are not conducive to the production of text, or at least not of the text that they deliver to us – for example, when the writer is starving on board a raft (as is the case of the narrator Kazallon in *Le Chancellor*), or when he is in darkness (as in *Face au drapeau*, where the narrator Simon Hart is held in captivity in a confined space and cannot even see what he is writing). The case of Axel is a particularly interesting one. In Chapter 33 of *Voyage au centre de la terre*, he claims to be reproducing his notes word for word in the narrative that we read, having been asked by Lidenbrock to take charge of the logbook entries. But, rapidly abandoning the style of the logbook and forgetting the adverse conditions in which he had to write, Axel launches into a description of his famous 'dream', in which prehistoric animals come to life. In this, one of the most famous episodes of the novel, it is clear that he has exceeded his brief and stepped well outside his diegetic space. Now these are problems that often arise in the case of first-person narratives, but if Verne sometimes strains the conventions to the very limits of plausibility it is because of his insistence on the centrality of that process involving the consumption and/or production of texts. Many characters in the *Voyages extraordinaires*, in addition to the first-person narrators, are also producers of texts, as we have seen. They write in circumstances which are sometimes not plausible, creating texts which themselves can be the object of a quest or a conflict in the subsequent development of the plot, or indeed the subject of further texts. If Verne's characters engage so consistently in the business of writing, it is often because others before them have produced texts on which their own texts can build, or because they intend their own texts to be instrumental in the creation of a new 'story'. They understand and accept implicitly that texts will circulate endlessly. The difference between consumption and production, or between reading and writing, is often minimal, because texts appear both as sources and as products of the story. Writing – like the extraordinary journeys it represents – involves both the retrieval of known sources and the creation of new documents which, in their turn, will go into circulation.

It has sometimes been observed that Jules Verne's texts appear to depend on the presence of other texts to get them going.[17] But, implausibly, this suggests difficulty and even implies that it was a tactic used by Verne to overcome writer's block. Patently, from what we know about Verne's writing habits, he never had the slightest difficulty either in planning his stories or in writing them out. So if he uses other texts at the outset — notably, for example, the cryptogram which has to be solved at the beginning of *Voyage au centre de la terre* before the explorers can set off on Arne Saknussem's traces, or the cryptogram which, read in three different ways in *Les Enfants du capitaine Grant*, sends the travellers off on three different searches — then surely it is because he wishes to draw attention to the fact that the story participates more generally in the circulation of texts of all kinds. Text emerges from text, interacts with it, and often returns to it at the end. In the course of a novel, many other texts are evoked and placed on display, some of them threatening to engulf or overshadow the very fiction which gives them space. Texts are always emphatically there in Verne, and usually from the very beginning of his stories. In such circumstances, it is understandable that many of the great adventures of the *Voyages extraordinaires* are sparked off by the reading of newspaper articles or other reports which point to the traveller's own textual engagement with a textual world. Fogg's calculation that he can get around the world in eighty days is made on the basis of an itinerary that he has seen in the *Morning Chronicle*, and his subsequent 'travel ledgers', in which he lists the distances covered and the time lost or gained, are essentially an elaboration (albeit in accounting mode) of this initial text. In *Vingt mille lieues sous les mers*, the hunt for the *Nautilus* is undertaken not only because of the fact that a gigantic object has been seen patrolling the seas, but more importantly because of the heated debate and discussion that has ensued in the newspapers. But the newspaper reports are, in the first instance, assessed alongside the more serious writings of Cuvier, Lacépède and others on the subject of marine monsters, so that the characters are emphatically involved with texts and their evaluation from the outset. The point is reinforced by the presence of Aronnax, a scientist and oceanographer who has gained credibility as an author on the subject, aboard the expedition to find out what the

17 On this subject, see in particular Martin, *The Mask of the Prophet*, pp. 27–54. Pointing to the example of the cryptogram as a typical case of Vernian dependency, Martin extends the point and argues that the authority of Verne's texts is often undermined by the presence of source material. This very negative view of indebtedness in Verne makes few concessions to the ways in which he problematises the question of borrowing, or exploits the idea of the circulation of texts.

Nautilus is. And with the early mention of Moby Dick, questions are implicitly asked too about 'literature' itself, and about the boundaries between fact and fiction. As soon as we find ourselves in a textual world, it is implied, we are likely to be involved in fictions. Fiction is everywhere, even in scientific text, just as scientific texts are so manifestly present in fiction. Aronnax is the master of ceremonies who ensures permanent continuity in this story between the texts of science and the text of fiction.

And just as Verne's stories appear to emerge from the many textual documents that circulate, so too at the end they frequently lead on to the production of new texts, with these texts in their turn generating further ones, and so on potentially ad infinitum. The new texts can, it is true, be circulated in oral as well as in written form, or both, and in some cases several different types of text simultaneously break out from the story. These may take the form of memoirs, or scholarly works, or public lectures, or even stories that are recounted and which, we are led to believe, bear an uncanny resemblance to the one we have just finished reading. At the end of *Voyage au centre de la terre* we read that the account of the travellers' underground adventures circulates under the title *Voyage au centre de la terre*, and that it has a fate apparently similar to that of Verne's own novel: '[Il] fit une énorme sensation dans le monde. Il fut imprimé et traduit dans toutes les langues; les journaux les plus accrédités s'en arrachèrent les principaux épisodes, qui furent commentés, discutés, attaqués, soutenus avec une égale conviction dans le camp des croyants et des incrédules.' (VCT, p. 391) ['It had a massive impact with the reading public, and was printed and translated into every language. The most respected newspapers disputed the rights to print its principal episodes, which were analysed, discussed, attacked or defended with equal conviction in the camps of both believers and sceptics.'] Is this a *clin d'œil* on the part of the author, a prediction about the fate of his own text? If so, it is one of the rare predictions that he got right! More importantly, however, the ending of the novel is a deliberate completing of the textual circle, suggesting that the new account in its turn becomes the subject of further readings, investigations and verifications, in a never-ending process of textualisation and re-textualisation. The point is made even more emphatically in *Cinq semaines en ballon*, where the various 'texts' that ensue from the balloon journey across Africa include newspaper articles about it, and a highly colourful version of events that is circulated by Joe. Then there is also the mandatory public lecture by Fergusson at the Royal Geographical Society which becomes the official account of the journey. But, as the final paragraph of the novel points out, just as Fergusson's report has provided the opportunity to control and refine the findings of Barth, Burton, Speke and others, so too this record of events will in its turn be subjected to the same processes, when new explorers return to the same region and come back with further accounts: 'Grâce aux expéditions actuelles de MM. Speke et Grant, de Heuglin de Munzinger, [...] nous pourrons avant peu contrôler les propres découvertes du docteur Fergusson' (5S, p. 362) ['Thanks to the expeditions currently being undertaken by Messrs Speke, Grant and Heuglin de Munzinger, we shall soon be able to verify Dr Fergusson's own discoveries']. The same or a similar journey will, it is implied, be undertaken by new explorers, who in their turn will write it up and turn it into a new text. The new texts, though dependent on previous texts, will also build upon and refine them endlessly, varying the findings in a process which is destined never to achieve completion though it constantly strives for perfection. And, equally, within that very process lurks the anxiety that it will ultimately prove regressive. This, as we saw earlier, is the fear expressed in *L'Eternel Adam*.

So the story, having emerged from texts and been supported by them throughout, finally returns into circulation as a text itself – sometimes indeed as the story we have just read. At the end of *Voyages et aventures du capitaine Hatteras*, Clawbonny's study of 'The English at the North-Pole' [sic] is published (CH, p. 622), the title bearing a remarkable resemblance to that of the first part of the novel itself, *Les Anglais au Pôle Nord*. Aronnax, for his part, claims in the final stages of *Vingt mille lieues sous les mers* that he is putting the finishing touches to the narrative we have just read: 'Je revois le récit de ces aventures. Il est exact. [...] C'est la narration fidèle de cette invraisemblable expédition.' (VML II, p. 614) ['I am now looking back over the story of these adventures. It is accurate. It is a truthful account of this improbable expedition.'] Much later Palmyrin Rosette, in the concluding chapter of *Hector Servadac*, publishes a memoir 'qui contenait [...] le récit des propres aventures de Palmyrin Rosette' (HS, p. 527) ['which contained the account of Palmyrin Rosette's own adventures']. But the diversification of the preceding story into different forms and media is also very common in the *Voyages extraordinaires*. Typically, at the end of *Deux ans de vacances*, the logbook kept by Gordon is published and sells widely, but in a further permutation this text itself becomes the basis of lectures given by another of the story's main participants, Doniphan. Subsequently, newspaper articles discuss and report the narrative in yet another form, so that the adventure is finally seen to circulate in various arenas where it is the subject of much comment and debate. As well as reinforcing the point about the essentially linguistic nature of our interaction with the world, the process of metatextual distancing serves a dual aesthetic and moral purpose here – the first by providing an exit and offering closure as we move beyond the diegesis, the second by showing as part of this very process that further lessons are drawn from the foregoing narrative. But although this may appear to seal off the story and to establish a boundary between its diegetic conclusion and its subsequent retelling, or between the text of the story and the 'reality' of the reader's world, that boundary is also seen to be crossed. As so often in Verne, bold transitions are made between different levels of discourse, creating a continuum between them and giving a very modern and self-conscious feel to his conclusions. Another typically self-referential example is the final line of *Les Frères Kip*, where the narrator, distancing himself from his own storytelling act, achieves closure through the mirroring of the story in his metatextual commentary on it: 'Tel est le dénouement de cette cause célèbre, – exemple fort rare, d'ailleurs, des erreurs judiciaires, – et qui eut un si grand retentissement sous le nom de *l'Affaire des Frères Kip*' ['Such was the outcome of this *cause célèbre* – a rare example, indeed, of judicial error – which, under the name of *The Affair of the Kip Brothers*, had such a major impact']. It is as if, going beyond fiction, the narrator creates a new fiction in the process, since his commentary now focuses on 'the story of the story'. The circulation of the text is ensured by another text, and the story begins all over again. Once more, we see Verne's fiction turning in on itself and appearing to go right back to its own origins, in the very image of circularity. But circularity is another mode of circulation.

While the beginnings and endings of Verne's novels are particularly rich in examples of the circulation of text, and if they demonstrate the interdependency of the story and its own textual sources, the presence of texts of all kinds is, as we have seen, attested throughout his writing. Such is the importance given to the interpolation of other texts that Verne is capable of veering quite suddenly, and often at crucial moments of the narrative, into overtly citational mode. It seems that the high profile given to 'text' at these critical points is itself an enthusiastic demonstration of the principle that no writing exists in isolation, that every narrative is surrounded by a host of other texts that permanently threaten its autonomy. Yet Verne accepts and indeed celebrates the inevitability of invasion, and rather than attempting to place his own writing in a literary fortress, he takes the risk of opening the gates to all-comers. Texts of all kinds are thus able to make frequent or indeed random incursions into his narrative. While this might appear as a threat to narrative stability or coherence, the process of investment by other texts also produces additional layers of meaning and a reflection on text itself. One striking example of this occurs when, in *Le Tour du monde en quatre-vingts jours*, Aouda is introduced into the narrative. As she returns to consciousness after her rescue in extremis from a suttee, the reader naturally senses the need for some kind of comment by the narrator about this beautiful woman and, more particularly, about Fogg's reaction to her. The conventional approach would be to focalise events through Fogg, but that is precisely what Verne refuses to do (in part because Fogg's thought processes are destined to remain inscrutable to the end). But there are other ways round the problem. What Verne does is have his narrator conspicuously hide from view and to allow the relaying of another, more exotic text, to perform the narrative function at one remove. Here is the moment at which he does this:

> Mrs Aouda commençait à revenir à elle [...] et ses beaux yeux reprenaient toute leur douceur indienne.
>
> Lorsque le roi-poète, Uçaf Uddaul, célèbre les charmes de la reine d'Ah-méhnagara, il s'exprime ainsi:
>
> 'Sa luisante chevelure, régulièrement divisée en deux parts, encadre les contours harmonieux de ses joues délicates et blanches, brillantes de poli et de fraîcheur. Ses sourcils d'ébène ont la forme et la puissance de l'arc de Kama, dieu d'amour...' (TDM, p. 108)

> [Mrs Aouda was beginning to return to consciousness, and her beautiful eyes were regaining their Indian softness.
>
> When the poet-king Ussaf Uddaul celebrates the charms of the queen of Ahmehnagara, he expresses himself in these terms:
>
> 'Her lustrous hair, divided into two regular halves, surrounds the harmonious shape of her delicate, white cheeks, so brilliantly polished and fresh. Her ebony eyebrows have the shape and the force of the bow used by Kama, the god of love, to fire his arrows...']

On one level, this intervention might be interpreted as an admission of failure by a novelist who, by his own admission, found it difficult to portray love in his novels. As Verne wrote to Hetzel in 1866:

> Je suis très maladroit à exprimer des sentiments d'amour. Ce mot-là seul 'amour' m'effraye à écrire. Je sens parfaitement ma gaucherie, et je me tortille pour n'arriver à rien. Aussi, pour esquiver la difficulté, je compte être très sobre de ces scènes. Vous me demandez de mettre *un mot du cœur* en passant! Rien que cela! Mais il ne me vient pas, *ce mot du cœur*, sans quoi, il y serait depuis longtemps![18]

> [I am very clumsy at describing sentiments of love. The very word 'love' fills me with dread at the thought of having to write it. I am perfectly aware of

18 In Dumas, Gondol della Riva and Dehs (eds.), *Correspondance inédite*, vol. I, p. 40.

my lack of skill, and I struggle desperately with it to no effect. And so, to get round the difficulty, I try to be very sparing with these scenes. You ask me to put in a *word from the heart* in passing! Is that all? The problem is that the *word from the heart* just does not come, otherwise it would have been there a long while ago.]

On another level, however, the tactic can be interpreted as a playful gesture by the elusive narrator, who makes it clear by his use of another text precisely how beautiful Aouda is and precisely how aware Fogg is of her beauty, and thereby gives the answer to the questions that the reader has implicitly asked. Beyond this, however, we might see an overt deconstruction of the narrative process, indeed a pointing up of the essentially conventional nature of the love intrigue as a requirement in such stories. If we want to know what Fogg's reaction to this beautiful woman is, Verne appears to be saying, we need only go as far as the historical celebration of love in literature. Almost any text will do, for there are so many instances of the poeticisation of love in words. Since the present story, it is further implied, has little to do with 'real' events in a 'real' world, but everything to do with the recycling of other texts, the best way that this narrative moment can be expressed is through the exaggerated use of another text. It is true that the example chosen by Verne conveys a sumptuously exotic image of beauty, and that it is particularly suited to the evocation of the beautiful Indian widow. However, the very exoticism of this text also highlights the abruptness of its introduction (the paragraph beginning 'Lorsque le roi-poète...' almost brutally challenges the reader to fill in the gaps and make up for what is unsaid). It draws attention to the fact that this is a textual strategy, a grafting of the story onto another text – or the grafting of another text into the story – by way of showing up its status as a textual artefact. The borrowing of another text thus has precisely the effect of reinforcing the notion that texts circulate at all times and that every narrative, every journey, uses them as a way to move forward. It is the high profile given by Verne to this idea that gives his narrative approach such a strikingly original quality and, let it be said, such problematic consequences.

The underlining of the textual nature of our reality does not, however, rely uniquely on the direct citation of sources in Verne. There are many different forms of text that make their incursions into the Vernian narrative, some of them improvised accounts such as the stories told by Joe in *Cinq semaines* or by Ned Land in *Vingt mille lieues*. While improvised texts do not rely on the use of particular, identifiable sources, they do gesture in the direction of well-known conventions, and often they will visibly compact multiple sources into a single account. In this sense they are recognisable products of or variations on a particular genre, and they draw attention to their links with it. In *Claudius Bombarnac*, the hero of the story makes the acquaintance of a Major Noltitz, a Russian army officer who speaks perfect French and who at every opportunity acts as guide and chaperone to the narrator, explaining the background, customs and history of the places they are passing through. Noltitz clearly has a phenomenal amount of knowledge – and, like so many of Verne's characters, a prodigious memory to rely on – which he reproduces in guidebook form for the narrator's benefit. Whether he is talking about the cities they pass through, the history of the railway, or the geographical and economic features of the various regions along its route, Major Noltitz continuously acts as a traveller's textbook, a speaking manual that is constantly open. Generically, his speech almost never leaves the category of travel manual, and in that sense it is a clear affirmation of its own dependence on textual sources and its reproduction of them. But this repetition and relaying of sources, aided by an exceptional power of recall, is perhaps most spectacularly exemplified in the figure of Paganel in *Les Enfants du capitaine Grant*, who dazzles his interlocutors with an extraordinary range of knowledge, most often reproduced in the form of the school textbook or manual. At critical points of the narrative, Paganel's improvised 'texts', like those of Major Noltitz, remind us of the problematic link between reality and language – or of the fact that our reality is linguistically constructed – and of the dependence of every account on multiple previous accounts. Like the journey undertaken by the intrepid travellers in that novel, text itself is a revisiting of places where others have been and whence they have returned to tell the tale.

The image of text as expedition or exploration, undertaken in the traces of previous journeys which are repeated or re-used as necessary, is nowhere clearer than in a highly colourful and dramatic episode in Part II, Chapter 6, where Paganel makes a bet with Mac Nabbs that he will be able to cite the names of fifty travellers who have influenced the history of the exploration of Australia. In the dizzying account that follows (ECG I, pp. 339–48), Paganel draws upon all his memorised knowledge to provide a schematic survey of the navigation of Australian coasts, and of the expeditions into the interior of the island-continent. Stringing together the names with loose and spontaneous narrative, usually a few words about the explorer's main achievement, he creates an entirely original and hugely entertaining account – the more so since, having reached the mark of fifty names, he continues to cite further explorers and finally arrives at a figure of 72, comprehensively winning his bet. What makes Paganel's account so interesting is his unabashed strategy of lifting and recycling material from the history books that he has read. A recital such as this could not take place unless it pointed in a conspicuous way to its own dependence on the books and sources in which the adventures referred to are documented. So Paganel's own journey through the names of Australian navigators and explorers is also a self-proclaimed journey through known textual territory, following the accepted and adopted routes, willingly and enthusiastically re-using established accounts to do so. It is, in every sense, a *répétition*, a rehearsal of what is known and has been learned, a bringing together of many different texts into a single discourse. But the fact that Paganel is recycling what he himself has read does not make his own improvised 'text' any the less exciting or spontaneous, and this episode reads as one of the funniest and liveliest in the novel. Punctuated by Mac Nabbs's growing anxiety that he is going to lose possession of his prized shotgun as a result of this wager, Paganel's recital is also regularly interrupted by the count of the current total of names, a job that has been assigned to the young Robert Grant. And when, finally, he has reached a figure of 56 names, Paganel then goes into negative enumeration with the remaining sixteen, telling Mac Nabbs that he has *not* recounted the stories of Duperry, Bougainville, Fitzroy, Wickam, Stokes and others. The obvious implication here is that the number of possible new narratives is endless, and that Paganel's story, though based on finite information, could in theory continue ad infinitum. For even though it may be dependent on previous texts, narrative is effortlessly self-generating, infinitely flexible. Thus does this crucial episode make the point that original narrative can also be a repetition and a recycling of its own sources, and that it can and should use this dependency to its own advantage. Here, it seems, is one of the most triumphant demonstrations that we will find in the *Voyages extraordinaires* of Verne's belief in the essential bookishness and textuality of our world. Like a hyperactive talking textbook, Paganel is a showman to the last and uses to his advantage the very feature that might on the face of it seem to militate against effective and original narrative: namely, the borrowing of previously used material for his own stories. He is an illustration of the endless circulation of text.

'Books' and how to read them

Throughout the *Voyages extraordinaires* the presence or the echo of the written word is fundamental. Books themselves abound, and, as physical objects, become the focus of many of Verne's stories. And where text is not graphically present in writing and words, it remains cognitively present in the characters' verbal interaction with the world. Reality is capable of ever-renewable textualisations, and is overlaid with endless discourses and words. It follows that there is no absolute path through and out of this textual jungle, only infinite possible paths within it. When Paganel relays the texts of Australian exploration, his performance suggests that in this cornucopian world of stories there is a multitude of possible variations on every narrative, all of which can go into further circulation in a never-ending process of verbal substitution and replacement. However, the dream of totalisation will never be realised, for Paganel's own account, it is suggested, is subject to the control and scrutiny of subsequent versions of events, and these in their turn will be submitted to a similar process. No single account can have the monopoly of truth; books and texts will circulate ceaselessly.

The point will be reinforced when Paganel and his travelling companions meet a young Aborigine named Toliné (Part II, Chapter 13). Toliné, who had been sent to a missionary school in Melbourne, is symbolically carrying that book among books, the Bible, a copy of which had been presented to him at the school as a geography prize. But the Bible is soon forgotten for a while. At the mention of geography, Paganel shows an interest in the Aborigine, who suggests that he question him on his knowledge. In the ensuing episode (ECG II, pp. 471-75) it turns out that Toliné too has an excellent memory and has learned his lessons well. The problem is, however, that his learning is based upon skewed books and manuals — to which he has, it seems, accorded the same veneration as to his Bible. For Toliné has learned an Anglocentric and demonstrably false version of geography, in which French territorial possessions have virtually no place, while the British colonies seem to have expanded to fill almost all the known parts of the globe. Under the persistent and increasingly stupefied questioning of Paganel, Toliné explains that Europe is under British rule, and that Spain, Russia, Prussia, France and other countries are mere provinces rather than states. France herself, according to Toliné, is ruled by a governor, Lord Napoleon, from his base in Calais. To the nonplussed suggestion from Paganel that perhaps even the moon is a British possession, Toliné replies with solemn certainty that one day it will indeed be part of Her Majesty's dominions.

The lesson here is that, while knowledge can be relayed in many different ways and based on many different sources, there is nonetheless good knowledge and bad knowledge. While our reality may be textually determined and may offer many different narrative pathways, the world is not simply a Babel of discourses in which there is no right and wrong. Toliné himself may have lost his way (without realising it) in a world of

Anglocentric discourses as a result of a biased education; but, Verne seems to be saying, the textual nature of our knowledge is always accompanied by the risk of error, so perhaps Toliné is not such an exception to the rule. Confronted with the well-meaning errors of the Aborigine, Paganel himself retreats momentarily into national stereotypes about the British and we are reminded that his knowledge too is, in spite of its greater range and sophistication, perhaps no less partial. At this point, 'the book' makes a symbolic reappearance. Glenarvan steps in and finds a copy of Samuel Richardson's *Précis de géographie*, which he gives to Toliné. It is, of course, just another book by another Englishman, and therefore no doubt another partial view of world geography. But it is at least, as Glenarvan maintains, 'plus au courant de la science que les professeurs de Melbourne' (ECG II, p. 475) ['more in touch with science than are the Melbourne teachers'], and is probably as good as any account in circulation. So another book now enters Toliné's possession – but not for long, since it will soon be abandoned. In what has to be interpreted as a comment by the young Aborigine on the French geographer himself, Toliné leaves during the night, placing the Richardson volume in Paganel's coat pocket before his departure. Meanwhile, he hangs on to the Bible that he had arrived with, no doubt believing that this book of books, at least, will provide him with some truths, even if all others are dispensable. Paganel himself, it is implied, perhaps needs to look afresh at geography from the point of view of a different text. There is no value-free, objective standpoint offering the complete and final perspective: there are only multiple texts, endless accumulations of different versions. This being so, even the great and the good of the scholarly community, like Paganel, are subject to error, and must constantly strive to correct it both by further reading and by a recognition of the potential fallibility of any of the texts they use. In this sense, Paganel has truly had the book thrown back at him. The episode is a reminder not only of the bookishness of all knowledge, but also of the corollary that all knowledge is subject to distortion, and perhaps that the possibility of error is its fundamental condition. Like many of Verne's heroes, Paganel is at times subject to the Bouvard and Pécuchet complex: the belief that knowledge might ultimately reach a final, absolute state from which it will have no further need to evolve. The placing of the book in Paganel's pocket by Toliné is a symbolic reminder that there is always more to be read and learned, but that all texts must be used with caution and with scepticism.

The powerful physical presence of books and libraries throughout the *Voyages extraordinaires* reinforces the point that we have never finished the business of reading, that texts will continue to circulate ad infinitum.

Like food, it is implied, texts have to be consumed and digested on a daily basis and integrated into our intellectual diet. It is no wonder that the two rooms at the heart of the *Nautilus* are the dining room and the library. Knowledge is consumption, and the implication is that the renewal of knowledge, like eating, must be a continuous process. In *Le Tour du monde en quatre-vingts jours*, Phileas Fogg moves from the reading room to the dining room in the Reform Club, where it appears that both his intellectual and his digestive faculties are subject to the same principle of contented rumination. Verne's point is that books themselves, as physical objects, are never far away, and that they are essential instruments in the business of modern life and travel. Naturally, Verne is talking about a society in which books are the unquestioned privilege of civilised and educated people, and it is evident that in his vision of the world those who do not read must be colonised, educated and raised to the level of civilised people. The active role that books play in daily life is attested again and again in Verne's depiction of travellers who carry libraries with them on their journeys (as does Glenarvan in *Les Enfants du capitaine Grant*), or who have the powers of recall to be able to summon up texts in their memory as required. In *Voyage au centre de la terre* we find another variation on this emphasis on the circulation of the book, when Lidenbrock is invited to dinner on his arrival in Iceland. Observing that the local library appears to have very few books, Lidenbrock is surprised by the response of his host, who proclaims proudly that, on the contrary, the library has some eight thousand volumes, many of them rare. However, he says, these are nearly all out on loan:

> On a le goût de l'étude dans notre vieille île de glace! Pas un fermier, pas un pêcheur qui ne sache lire et qui ne lise. Nous pensons que des livres, au lieu de moisir derrière une grille de fer, loin des regards curieux, sont destinés à s'user sous les yeux des lecteurs. Aussi ces volumes passent-ils de main en main, feuilletés, lus et relus, et souvent ils ne reviennent à leur rayon qu'après un an ou deux d'absence. (VCT, pp. 89–90)

> [We like studying in our old island of ice. There is scarcely a farmer or a fisherman who does not know how to read, and who does not read. We consider that books, rather than going mouldy behind an iron grille far from curious eyes, should be subjected to the wear and tear of the gaze of readers. So it is that these volumes pass from one person to another. They are opened, read and re-read, and often they will return to their shelf only after an absence of a year or two.]

The reality of the circulation of texts is summed up neatly in this episode, which both illustrates it as a fact and promotes it as an ideal for which all educated societies should aim. The democratisation of reading has, in this remote community, been effortlessly achieved, and the text is an integral part of the daily life of the fisherman or the farmer. It is a society that lives and defines itself through reading, and for Verne there is something truly utopian in this.[19]

The symbolic presence of reading in our lives, if not always represented in the physical form of the book itself, is conveyed in many ways in the *Voyages extraordinaires*, for reading takes on many different forms. As we have seen, numerous Vernian characters are seen either to read or to have read, and like Dick Sand in *Un capitaine de quinze ans* they use their reading knowledge as a survival instrument in extreme circumstances. The traveller is a reader, just as the reader, in another no less obvious sense, is a traveller. But since reality is so abundantly textual, it is clear that there are many different types of 'text' to be read and deciphered, so the Vernian character reads his reality in many ways and on many levels. This reading activity may involve the deciphering of cryptograms or other clues, or it may involve applying the cognitive processes of reading to physical objects, natural phenomena or indeed to human behaviour by way of decoding its messages. There is always something or someone to be 'read' in Verne, for there are open books everywhere. Understandably, in the light of the example of the Icelandic library cited above, one of the texts that most conspicuously profiles the notion of reading in all its senses is *Voyage au centre de la terre*. Not only does the story start out with the deciphering of a cryptogram, it suggests throughout that the world itself is a vast cryptogram that has to be understood. If this novel gives such a significant place to figures such as Cuvier, it is because France's most celebrated zoologist possessed a legendary ability to reconstitute the history of species through the careful 'reading' of a few fossilised fragments – thus deducing the full story from what initially appear to be random elements.[20] The good reader is the one who is able to

---

19 We should note that this detail about Icelandic libraries is also highlighted in one of the sources for Verne's text, an account by the journalist Charles-Edmond. See Charles Edmond Chojecki, *Voyage dans les mers du nord à bord de la corvette la Reine Hortense et Notes scientifiques communiquées par MM. les membres de l'expédition* (Paris: Michel Lévy, 1857), p. 97: 'On croit, à juste titre, en Islande, qu'un livre n'a de valeur qu'autant qu'il circule' ['In Iceland they rightly believe that a book has value only in so far as it circulates'].

20 Georges Cuvier (1769–1832) succeeded Lamarck as holder of the prestigious Chair of Comparative Anatomy at the Muséum d'Histoire Naturelle in 1795, becoming a member of the Académie Française in 1818. Among his best-known works were *Tableau élémentaire de l'histoire naturelle des animaux* (1798), and *Leçons d'anatomie comparée* (1800–1805). The view of Cuvier as a 'reader' of reality, and consequently as a creative artist who relays the story that he has uncovered, is famously developed

extract the story that is written in nature. In explicit imitation of Cuvier, Lidenbrock and his nephew find themselves involved in a continuous act of reading, and consequently of reconstitution of the earth's prehistory, as when they come across a vast plain of fossilised skeletons and realise that 'là, sur trois milles carrés, peut-être, s'accumulait *toute l'histoire* de la vie animale, *à peine écrite* dans les terrains trop récents du monde habité' (my italics) ['there, over an area of perhaps three square miles, was the entire accumulated story of animal life, one that is scarcely yet written in the all too recent terrains of the inhabited world']. But the business of reconstitution is huge, and would, says Axel, require the efforts of a thousand Cuviers simply to carry out the work (VCT, pp. 320–21). While the underground world they visit may not be a text in the literal sense, it is very much the locus of a story, even of many stories which have to be wrested from it. Repeatedly, the status of the travellers as readers and the status of the natural world as a story is emphasised, as here: '*Toute l'histoire* de la période houillère *était écrite* sur ces sombres parois, et un géologue en pouvait suivre facilement les phases diverses' (VCT, p. 182, my italics) ['The entire history of the carboniferous age was written on those dark walls, and a geologist could easily follow its various phases']. As Lidenbrock and Axel penetrate ever more deeply through the different layers of the earth's prehistory, they thus come across different levels of a story that they are trying to put together, and understand more fully both the 'text' and the 'texture' of the reality with which they are dealing.

However, it is not only nature that has to be read and decrypted. Human creations too have their 'story', and often the Vernian narrator suggests that the scenes or the objects he represents must be read correctly – a rhetorical strategy, which establishes a link between the physical act of reading and the symbolic process of interpretation that is carried out within it. At the beginning of the unfinished early novel *Un prêtre en 1839*, the description of the Eglise de Saint-Nicolas – about to be ruined

---

by Balzac in the 'éloge de Cuvier' in the early pages of *La Peau de chagrin*: 'Cuvier n'est-il pas le plus grand poète de notre siècle? [...] Il est poète avec des chiffres, il est sublime en posant un zéro près d'un sept. Il réveille le néant sans prononcer des paroles artificiellement magiques, il fouille une parcelle de gypse, y aperçoit une empreinte, et vous crie: "Voyez!" Soudain les marbres s'animalisent, la mort se vivifie, le monde se déroule!' (Balzac, *La Peau de chagrin*, in *La Comédie humaine*, vol. X (Paris: Gallimard, 1979), p. 75) ['Is not Cuvier the greatest poet of our century? He is a poet with figures, sublime when he places a zero next to a seven. He revives nothingness without having to pronounce artificially magic words, he examines a piece of gypsum, sees a footprint on it, and announces: "Look!" Suddenly marble becomes animal, death becomes life, the world passes before your eyes!']

when its belfry comes crashing through the roof of the building – emphasises that many episodes of an architectural story are contained in this composite edifice: 'Et toute l'histoire d'une longue suite d'architecture était écrite dans cette incroyable structure; on y voyait la primitive charpente avec ses poutres à peine équarries, chantournées en quelques endroits, raboteuses et noueuses en d'autres.' (P39, p. 10) ['And the whole story of a long architectural development was written in that incredible structure. You could see the original frame with its roughly hewn beams, carved out in certain places, rough and knotty in others.'] By suggesting, in Balzacian manner, that the scene he describes is the site of a text that is to be extracted from it, Verne reinforces his own narrative authority and pushes the reading process into the front line of his narrative (there are also obvious echoes of Hugo's *Notre-Dame de Paris* in this text). This is a ploy he will use again and again. Later in the same story, we are told that a character whose face is apparently a closed book can nonetheless be read and understood, as long as the clues are correctly observed and interpreted: 'Il n'y a pas besoin d'être bon physionomiste pour deviner ces choses-là; il suffit de lire, c'est encore une lecture naturelle, synthétique, comme le geste qui, délaissant l'analyse, résume toute une pensée dans son signe.' (P39, p. 80) ['You do not need to be a good physiognomist to guess such things. It is sufficient to read, and it is a natural, synthetic form of reading, like a gesture which, putting analysis aside, summarises a whole series of thoughts with the sign it makes.']

The stress placed on human physiognomy throughout Verne's writing is another very obvious sign of his debt to Balzac. What is interesting in Verne's case, as in the last example, is the implicit or explicit link made between human behaviour and the idea of reading itself. This point will be well made in a one-act drama that Verne began writing in 1851 under the title *Léonard de Vinci*, retitled *Monna Lisa* in 1855. In one exchange between the artist and his model, the centrality of the reading process in our interpretation of human sentiments is highlighted:

LEONARD   Vous avez dans mon cœur lu les pages d'amour,
           Mais dans le vôtre il faut que je lise à mon tour.
MONNA LISA Le livre de mon cœur vaut bien qu'on le médite;
           Peut-être, Léonard, le liriez-vous trop vite.[21]

[LEONARD   You have read the pages of love in my heart,
           But of yours, now, my own reading must start.
MONA LISA Consider with care my heart as a book;
           Do not, Leonardo, cast too hasty a look.]

---

21 Verne, *Monna Lisa* suivi de *Souvenirs d'enfance et de jeunesse*, pp. 71–72.

Although here it is the human heart that has to be read as a book, in Verne it is most often the face which reveals the heart and contains the clues that must be deciphered. Faces are books, and human physiognomy is a text which the narrator conspiratorially reads for us and with us, thus hinting at the likely development of his own text. In this way, the text of human behaviour is clearly linked to the text of the story that we are reading, and these two levels of the interpretative process become symbolic equivalents. This is most often the case, though not uniquely so, with the rogues, the infiltrators and the traitors in Verne's stories. As he describes the faces of such men, he or his narrator invites us to use this reading of character as a clue to our actual reading of the text, and to predict the direction the story might take as a result. The process can be distinctly lacking in subtlety at times, for the evil-doers in Verne are painted in the blackest of colours from the outset, their faces totally 'readable'. In *Le Chancellor*, which is typical, we know beyond all doubt that the ship's hand Owen is up to no good and will play a damaging role in events, when we read: 'Sa face se termine en pointe par une barbe rougeâtre, presque nulle ou rase sur les joues, ses lèvres sont repliées en dedans, et ses yeux fauves sont marqués d'un point rouge à la jonction des paupières' (C, p. 100) ['His face narrows to a point at its reddish beard, which is almost absent from the cheeks; his lips are turned inwards, and his wild eyes have a red mark where they join with the eyelids']. Or, similarly, in *La Jangada*, we know that Torrès will prove to be a deeply untrustworthy character, when we come across this description: 'Il y avait, en effet, un manque absolu de franchise dans les yeux de cet homme, dont le regard fuyait sans cesse, comme s'il eût craint de se fixer' (J, p. 157) ['There was, indeed, an almost complete lack of frankness in this man's eyes, and his gaze continually took flight, as though it were afraid to settle']. Again and again, such descriptions contain clues that alert the reader to a character's subsequent role in the story, and in that sense they put the reading process itself at the very forefront of Verne's own representation of human behaviour. Naturally, the possibility of misreading is always there too, and Verne plays on this by way of varying the theme, either giving us the wrong clues or indicating that the clues cannot always be read as we might expect. At the beginning of *Mathias Sandorf*, the following reflection on Sarcany is offered by the narrator:

> Si les physionomistes prétendent, – et ils ont raison en la plupart des cas, – que tout trompeur témoigne contre lui-même en dépit de son habileté, Sarcany eût donné un démenti formel à cette proposition. A le voir, personne n'eût pu soupçonner ce qu'il était, ni ce qu'il avait été. Il ne provoquait pas cette irrésistible aversion qu'excitent les fripons et les fourbes. Il n'en était que plus dangereux. (MS, p. 4)

[If physiognomists claim – and they are usually right – that every deceiver bears testimony against himself despite his skill, Sarcany was a living challenge to this idea. To look at him, nobody would have suspected what he was or what he had been. He did not incite that irresistible sense of antipathy we feel towards scoundrels and deceivers. But this merely made him more dangerous.]

This is the classic case of the criminal having learned the famous lesson offered by Laclos's Madame de Merteuil in *Les Liaisons dangereuses*: he suppresses all facial clues that suggest anything other than the purest of motives, and adopts the mask of virtue at all times. However, since we as readers have been informed that Sarcany has this faculty, our negotiation of the story will be marked by a suspicion of him. On other occasions, though, it is the novelist himself rather than the character who obscures the clues, so the process is further complicated. In the same novel, we are given to understand that the beautiful Sava is the daughter of the banker Silas Toronthal who had betrayed Sandorf. This puzzles us, for everything about the girl suggests a noble character, completely at odds with that of Toronthal himself. How could such a wretched specimen of a man have fathered such a dignified and admirable daughter? The comments that the narrator offers about Sava make for a puzzling incompatibility: 'Mais, ce qui frappait surtout dans sa personne, ce qui devait plus vivement impressionner les âmes sensibles, c'était l'air grave de cette jeune fille, sa physionomie pensive, comme si elle eût toujours été à la recherche de souvenirs effacés, c'était ce on ne sait quoi qui attire et attriste' (MS I, p. 313–14) ['But what was striking above all about her, and would have had the strongest effect on sensitive souls, was the solemn look and the pensive features of this young girl, as if she had always been searching for lost memories; for there was about her that mysterious something that fascinates and saddens']. In fact, as it subsequently turns out, Sava is not the daughter of Toronthal at all, a fact which has major consequences since it makes her love for Pierre Bathory acceptable and, indeed, 'readable' in the light of what we know about her character. In this case, the physiognomy was a clue that we needed to read against the apparent momentum of the narrative. The 'text' that Sava's physiognomy offers is, in the end, the true story that emerges against and in opposition to the wrong story that so nearly obliterated it, and it offers a direction through and out of this complex adventure. This struggle between different stories for the right to win through in the long Vernian narrative is one of the many interesting issues that are highlighted by the emphasis on physiognomy.

Another novel in which there are many links between the physiognomy of characters and the reading clues that are given in the text is *Le*

Superbe Orénoque. At the beginning of the second part of that novel, a character by the name of Jorrès is taken on board by Valdez, the ship's captain, who requires an extra hand. But we are immediately alerted as to how to read this newcomer's appearance: 'Cet Espagnol paraissait être doué d'intelligence, bien que la dureté de ses traits, le feu de son regard, ne prévinssent pas trop en sa faveur' (SO, p. 391) ['This Spaniard seemed gifted with intelligence, although the hardness of his features and the fire of his gaze did not augur too well in his favour']. If we need confirmation that we have correctly read the clues, this is provided later, when we learn of the story of a Spanish thief Alfaniz who, after being jailed in France, subsequently escaped and made his way to Venezuela. Naturally Jorrès is that man, and this is his story. Though his cover has not yet been blown, the narrator tells us: 'Si Jacques Helloch eût regardé Jorrès à cet instant, il aurait certainement surpris sur ses traits un tressaillement que celui-ci n'avait su dissimuler' (SO, p. 423) ['If Jacques Helloch had looked at Jorrès at that moment, he would certainly have seen a facial movement that the latter had been unable to conceal']. Jorrès's face is a book, and tells the story that he wishes to conceal. Here again is the alternative narrative lurking between the textual and facial lines, another world that the text or the face might reveal at any point. The reader, who is given information about the face, is placed in a privileged position.

Later, another character provides through his physiognomy a fore-warning of how the story is going to unfold. Père Espérante is the founder of a mission at Santa-Juana. His past appears to be a closed book to those who do not know him. However, he will turn out to be none other than Colonel de Kermor, the father whom Jeanne de Kermor has set out to find in Venezuela. His past life, and the reasons why he left France, are yet another of the potential alternative stories that are hidden within the plot of this novel – those texts within the text that so often reveal themselves at moments when an attempt is made to conceal their existence. The presence of this other story is revealed fleetingly in the face of the missionary to those (like the narrator himself) who know how to read it: 'Quelle avait été l'existence de ce missionaire avant qu'il l'eût vouée à cet apostolat si rude, personne ne l'eût su dire. Il gardait à cet égard un absolu silence. Mais, à de certaines tristesses dont se voilait parfois sa mâle figure, on eût compris qu'il portait en lui les douleurs d'un inoubliable passé.' (SO, p. 503) ['What the missionary's life had been, before he had devoted it to this harsh calling, was impossible to say. He maintained absolute silence on that front. However, a certain sadness that occasionally clouded his manly face might have suggested that he bore within himself the pain of an unforgettable past.'] Here, as so often, Verne links the reading of a human face to the very process of narration, making of this symbolic text with its concealed story a clue as to how his own narrative should be processed. The text of the face becomes, momentarily, the face of the text.

Fiction and literature

The reading of events, objects, artefacts or even people as texts within Verne's narratives reinforces the impression that the world he represents is abundantly and irrepressibly textual. Within the outer framework of the story, or that actual narrative that we negotiate as readers, Verne processes all manner of other texts – both real and symbolic. Everywhere in the text are further texts, mirroring the narrative process or providing the means to move the story forward. But within this 'texture of textuality' that Verne so comprehensively creates, a special place is accorded to the fictional and the literary. Since our knowledge of the world is so often mediated by fictional accounts, or by our readings and speculations about the facts as we perceive them, there is for Verne a sense in which reality and fiction must be seen to overlap. If reality is so often a fiction, then perhaps too fiction is reality, and the works of the great writers are themselves a key to our understanding of the world. Literature, in Verne's novels, works in continuum with the great strides forward made by science and technology. The progress of humanity in the nineteenth century – famously derided by authors such as Baudelaire or Flaubert, who saw so-called 'progress' as an enemy of the arts[22] – is seen by Verne to be as much the responsibility of fiction and literature as of any other area of human endeavour. In *De la terre à la lune*, fictional sources are liberally quoted as a justification and a reason to undertake the lunar expedition. In his speech to the Baltimore Gun Club, Barbicane sees no inconsistency whatsoever in citing literary texts alongside scientific ones – the implication being (and Ardan will later make the point more emphatically) that exploration itself is perhaps the greatest of all fictions and the quintessential subject of all literature. Thus Barbicane's range of references

---

22 Baudelaire, who is emphatic about the incompatibility of art and journalism – that key locus of the nineteenth century's sense of its modernity – writes memorably on one occasion: 'Je ne comprends pas qu'une main pure puisse toucher un journal sans une convulsion de dégoût' (*Mon cœur mis à nu*, in *Œuvres complètes*, ed. Claude Pichois, vol. I (Paris: Gallimard, 'Bibliothèque de la Pléiade', 1975), p. 706) ['I cannot understand how a pure hand is able to touch a newspaper without a convulsion of disgust']. Flaubert's contempt for the press, as a sign of modern 'progress', is also abundantly documented, and is powerfully expressed in the figure of Homais and his articles for the *Fanal de Rouen* in *Madame Bovary*.

includes Cyrano de Bergerac and Edgar Allan Poe, whose Hans Pfaall is referred to almost as though he were a real person. But the fictional accounts are placed alongside references to travellers, scientists and philosophers, including Fabricius, Baudoin, Fontenelle, Locke, Herschell and others (TL, pp. 19–20). The boundaries between different types of writing are dispensed with, as the literary and the fictional are fully integrated into the business of exploration, technology and travel. The point is subsequently reinforced in Chapter 5, entitled, in a playful *mise en abyme* of Verne's own text, 'Le Roman de la lune' ['The Story of the Moon']. Here, science, philosophy and poetry mingle in a sumptuous evocation of the moon, in such a way that the texts of the scientists and philosophers take on an exotic and poetic aura, thus giving this new quest a powerfully verbal status. In one of his famous enumerations, Verne details the history of lunar observation and once again puts the whole question of texts at the forefront of his approach. Self-consciously, he turns knowledge of the moon into a specifically literary affair:

> Ainsi, Thalès de Milet, 460 ans avant J.-C., émit l'opinion que la Lune était éclairée par le Soleil. Aristarque de Samos donna la véritable explication de ses phases. Cléomène enseigna qu'elle brillait d'une lumière réfléchie. Le Chaldéen Bérose découvrit que la durée de son mouvement de rotation était égale à celle de son mouvement de révolution, et il expliqua de la sorte le fait que la Lune présente toujours la même face. Enfin Hipparque, deux siècles avant l'ère chrétienne, reconnut quelques inégalités dans les mouvements apparents du satellite de la Terre.
>
> Ces diverses observations se confirmèrent par la suite et profitèrent aux nouveaux astronomes. Ptolémée, au IIe siècle, l'Arabe Aboul-Wéfa, au Xe, complétèrent les remarques d'Hipparque sur les inégalités que subit la Lune... (TL, p. 43)

> [And so, in 460 BC, Thales of Miletus put forward the idea that the moon was illuminated by the sun. Artistarchus of Samos gave the true explanation of its different phases. Cleomenes taught that it shone with reflected light. Berose the Chaldean discovered that the time the moon took to rotate on its own axis was equal to the time it took to complete an orbit around the earth, and thus explained that only one side of it is ever visible. Finally Hipparchus, two centuries before the Christian era, recognised certain inconsistencies in the apparent movements of this satellite of Earth.
>
> These various observations were subsequently confirmed, to the advantage of later astronomers. Ptolemy, in the second century, and the Arabian Aboul Wefa, in the tenth, completed Hipparchus's observations concerning the moon's inconsistencies.]

Texts are everywhere, but if ever there were a celebration of that fact, Verne provides it here. Passages such as the above in the *Voyages extraordinaires* benefit from being read aloud and savoured for their phonetic resonance and their richly cascading rhythms. Verne makes literature out of the abundance of text, turning these lunar speculations into a positive feast of words, revelling in the strange-sounding names quite as much as in the enumeration of the different contributions that each has made to the overall understanding of the subject.[23] Unashamedly, literature appropriates the texts of science and philosophy. Reality is not merely textual, it is also a resplendently literary phenomenon.

Verne's highlighting of the literary is achieved not only through the deployment of stylistic techniques and strategies designed to enhance the pleasure of the text. The *Voyages extraordinaires* do indeed contain many passages that are models of literary style, notwithstanding Verne's own feeling late in life that he had failed to make an impact as a serious author.[24] But more than this, Verne repeatedly uses the strategy of placing his own work conspicuously within the 'literary field' and of making his reader process it as such. He creates a vast network of literary references that puts him in the company of other figures of world literature and suggests that his own texts move effortlessly in and through this sphere.[25] Far from being mere passing allusions, literary references often become keys to the furthering of the plot, and this technique is particularly evident in the stories which use the Robinson legends or in those which refer to Poe. I shall discuss the question of the re-use and rewriting of certain specific literary texts in more depth later, but the point to be made here is that such texts are liable to figure in Verne's stories as maps or guidebooks or as keys to the unlocking of a mystery. In this sense, literature is integrated dynamically into Verne's representation of the world, and the texture of literariness is created. Not only does this further break down the boundaries between 'fiction' and 'reality' – for literary texts are themselves part of the characters' reality – it also gives a message about the framework of literary reference through which we must approach Verne's fictional world. Literature itself is fictionalised and even dramatised in Verne, so that it becomes its subject as well as its context. One striking example of

---

23 The presence, in particular, of the Spartan king Cleomenes in this list seems to be more for the sound of the name than for any documented contribution to astrology. Virtually all that is known about this figure comes from Plutarch's *Lives*.

24 See the interview, previously quoted, with Sherard ('Jules Verne at Home').

25 For further consideration of this question, including references to some of the many authors Verne cites, see Arthur B. Evans, 'Literary Intertexts in Jules Verne's *Voyages extraordinaires*', *Science Fiction Studies*, 23 (1996), pp. 171–87.

this double role of the literary is the use made of Poe's story 'The Gold-Bug' in *La Jangada*. In Part II, Chapter 12 of Verne's novel, Judge Jarriquez, entrusted with solving the riddle of a murder, is faced with a cryptogram. To decipher it he has recourse to the method of 'ce grand génie analytique, qui s'est nommé Edgard Poë [sic]' (J, p. 341) ['that great analytical genius named Edgar Poe'], whose story we are told he has often read and re-read. Not only does this episode of Verne's novel provide an example of the way in which the story reminds us of its dependence on other texts, it also establishes a relationship, perhaps a sense of parity, with the work of an acknowledged great literary author (and the one whom Verne himself admired above all others). The plot moves forward, and the mysterious cryptogram is eventually solved, partly as a result of the use of Poe's story, which is seen to have as much practical value as any map or manual. So literature, it is implied, contains helpful truths that can also be used as a guide in our dealings with the so-called 'real' world, and at the same time Verne's story implicitly puts itself on a level with Poe's as it works with and through the other text. As we shall see in the final chapter, this double process will be taken to its final and most fascinating conclusion in *Le Sphinx des glaces*, which uses Poe's *Narrative of Arthur Gordon Pym*. The process enhances the overall texture of literariness that Verne so obviously wishes to create, and cleverly requires that we judge his novel in relation to that of Poe. As an author, Verne seldom fails to seek out influential company.

While the use of Poe has an exceptional place in Verne, his overall range of literary references shows him to be an alert and keen reader of world literature, always on the lookout for parallels and points of contact with his own stories. The range of authors referred to is vast, the echoes almost endless. Naturally, the texts of antiquity are present, both as authorities to be quoted and as models of writing, for, as Michel Serres points out, Verne's entire corpus can be read as an echo of Homer's *Odyssey*.[26] Similarly, Verne alludes variously to the classics of modern civilisation (Dante, Rabelais, Shakespeare, Molière, Sterne, Diderot, Defoe and many others), or to great poets and writers of the contemporary era (Wordsworth, Poe, Hoffmann, Balzac, Hugo and Zola). Often these references are introduced as mere asides, and as points of comparison or simple curiosities which among other things demonstrate the extent of the author's literary culture. In Chapter 5 of *Le Chancellor*, for example, when

---

26   Serres, *Jouvences sur Jules Verne*, p. 150. Simone Vierne, in her reading of Verne as a modern recycler of myths (*Jules Verne: Mythe et modernité*), also emphasises how closely his writing models itself on the texts of antiquity.

it becomes apparent that the ship is heading in an easterly direction and might be nearing the Bermudas, the literary mentions of that group of islands are enumerated, in a manner reminiscent of Verne's allusions to scientific texts: not only have the Bermudas been evoked by the poets Thomas Moore and Walter, but we are reminded that they are also famously alluded to in Shakespeare's *The Tempest*. On other occasions, literary references are seen to figure as part of the characters' dialogue. In *Un capitaine de quinze ans,* one day Bénédict the eccentric entomologist is telling a story about Sir John Franklin who, on being bitten by an insect, swept it away and said: 'Le monde est assez grand pour vous et moi!' ['The world is big enough for you and me!'] Whereupon, Captain Hull tells Bénédict that Sterne's Uncle Toby had come out with the same remark well before Sir John Franklin, but had used the familiar second-person singular form (C15, p. 52). Bénédict naïvely asks whether Uncle Toby is still alive, and is told that he never even existed. Apart from its familiar suggestion that all human experience can be found in previous texts, or the equally important notion that in Verne's work textual events seem as 'real' as lived events, this reference to Sterne is an obvious example of the way in which, through his characters, our author bolsters his own literary credentials. References to living authors take the same form, and sometimes also help to add a humorous touch. In *L'Ile à hélice*, the inhabitants of the floating island one day leave their domain to visit the small kingdom of Upolo, where they learn that the king has been deposed and, curiously, that the character considered the best replacement candidate is 'un Anglais, l'un des personnages les plus considérables de l'archipel, un simple romancier' (IH, p. 211) ['an Englishman, one of the most notable characters of the archipelago, a simple novelist']. The novelist in question turns out to be none other than Robert Louis Stevenson (not an Englishman, as it happens, but a Scotsman). To reinforce the point that literature and life seem to overlap in many ways, the musician Yvernès exclaims: 'Voilà donc où peut mener la littérature' ['Look where literature can lead']. Meanwhile, to complete the picture, Pinchinat conjures up an image of Zola I, king of the Samoans. Zola himself gets another, less flattering mention in the *Voyages extraordinaires,* when in *Clovis Dardentor* Patrice, the eponymous hero's very proper and correct manservant, fantasises about finding a new master, one who might be less prone to vulgarity and bad language than Dardentor himself. Pursuing his trail of thoughts, Patrice decides that a member of the Académie Française might be suitable – though definitely not a writer like Zola, he decides (CD, p. 195), the implication being that the author of the *Rougon-Macquart* novels lacks the linguistic delicacy of a true *académicien*. Famously, from 1890–91 onwards

Zola tried and failed on several occasions to gain entry to the Académie. Could it be that Verne saw an opportunity in his 1896 novel to get back at the author who had been so disparaging about his own work in the late 1870s?[27]

On occasions we get a sense of competitiveness and rivalry in the *Voyages extraordinaires* when Verne refers to the works of some of his contemporaries or to authors of a recent generation. *Le Sphinx des glaces* is undertaken partly in order to complete the story for which Poe had failed to find a satisfactory ending, as Verne himself points out in a letter to Louis-Jules Hetzel of 1 September 1896.[28] Something of the same competitiveness informs the writing of *Le Secret de Wilhelm Storitz*, in which Verne is wrestling not only with the ghost of Poe, nor even with the equally important legacy of Hoffmann, but also with the very real success of his contemporary, H. G. Wells. The manuscript of the novel – handed to Hetzel *fils* on 5 March 1905, less than three weeks before Verne's death – was originally entitled *L'Invisible Fiancée*, in an unmistakable response to Wells's *Invisible Man*, published in 1897. As for the legacy of Hoffmann, Verne confirms its significance in a letter to Hetzel accompanying the manuscript, but adds by way of distinguishing his own achievement from that of his predecessor: 'Hoffmann n'aurait pas osé aller si loin'[29] ['Hoffmann would not have dared go as far'] – a point which is also made on the first page of the novel when the narrator says that Hoffmann 'n'eût peut-être pas osé publier ce récit, et qu'Edgar Poe même dans ses *Histoires extraordinaires* n'eût pas osé l'écrire!' (WS, pp. 23–24) ['would perhaps not have dared to publish this story, and that even Edgar Poe would not have dared write it in his *Extraordinary Tales*'].

In other instances, literary echoes in Verne take the form of pastiches of well-known styles or genres. In *Le Chancellor*, the description of the American businessman Mr Kear is done in terms of the popular early-nineteenth-century genre of the 'physiology'. This recalls Balzac and other realist authors, but also reminds us conspicuously that Verne is capable of writing in the tradition of La Bruyère (an author with whom the readers of the *Voyages extraordinaires* would certainly have been familiar), notwithstanding the fact that he also takes the opportunity to quote a much less famous writer: 'Orgueilleux, vaniteux, contemplateur

27 See above, p. 14.

28 See Jean Richer, 'Deux lettres à Louis-Jules Hetzel' (précédées de 'Note sur la Constellation du Marin'), *L'Herne: Jules Verne*, 25 (1974), pp. 71–74.

29 *Le Secret de Wilhelm Storitz*, version d'origine présentée et annotée par Olivier Dumas (Paris: Folio, 1999). See the introduction by Dumas, p. 12.

de lui-même et contempteur des autres, il affecte une suprême indifférence pour tout ce qui n'est pas lui. Il se rengorge comme un paon, "il se flaire, il se savoure, il se goûte", pour employer les termes du savant physionomiste Gratiolet. Enfin, c'est un sot doublé d'un égoïste.' (C, p. 12) ['Proud, vain, filled with the contemplation of his own person and contempt for others, he affects supreme indifference for anything that is not himself. He puffs himself out like a peacock, "he smells, savours and tastes his own being", to use the language of the expert physiognomist Gratiolet. In sum, he is a fool combined with an egotist.'] This technique will elsewhere be extended into an explicit pastiche of well-known texts. One example of this is the penultimate chapter of *L'Etoile du sud* entitled 'La Statue du Commandeur' ['The Commander's Statue'] – a deliberate echo of the ending of Molière's *Don Juan*. As in Molière's play, this is a classic scene of come-uppance, as John Watkins, holding a dinner to celebrate his wealth and fortune (though definitely not his sexual prowess), suddenly receives a very unwelcome visit and learns that someone else is making a valid claim on his riches.

The symbolism of literary texts is a significant aid to the development of narrative, and Verne uses it in many ways. In *Le Rayon vert*, shortly before the narrator introduces Helena Campbell, he quotes in translation William Wordsworth's line in which a swan is described as a double creature that includes or contains its own shadow (RV, p. 15).[30] Later in this chapter, as he is evoking Miss Campbell's charms, he returns to the idea of the double within, this time quoting De Maistre, and pointing out that the practical young heroine seems to contain some other Romantic being in her. It is no accident that the key episode in the story will later take place in Fingal's Cave, that most intensely Romantic of places made famous, we are reminded, by Ossian (RV, p. 194). Nor is it coincidental that, as the party is setting out for Fingal's Cave, a passing reference is made to one of the saddest and most beautiful poems in Hugo's *Les Contemplations*. As they decide on the timing of their journey, which is to be early the following morning, one of Helena's uncles cheerfully intervenes with the line: 'Demain dès l'aube' (RV, p. 170) ['Tomorrow at daybreak'], replicating with no more than a comma's difference the opening words of 'Demain, dès l'aube, à l'heure où blanchit la campagne' ['Tomorrow, at

---

30 The lines referred to are from Wordsworth's poem 'Yarrow Unvisited' (ll. 41-44), written during a visit to Scotland in 1803 (first published in 1807):
  Let beeve and home-bred kine partake
  The sweets of Burn-mill meadow,
  The swan on still St Mary's Lake
  Float double, swan and shadow!

daybreak, when the countryside grows pale']. Hugo's poem is a requiem to his much-loved daughter Léopoldine, who had drowned in the Seine in 1843. Though Helena Campbell will herself come close to drowning in this story, she is rescued by the hero Olivier Sinclair with whom she will also find love, so in the end the story is a celebration of life rather than a mourning of death. However, death by drowning is one of the possible directions that the narrative might have taken. It is the alternative story that accompanies the text in its crucial phase and, like the upside-down reflection of the swan in the water, offers a reverse image of it. The fleeting reference to Hugo combines with the earlier reference to Wordsworth and confirms that Verne's use of literary texts is carefully thought out. Overall, the literary references in this text not only help to define and explain the heroine's temperament, they also give clues about the unfolding of the story, while situating the narrative in a context of poetic sentiment and Romantic literature. Of course, Verne plays some of his characters off against this highly charged Romanticism (as is confirmed by his putting the words of Hugo's poem into the mouth of a glib and entirely unsentimental figure), but this serves only to reinforce the fact that he is using literary reference as a means of adding an additional layer of irony to his story.

The power of words

Traditionally literary texts, and especially poetic ones, place a premium on the power of words. Words cast spells, work magic through their incantatoµry force or special properties, and can even change the nature of our visible reality. They can draw attention to their status as graphic or phonetic objects existing in a sphere of their own, often substituting themselves for the 'real' world or, at the very least, mediating it through and into the Verb. This attention to the power of words, to the almost surreal properties that they have, is one of the most striking and consistent features of the *Voyages extraordinaires*. Words are the ultimate refuge and comfort, and text itself (in all its forms, spoken or written) the final reality. This is, perhaps, the quality that Roussel and others so admired in Verne,[31] for again and again in his writing we have a sense that the most extraordinary journey of all is that of words themselves.

Nowhere is this more clearly exemplified than in the 'naming and claiming' rituals that take place in so many of Verne's novels, where a

---

31 See above, pp. 17–19.

group of castaways familiarise themselves with their surroundings and, as part of their physical reconnaissance of the territory, immediately turn it into identifiable text. Islands become words and acquire a satisfying aura of familiarity; unknown domains are 'textualised' at the very moment when they become physically negotiable; remote regions are opened up like books. Here we have a small-scale image of Verne's own writing enterprise, in which the known world is covered by words that familiarise and contextualise, making it understandable, negotiable, 'readable' in every sense. And along with the ritual of colonising unknown places by naming them and giving them a recognisable identity, Verne's characters also create maps, for the verbal and the visual are considered to be continuous. The archetypal episode of naming and claiming, so often echoed elsewhere in the *Voyages extraordinaires*, occurs in *L'Île mystérieuse*. In Part I, Chapter 11 of the novel, the castaways are conducting their first major exploration of their new domain and, prior to establishing an illustrated map of it, they turn it first into a word-map. In a revealing comment that initiates the naming ceremony (referred to as a 'baptême' ['baptism'] in the chapter summary) Cyrus Smith suggests to his companions that it is time they considered themselves not as castaways in their new domain, but as colonisers (IM I, p. 140). Words are a means, among other things, of establishing control over the unknown (a process which will be further developed by Proust some decades later, when his narrator savours the strange resonances of words and discovers their mysterious links with his deeper intuitions). The naming ritual then gets under way, for they are all in agreement that this will be of real practical benefit, with Pencroff alone intimating that there may be an element of self-deception about the process ('Au moins, on a l'air d'être quelque part', he interjects ['At least it gives the impression that we are somewhere']). The castaways proceed to turn their island into a word-map, fully convinced that this act is every bit as important as that of building a house, rearing animals or planting crops. The island is consequently rendered more inhabitable. In the event, the novelist himself then has the convenience of being able to use the new nomenclature, so quite apart from the symbolism of naming, this is an extremely useful device from his point of view: 'Tout était donc terminé, et les colons n'avaient plus qu'à redescendre le mont Franklin pour revenir aux Cheminées...' (IM I, p. 144) ['So everything was now done, and it merely remained for the castaways to go back down from Mount Franklin to The Chimneys']. In the beginning was the Word. From now on, Lincoln Island will be a textual reality, an identifiable verbal terrain.

Almost every one of Verne's numerous *robinsonnades* offers a variation on this scene, as an island is invested with words that make it recognisable and turn it into text. The process is extended to many of the novels involving reconnaissance (i.e. 'recognition') of unknown territories. Often, the names will be chosen for sentimental reasons, perhaps in honour of a loved one: in *Voyage au centre de la terre*, the point at which the explorers set out on a vast underground sea is named 'le Port Graüben' in honour of Axel's fiancée; and, in *L'Ecole des Robinsons*, Godfrey also uses the name of his fiancée and names his new abode Phina Island. Interestingly, however, the names conferred will often be those of the principal characters themselves – aware as they are that 'what's in a name' can be hugely significant, and that the word has power to ensure a reputation for posterity. Sometimes it will be the scientists or explorers who are keen to use their own name in this way. The underground sea of *Voyage au centre de la terre* is named 'la mer Lidenbrock', and in *Voyages et aventures du capitaine Hatteras*, the volcanic mountain which the captain ascends at the North Pole will be named 'le mont Hatteras'. In *Un capitaine de quinze ans*, the eccentric Cousin Bénédict, eager to put his name to a new entomological discovery, finally decides after many failures that he will confer the grandiose title of *hexapodes Benedictus* on a common spider. The word is everything, and if the word sounds exotic, so much the better. But Verne's scientists will sometimes risk everything to have their name associated with a discovery – not so much because of the discovery itself, but because of the magic of the name. In *La Chasse au météore* two amateur astronomers, Hudelson and Forsyth, both want to put their name to the comet that they have separately observed in the skies, and are prepared to engage in a bitter rivalry for the privilege of doing so. For them, the word and the name are more important than what the comet actually is – a point borne out by subsequent events, when many others become interested in the comet because it turns out to be made of gold. The astronomers themselves have little interest in the wealth-creating possibilities of their comet, believing that possession of an intangible verbal wealth is of far greater consequence.

The turning of objects and places into names and words is fundamental to the wider process of textualisation in Verne. The world, if not actually made up of words in the first place, must at least be turned into words, for words themselves are the first and most significant dimension of the real, and their power to shape lives and alter events is seen to be overwhelming. The huge importance of words is sometimes reinforced by the misunderstandings which take place in Verne's texts. In *Clovis Dardentor*, as the vessel carrying the eponymous hero and his travelling companions crosses the Mediterranean sea, the entire group is confused by the silent but intense presence in the dining room of one character,

M. Eustache Oriental. Oriental is, we are led to believe, President of the Société astronomique de Montélimar, yet curiously he evinces not the slightest interest in the heavenly firmament, nor does he do anything else but eat. Indeed, he chomps his way right through the narrative, regularly taking his seat first in the dining room and partaking of everything on the menu, with an almost heroic commitment. But finally, the mystery is explained. Eustache Oriental is not President of the Société *astronomique* de Montélimar, but of the Société *gastronomique* de Montélimar. A single letter changes a word and alters the entire perception of the man. Dardentor, eager to point out that this is not such a huge difference, chips in with one of those untranslatable puns that so often enliven our reading of Verne, claiming that Oriental is an 'astronome doté des plumes d'un *g*' (CD, p. 196) ['an astronomer endowed with a *g*'; literally: 'endowed with the feathers of a jay']. In one sense the difference is indeed minimal, but that is precisely the point. A tiny difference between words can have huge consequences in the way we view people or events, for words are everything. Another example of the power of words to mislead or to deceive occurs in *Kéraban-le-têtu*, where Kéraban's travelling companion Van Mitten believes on the evidence of a telegram that his wife is dead, 'décédée il y a cinq semaines' ['deceased five weeks ago']. However, like so many of the texts that Vernian characters find themselves trying to decipher, this one reveals its secrets much later, when Van Mitten looks again at the telegram in the final chapter of the novel and sees that the phrase apparently announcing his wife's death was followed by the words 'à aller rejoindre son mari' ['to go and join her husband']. 'Décédée' ['deceased'] was, he now correctly deduces, a misprint: the word should have been 'décidée' ['decided']. Van Mitten's wife had decided five weeks earlier that she would go and join him, and his marital tribulations, we suppose, are about to start all over again. A word, a single letter, proves in the end to have immense consequences, at least for the hapless Van Mitten.

There is one other instance in the *Voyages extraordinaires* where a single letter proves to be of the utmost significance, a truly life-and-death matter, and it returns us to the central question of writing itself. In *Les Cinq Cents Millions de la Bégum*, the evil tyrant Schultze dies pen in hand as he is writing a letter ordering the destruction of France-Ville. The letter is almost complete, and all that it lacks is the final 'e' of Schultze for the order to be enacted. As it is, the words in the letter remain frozen, suspended, incomplete. They are unable to set out into the world where their impact will be felt, and, in the last analysis, the evil scientist is also the blocked writer whose work does not come to fruition. Through this image of failure and death, we also read a powerful message: that text has potentially devastating power, that writing itself can determine the outcome of humanity's greatest crises. If we needed further confirmation of Verne's belief in the supremacy of words, this is it. The world is a text – and the text itself, for all its susceptibility to error and distortion, can change the world.

Chapter 4

Theatre and Theatricality

Jules Verne and the stage

'Mais, dira-t-on, cela finit comme un vaudeville... Eh bien, qu'est ce récit, sinon un vaudeville sans couplets, et avec le dénouement obligatoire du mariage à l'instant où le rideau baisse?' (CD, p. 211) ['But, you will say, it all finishes like a vaudeville. Well, what is this story if not a vaudeville without verse, and the obligatory ending with a marriage as the curtain falls?'] Thus reads the final, self-reflexive line of *Clovis Dardentor*. Not only does it make absolutely explicit the link between the style of the vaudeville and the plot of the narrative just completed, it also uses the comparison itself as a means of closure. Young love and family interests, marriage, wealth and inheritance, conflict occasioned by the presence of an unwelcome suitor – these are the ingredients not only of *Clovis Dardentor*, but of many of Verne's novels, and they return us directly to the apprenticeship years of the 1850s when he learned the craft of the vaudeville through his involvement in the Parisian stage. As secretary of the Théâtre Lyrique from 1852 until the death of its director Jules Seveste in 1854, Verne met and fraternised with many of the best-known dramatists and actors of the day, and wrote numerous plays himself. He also made important contacts with influential critics and journalists, notably Théophile Gautier and Emile de Girardin. One of the most significant friendships he formed during this period was with Alexandre Dumas *fils*, who collaborated with him on two plays and also introduced Verne to his father, who was director of the Théâtre Historique. In 1894 Verne reminisced:

> The friend to whom I owe the deepest debt of gratitude and affection is Alexandre Dumas the younger, whom I met first at the age of twenty-one. We became chums almost at once. He was the first to encourage me. I may say that he was my first protector. I never see him now, but as long as I live I shall never forget his kindness to me nor the debt that I owe him. He introduced me to his father; he worked with me in collaboration. We wrote together a play called *Les Pailles Rompues*, which was performed at the

Gymnase; and a comedy in three acts entitled *Onze Jours de siège*, which was performed in the Vaudeville Theatre.[1]

The theatre remains a constant presence throughout Verne's writing: not just in its gusto and pacy crescendos, its dramatic confrontations, its reversals and surprises, its complicated but neat solutions and its happy *dénouements*; but also in its contrived virtuosity and stagey artificiality, its humour and word-play, its colourful dialogues and eccentric characters, its ludic convolutions, and its rhythms of disguise, revelation and reconciliation. The sheer theatrical self-consciousness of Verne's writing in the *Voyages extraordinaires* often takes it right out of the so-called 'realist' mode and back into the simulated, factitious world of the vaudeville. While, as we have seen, Verne's technique is based on the extensive and scrupulous use of documents and other sources that validate its content, the very seriousness of the endeavour sometimes appears to be undermined by the exuberantly theatrical qualities of the characters, situations, plot developments and language. But it is the confrontation and the coexistence of different genres and influences that gives his narrative style such resonance and richness, for it points to the artifice of writing itself and suggests a deeply ironic attitude towards the question of authorship. Such self-consciousness is Verne's hallmark, and no true understanding of his literary originality can be achieved without an assessment of its origins and links with the theatre.

'I adored the stage and all concerned with it, and the work that I have enjoyed the most has been my writing for the stage', declared Verne to the journalist R. H. Sherard in the interview quoted above. Like those Vernian islands in their seas, the *Voyages extraordinaires* are completely surrounded by the theatre and, occasionally, immersed in it. They grow naturally out of Verne's early experiments as a writer of *opéras-comiques*, *comédies-proverbes*, *opérettes* and so on, and they maintain many of the qualities of the theatre in narrative form. Frequently, they point up their own theatrical qualities and origins. And subsequently, they return to the theatre, with the staging of some of the most successful novels in the corpus – notably *Le Tour du monde en quatre-vingts jours* in 1874, *Les Enfants du capitaine Grant* in 1878, and *Michel Strogoff* in 1880. The dazzling and miraculous world of the *Voyages extraordinaires* is, for some, ideally suited to the stage. Julien Green was to remember being delighted as a child by the magical qualities of *Strogoff* when he went to see the play in 1911:

---

1 See Sherard, 'Jules Verne at Home'.

Sorti du théâtre, j'étais dans un tel état qu'il fallait me calmer en essayant de me faire comprendre que tout cela était faux. On ne comprenait pas que pour moi tout cela était plus vrai que vrai. Je voulais être ce que je voyais sur la scène, et, rentré chez moi, je lançais un regard boudeur sur ma chambre qui avait le grand tort de n'être ni à Pétersbourg, ni à Irkoutsk, ni à Omsk, ni même à Tomsk. [...] J'aurais voulu à la fois des steppes avec une meute de loups haletants derrière mon traîneau et des salons impériaux éclairés de lustres gigantesques.[2]

[Once out of the theatre, I was in such a state that it was necessary to calm me down by trying to make me understand that it was all false. What they did not understand was that, for me, all of that was more real than reality. I wanted to be what I saw on the stage, and, back at home, I looked sulkily around my room, the great fault of which was not to be in St Petersburg or in Irkutsk or in Omsk or even in Tomsk. I wanted steppes with a pack of panting wolves chasing behind my sledge, and, at the same time, imperial salons ornate with giant candelabras.]

Although plays such as *Strogoff* and *Le Tour du monde* had spectacular commercial success (*Le Tour du monde*, notably, ran to 415 performances in 1874–75 at the Théâtre de la Porte Saint-Martin, and later figured regularly in the repertory of the Théâtre du Châtelet right up until the Second World War), they were of course re-conversions of Verne's novels back into dramatic form, usually in collaboration with Adolphe d'Ennery.[3] The emphasis was on grand, stagey effects and greater complexity of plot, and in one production of *Le Tour du monde* (whose stage version contains many more characters and sub-plots than the novel) a live elephant was used.[4] It might be argued that this mature phase of Verne's stage career, driven by commercial constraints and the desire to achieve blockbuster success, is of less intrinsic interest than the earlier apprenticeship phase, to which we shall shortly return. It does, however, reinforce the point that, for Verne, the theatre was an abiding obsession, a form of writing to which he returned not only with pleasure, but also with consummate ease because

2 Julien Green, *Partir avant le jour* (Paris: Gallimard, Bibliothèque de la Pléiade, 1977), p. 732.

3 D'Ennery was co-author of the stage versions of *Le Tour du monde*, *Les Enfants du capitaine Grant* and *Michel Strogoff*. These three plays were subsequently reissued as a publication in volume form by Hetzel (*Les Voyages au théâtre*, 1881). Authorship of *Le Tour du monde* was famously contested by Edouard Cadol who, on the basis of Jules Verne's plan for the novel, had sketched a scenario for the theatre in 1871. For further remarks on the 'Affaire Cadol', see pp. 189–90.

4 For a detailed account of the differences between the novel and the play, see Pierre Terrasse, 'Le *Tour du monde* au théâtre', in *Jules Verne 1: 'Le Tour du monde'*, ed. François Raymond (Paris: Minard, 1976), pp. 109–22.

it was intrinsic to his whole approach. And while many of the plays written by Verne were collaborative ventures, he also rewrote a number of his novels independently as theatrical works, notably *Kéraban-le-têtu* in 1883 and *Mathias Sandorf* (his last completed play) in 1887. In addition to the completed texts, fragments of other theatre scenarios on which Verne worked have survived and have been published in recent years – for example, an adaptation of *Voyages et aventures du capitaine Hatteras* entitled *Le Pôle nord* (1871–72), and a stage version of *Les Tribulations d'un Chinois en Chine* (1888–90).[5] Another major success for Verne was the play *Voyage à travers l'impossible*, also written in collaboration with d'Ennery, which ran to 97 performances at the Théâtre de la Porte Saint-Martin in 1882-83. Occupying a slightly unusual place in the corpus, this play is an extravagant fantasy based not on one but on several of the best-known novels of the *Voyages extraordinaires* (notably *Voyage au centre de la terre*, the Gun-Club trilogy and *Vingt mille lieues*) and introducing a range of characters from further texts (for example Tartelett from *L'Ecole des Robinsons*, and the eponymous hero of *Une fantaisie du docteur Ox*). The impossible journey undertaken in this play is that of George Hatteras, introduced as the son of the famous captain, who under the guidance of a certain Volsius covers a number of different journeys from the *Voyages extraordinaires* and, unlike his father in the 1864 novel, makes a return journey from madness back to sanity.[6] For all its interest, a play such as *Voyage à travers l'impossible* is not at the cutting edge of Vernian creativity: rather, it is a spin-off from it. Yet it exemplifies two things: first, Verne's sustained interest in the theatre long after he had become successful as a novelist; and second, the obvious adaptability to the theatre (once issues of transport and changing geographical locations have been

---

5   A helpful list of Verne's theatrical works will be found in Volker Dehs, *Bibliographischer Führer durch die Jules-Verne-Forschung. Guide bibliographique à travers la critique vernienne. 1872–2001* (Wetzlar: Phantastische Bibliothek, 2002), pp. 339–48. See also Volker Dehs, Jean-Michel Margot and Zvi Har'El, *The Complete Jules Verne Bibliography* (work in progress), Section V (Plays), available online at http://jv.gilead.org.il/biblio/plays.html .

6   Found in the Censorship Office of the Third Republic as recently as 1978, the play was first published three years later: Jules Verne, *Voyage à travers l'impossible*, ed. François Raymond and Robert Pourvoyeur (Paris: J.-J. Pauvert, 1981). An English-language version has recently been made available, with the addition of a scene missing from the first edition: Jules Verne, *Journey Through the Impossible*, translated by Edward Baxter, introduction by Jean-Michel Margot (Amherst: Prometheus Books, 2003). The play had, however, made a much earlier appearance in a different medium, when it was adapted by Georges Méliès for his 1904 silent film, *Voyage à travers l'impossible*.

resolved) of many of the texts of the *Voyages extraordinaires*. Extravagant and eccentric characters like Tartelett are eminently suited to the theatre because, in a sense, they came from it in the first place.

It is, though, Verne's early involvement in the theatre that 'sets the scene' for his writing and teaches him the techniques that will remain and influence the style of his greatest novels. The two decades from 1847 through to 1867 see a huge range of theatrical works flow from Verne's pen. Apart from Dumas *fils*, the best-known of his co-authors, he collaborates with Georges Schwob, Pitre-Chevalier, Charles Wallut, Michel Carré and, for the musical scores, with Aristide Hignard, the friend who will accompany him on his journey to England and Scotland in 1859 (written up as *Voyage à reculons en Angleterre et en Ecosse*). What is striking in any survey of Verne's writing during this period (which stretches into the first hugely successful years of the *Voyages extraordinaires*) is his readiness to experiment with different artistic combinations – prose or verse, ballet, music and libretti – and with different authors and musicians. The plays he writes vary in length from the single-act 'filler' to the fully-fledged five-act drama. Though the vaudeville is dominant, signalling the word-play and the levity which are to be such important features of Verne's writing, there are also more serious dramas. Set alongside the later adaptations of his novels to the theatre that I have mentioned, this amounts to a very substantial corpus of theatrical writings, either from Verne's pen alone or in collaboration.[7] By way of setting these in context, here is a list of Verne's most important theatrical works written, performed or published in the crucial twenty-year period 1847–67 (only complete works are listed here):[8]

---

7 A number of important studies of Verne's theatrical works have been carried out, notably Robert Pourvoyeur, 'Jules Verne et le théâtre', preface to Jules Verne, *Clovis Dardentor* (Paris: Union générale d'éditions, 1979), pp. 5–30; Daniel Mortier, 'Le récit et le spectacle: Jules Verne au théâtre', in *Modernités de Jules Verne*, études réunies par Jean Bessière (Paris: Presses Universitaires de France, 1988), pp. 107–22; and Jean-Michel Margot, 'Jules Verne, Playwright', *Science Fiction Studies*, 32 (2005), pp. 150–62. Recent editions or re-editions of texts such as *Le Colin-Maillard*, *Un fils adoptif* and *Les Compagnons de la Marjolaine* in the *Bulletin de la Société Jules Verne*, and the re-edition of *Les Pailles rompues* in the *Revue Jules Verne*, have refocused attention on the theatrical corpus and its importance, and further texts are being edited by Volker Dehs and other scholars.

8 A more comprehensive survey is provided by Alexandre Tarrieu, 'Théâtre de jeunesse', *Revue Jules Verne*, 11 (2001), pp. 11–24. A survey of Verne's complete theatrical output is provided by Jean-Michel Margot in 'Jules Verne, Playwright'.

1847   *Alexandre VI* (five-act drama)
1848   *La Conspiration des poudres* (five-act verse drama)
       Une promenade en mer (one-act vaudeville)
       Le Quart d'heure de Rabelais (one-act vaudeville)
1849   *Abd'allah* (two-act vaudeville, in collaboration with
       Georges Schwob)
       Un drame sous Louis XV (five-act verse drama)
       Quiridine et Quidinerit (three-act verse *comédie italienne*)
1850   *La Guimard* (two-act comedy)
       La Mille et Deuxième Nuit (one-act *opéra-comique*)
       Les Pailles rompues (one-act verse comedy, in collaboration with
       Alexandre Dumas *fils*)
1851   *De Charybde en Scylla* (one-act verse comedy)
       Monna Lisa (one-act verse drama)
1852   *Les Châteaux en Californie ou Pierre qui roule n'amasse pas mousse*
       (one-act *comédie-proverbe*, in collaboration with
       Pitre-Chevalier)
       La Tour de Monthléry (five-act drama, in collaboration with
       Charles Wallut)
1853   *Le Colin-Maillard* (one-act *opéra-comique*, in collaboration with
       Michel Carré)
       Un fils adoptif (one-act comedy, in collaboration with Charles
       Carlut)
       Les Heureux du jour (five-act verse comedy)
1854   *Guerre aux tyrans* (one-act comedy)
1855   *Au bord de l'Adour* (one-act verse comedy)
       Les Compagnons de la Marjolaine (one-act *opéra-comique*, in col-
       laboration with Michel Carré)
1858   *Monsieur de Chimpanzé* (one-act *opérette*, in collaboration with
       Michel Carré)
       Le Page de Madame Malbrough (one-act *opérette*, dubious attribu-
       tion to Verne)
1860   *L'Auberge des Ardennes* (one-act *opéra-comique*, in
       collaboration with Michel Carré)
1861   *Un neveu d'Amérique ou Les Deux Frontignac* (three-act comedy)
       Onze Jours de siège (three-act comedy, in collaboration with
       Dumas *fils*)
1867   *Les Sabines* (*opéra-bouffe*, in collaboration with Charles Wallut)

Many of these texts exist in manuscript form at the Bibliothèque Municipale de Nantes,[9] and, since Jules Verne's involvement with the theatre is an area that scholars have begun to explore more fully in recent years, we can expect that they will now be subjected to increased scrutiny. What we should remind ourselves of here is, first, that in the 1850s Verne's plays outnumbered his narrative works; and second, that many of Verne's subsequent characters are to be found in the dramatis personae of these early comedies, notably the young suitors and their inevitable antagonists. Christian Chelebourg makes the important point that Vernian humour has its true origins in these works: 'L'humour du théâtre de jeunesse influence […] la narration romanesque par la place qu'y occupe le jeu'[10] ['The humour of the early theatrical writings has an influence on the narrative style of the novels, because of the important ludic dimension']. Clearly, the early theatrical writings are a crucible in which Verne works towards a style that will ultimately become his own, and in this respect their importance cannot be overestimated. I shall now make brief comments on three of the best-known early plays, by way of establishing some of the basic elements that will remain and influence the highly self-conscious narrative style of the *Voyages extraordinaires*. I shall then move on to look more generally at theatrical elements that remain in Verne's fiction as a result of this apprenticeship in the theatre.

Three early plays

Les Pailles rompues, for which Jules Verne acknowledged – but could have exaggerated – the collaboration of Dumas *fils*, was first performed as a late-night 'filler' at the Théâtre Historique on 12 June 1850. Although it was by no means Verne's first play, it was his first major break. The play was later staged at the Théâtre du Gymnase (referred to by Verne in the Sherard interview previously quoted), and in Nantes, where it was acclaimed in the press and gave the still unknown Verne some local notoriety. As Jean-Paul Dekiss puts it: 'Le plaisir de briller par le calembour, la rime et l'allitération, le goût de l'auteur pour les dialogues humoristiques font le succès d'estime de ce premier spectacle'[11] ['The pleasure of

9 For a complete list of the Nantes manuscripts see Dehs, Margot and Har'El, *The Complete Jules Verne Bibliography*.

10 Christian Chelebourg, 'Pour une réhabilation de l'humour vernien', in *Jules Verne 8: Humour, ironie, fantaisie*, ed. Christian Chelebourg (Paris: Minard, 2003), pp. 5–15 (p. 10).

11 Jean-Paul Dekiss, *Jules Verne l'enchanteur* (Paris: Editions du Félin, 1999), p. 29.

making brilliant puns, the presence of rhyme and alliteration, and the author's enjoyment of witty dialogues result in this first play being highly esteemed']. In addition to its racy and playful exchanges, the play is interesting on three counts for the reader of Verne's later work: first, its focus on love, marriage and the conflicts of interest that arise between them; second, its use within the plot of a ludic convention (the *pailles rompues* of the title); and third, its neat and clever *dénouement*.

At the start of this one-act comedy we learn that the recently married, nineteen-year-old Henriette and her husband d'Esbard have fallen into disagreement. Henriette has asked her husband for a diamond necklace, while d'Esbard has asked his wife to go and live in the country with him. Neither is prepared to grant the other's wish. However, they have agreed to *rompre la paille* ['break the straw'] – a game in which a disagreement is settled when one party inadvertently accepts something from the hand of the other. Henriette's maidservant Marinette, a smart and spirited character in the tradition of Molière's servants, accurately predicts that her mistress will outwit her husband and get her way. Meanwhile, we learn of a secret visit to Henriette by her former suitor, Raoul, who extracts from her the admission that she still loves him. However, Raoul tells her he has to depart with the dragoon guards for Lorraine the next day. As their conversation is ending, a jealous d'Esbard returns, and the lover is hastily bundled into a cupboard. D'Esbard insists he knows that a man is hiding. Seeing this as an opportunity, his wife admits it, gives him the key, and, as he takes it from her hand, declares triumphantly that she has now won the game of *pailles rompues* ['broken straws']. Fooled by this piece of daring, d'Esbard accepts his defeat, neglects to look in the cupboard, and goes out to buy diamonds for his wife. During his absence, the lover is hastily spirited away, and when the husband reappears with his gift, the wife accepts his proposal to live in the country, since he now talks of heading to Lorraine. So the play ends on this neat double-trickery, the husband feeling falsely vindicated that his wife has acceded to his wishes, the wife knowing that she will be able to meet up with her lover in their country retreat.

The jealous but outwitted husband, the lover hidden in a closet, the conniving maidservant – these have long been the stock-in-trade of comedy, and Verne uses the conventions well. The fact that there are two entirely separate points of disagreement between husband and wife, or the possibility that the husband could have solved everything and won at *pailles rompues* by giving his wife a diamond necklace in the first place, are issues neatly side-stepped for the purposes of the plot. Verne also finds his own trademark here, with the tongue-in-cheek artfulness by which the plot reunites separated lovers and marginalises the third party. Later, marriage itself will nearly always, after many obstacles, be the institution that reconciles lovers in Verne: here, marriage is what separates them. But effectively d'Esbard, the husband, in similar fashion to so many of Verne's later characters, is the interfering outsider whose presence serves only to reinforce the true feelings of the lovers. Trickery and gamesmanship are essential: Henriette extends the game of *pailles rompues* to a more general 'game' of outwitting her husband, which turns out to be an easy thing to do. The ludic dimension is thus thematised within the text, as it will be much later with, say, *Le Tour du monde en quatre-vingts jours*, where Phileas Fogg's journey around the world is undertaken because of a bet, and where the constant games of whist that the hero plays are a continuing reminder of the gamesmanship that is at the heart of this text. The end of the play unites the lovers, in prospect at least, and suggests that the heroine will continue to outwit her foolish husband. It leaves us with that contrived and self-conscious sense of justice which will so often mark closure in Verne's work.

Les Châteaux en Californie, ou Pierre qui roule n'amasse pas mousse, is a one-act *comédie-proverbe* about financial speculation in California. It was published in the *Musée des Familles* in 1852, and written in collaboration with its director Pitre-Chevalier, but was never performed on stage. Again light-hearted in tone, the 'wisdom' that it dispenses is that wealth is an illusion and that there is, as the main character admits at the end of the play, no worthier occupation and no truer wealth than being able to exercise a profession which defies the ups and downs of fortune. As Marc Soriano points out in his study of this and other early works by Verne, the Californian gold rush was a highly topical matter in the early 1850s and was an obvious choice of subject for the young Verne.[12] But the folly of the gold rush (in Africa, America, Australia and New Zealand) is a theme that will recur throughout Verne's work, from *Cinq semaines en ballon*, in which Joe wants to fill up the balloon's basket with gold nuggets but is forced by Fergusson to jettison them for aerodynamic reasons, through to posthumously published texts such as *Le Volcan d'or* and *La Chasse au météore*, in which a volcano and a comet are respectively made of gold. And the madness of Mammon, in *Les Châteaux en Californie* as in so many of Verne's other works, will raise wider questions about the currencies of truth and falsehood in human emotions.

12 Marc Soriano, 'Portrait de l'artiste jeune, ou actualité, antisémitisme et jeux de mots dans les quatre premières œuvres publiées de Jules Verne', in *Portrait de l'artiste jeune*, pp. 9–49. See especially p. 28.

The plot of the play is lively if a little convoluted. Dubourg, a Parisian architect, has abandoned his profession and left for California to try to make his fortune. Madame Dubourg, convinced that her husband will return with immeasurable riches, runs up large debts (the title of the play is of course a play on the French expression 'châteaux en Espagne', conveyed in English by the metaphor 'castles in the air'). Confident, too, that her daughter Henriette will soon be a rich heiress, she turns away the young suitor Henri, despite the fact that Henriette loves him. Then Dubourg reappears in a dishevelled state. He tells his wife that he has lost everything, and goes through the catalogue of his woes. Almost immediately, however, we learn that he is playing a game with her – in order to put her and the rest of the family to the test. He is in fact rich (or so he believes at this stage), and wishes to arrange the marriage of his daughter to a young Russian prince, Alexis Salsificof. Alas, though, neither the rich man nor the young prince are what they seem. Dubourg has lost his entire fortune because his bank has crashed. Salsificof turns out not to be a prince at all, nor even Russian, but an ordinary young man who had assumed a new identity in search of fortune. He is, moreover, the nephew of the maidservant Catherine. We learn that Henriette will, after all, end up marrying Henri, and in a parallel development the maidservant's daughter Clara will end up marrying the 'Russian prince'. The moral of the play: there is no wealth greater than that of true love, no currency more false than that of pretence. In the typically happy *dénouement*, everything returns to its orderly state.

In a move that will again be typical of the later Verne, the young playwright here extends the notion of 'playing games' (as when Dubourg initially tricks his wife into believing he has returned a pauper) to include the question of disguise. Disguise, and its theatrical ally, revelation, here links up with the question of marriage, love and the validity of human emotions. As we shall see, disguise in Verne will often be the device that reveals the underlying but initially concealed truth, and pretence of all kinds – social, emotional or sartorial – will ultimately be exposed. The quest for gold is also a form of pretence, for it is an obsession with something of false value which brings with it false modes of behaviour, and those who pursue such quests are shown up as fools. Verne is merciless in his chastisement of characters such as Salsificof, who, like many later characters in the *Voyages extraordinaires*, is ridiculed not only through his unwieldy name, but also for his pretentiousness and his falsehood. His marriage to Clara is, in some senses, a punishment and a bringing-into-line of a character who attempted to disregard his origins and forget those closest to him.

What is noticeable, given the weighty (if conventional) moral content of this play, is the levity that the young Verne sustains within it. Again, this will be typical of the later work, and it presages the mixture of tones and styles that will be such an important feature of the *Voyages extraordinaires*. Verne creates humour partly because the characters are larger than life, caricatured in their excesses, and partly because he is so adept at handling the dialogues, which move swiftly and depend on well-honed repartee. But one of the most important features of this play is the extravagant, exuberant and sometimes quite excessive word-play in which the author indulges. The maidservant Catherine is prone to constant malapropisms and misquotations, which give her speech undertones ranging from the absurd to the scurrilous to the blatantly sexual. In the first scene of the play, she comes out with a series of misremembered sayings, the result being that the comedy of language itself moves centre-stage. The following are typical examples: 'Toujours franc […] et la queue sur la main' ['always straightforward, with tail in hand'] instead of 'le cœur sur la main' ['heart in hand']; 'vous avez pris le chemin des espaliers' ['you took the route by the espalier trees'] instead of 'le chemin des écoliers' ['the schoolchildren's route', i.e. the longest way round]; 'mieux vaut lard que navet' ['better lard than turnip'] for 'mieux vaut tard que jamais' ['better late than never']; 'il a pris les saucisses pour les lanternes' ['he mistook sausages for lanterns'] instead of 'prendre des vessies pour des lanternes' ['to be completely deluded'], or 'rira bien qui rira derrière' ['he who laughs last laughs from his backside'] for 'rira bien qui rira dernier' ['he who laughs last laughs longest']. In the next chapter we shall look again at the important question of language and word-play in Verne. In this early drama it creates a mood of self-conscious exuberance and reminds us of the artificiality – and therefore the malleability – of the writer's own building blocks, namely words themselves. Soriano and others have stressed, with some justification perhaps, that such word-play seems almost to be an invitation to psychoanalyse the sexually confused young Jules Verne.[13] However, it is easy to pursue such speculations into areas where there are simply no answers, since we do not have a living subject to confirm whether our intuitions might be correct. What is beyond doubt is that the writing of *Les Châteaux en Californie* coincides with a troubled period in Verne's life, as he wrestles with the problem of finding a wife, and takes refuge from his fears and disappointments in puns that are sometimes an underhand challenge to the prevailing standards of 'decency' in his own society. Word-play enables him to get away with all

13 Soriano, *Portrait de l'artiste jeune*, pp. 37–47.

kinds of suggestiveness – as he will throughout the *Voyages extraordinaires* – but it is also, and most fundamentally, a form of fun. The fear of disappointment and the joy of words come together in a significant alliance in *Les Châteaux en Californie*. They will also coalesce memorably in real life on one occasion at about this time, when the young Verne goes back to his native Nantes. At a reception held in a local bourgeois household, he meets the attractive Laurence Janmar who, according to Verne's first biographer Marguerite Allotte de la Fuÿe, complains that the whalebones of her corset are too tight on her ribs ('son corset, trop baleiné, lui meurtrit les côtes'). As quick as a flash, the gallant but impudent young Verne, playing on the double meaning of the French word *côtes*, exclaims: 'Que ne puis-je pêcher la baleine sur ces côtes?'[14] ['Would that I could go fishing for whales on those ribs/coasts!'] And that, it appears, puts paid to his chances of becoming the fiancé of Mademoiselle Janmar. But it does establish Verne as a master-punner, and henceforth this will be one of the most important features of his writing. Life and literature overlap interestingly here. Life is being turned into words, its difficulties and dilemmas kept at a distance. Verne is already very much a wordsmith, as is abundantly clear from a play such as *Les Châteaux en Californie*.

Our third play, *Le Colin-Maillard*, is a one-act *opéra-comique* written by Verne in collaboration with Michel Carré, and first produced at the Théâtre Lyrique on 28 April 1853. As with the two plays previously discussed, the plot revolves around love, marriage and the eternal problem of pairing up the right people. In this play, set in the Bois de Meudon in 1744, three handsome young suitors woo three beautiful young sisters. However, the latter's prospects of marriage are impeded by their aunt Pélagie (also their guardian) who has set the condition that she herself should be married before she gives away her nieces. As the play opens, a threefold tryst of lovers is due to take place in the woods, opening the way for confusion and trickery. The three girls are due to meet up with their young suitors, but Pélagie has also arranged a meeting (or so she thinks) with a *vieux seigneur* from whom she has received a letter. The *vieux seigneur*, who goes under the title Le Baron de la Verdure, has, however, been propositioning one of the young sisters, and Pélagie has received his letter in error. He now comes strolling into the woods in the hope of meeting up with the girl to whom he has written. The problem, for the three young and very much in love couples, is how to pair off Pélagie and the baron, thus leaving them free to marry as they wish. In concert with their

14 Marguerite Allotte de la Fuÿe, *Jules Verne, sa vie, son œuvre* (Paris: Hachette, 1953 [1928]), p. 61.

uncle – who himself is eager to see his sister married – the girls arrange a game of blind man's buff with the baron while Pélagie is absent. As soon as he has put on the blindfold, they disappear, just as Pélagie is returning to the scene. Alone with Pélagie, but still blindfolded, the baron seizes her and – because of the compromising situation he has put her in, which is witnessed by the other characters on their return – is forced to make amends by offering to marry her. Pélagie willingly and rapidly consents to the marriage, and consequently gives her blessing to the proposed alliances of the three girls with their three suitors. Problem solved.

Once again Verne has used the idea of a game within the plot – this time the *colin-maillard* or 'blind man's buff' of the title – thus doubly stressing the artificiality of his medium by using 'play' within a play. Once again, alliances are forged and resolved in marriage, but not before there has been a threat from an outside party. And once again, everything resolves itself happily and order is restored in the happiest of *dénouements*. Trickery, craft and gamesmanship are central to the unfolding of the plot, which depends on the forces of 'true love' outwitting the machinations of the seducer or the interferer. The theme of being tricked into marriage – as the Baron de la Verdure is – is one that will reappear years later in the *Voyages extraordinaires*, for example when Van Mitten, the Dutch friend of Kéraban-le-têtu, is very nearly forced into an alliance with 'la noble Saraboul', only to be rescued from it in extremis by the news that his former wife is still alive after all. But the tone of this play, as ever when Verne deals with the question of marriage, is light-hearted and bantering. The playful style mirrors the very subject of the comedy, which is that of a game. But the game, frivolous though it may be, is seen to be the thing that ultimately resolves the deeper human issues, corrects potential injustices and settles the various alliances as they should be settled. Pretence, or disguise, leads to the truth, and the business of righting wrongs has, it is implied, to be carried out by artificial and ludic means. The game of blind man's buff is, then, a contrivance, artfully 'staged' by the three sisters and their uncle, but beyond the blindfold there is the truth of real emotions. So too, it is implied, the play itself is a self-consciously imaginary creation, a light-hearted diversion on the margin of real human drama, but which nonetheless leads to important revelations and appropriate conclusions. The neat *dénouement* once again leaves us feeling that in the end there will always be justice in Verne's world. It is reassuring and comforting, as well as being highly self-conscious and extravagantly contrived. It is a theatrical world par excellence.

From stage to fiction

The three plays we have just examined are typical of Jules Verne's early output, and show his love of theatrical contrivance, with exaggerated plots, eccentric characters, misadventures and peripeteia, racy repartee, colourful (sometimes outrageous) humour and word-play. These qualities remain apparent throughout the theatrical writings of the 1850s. Though the early years of the decade see, alongside the high-spirited and energetic writings for the stage, the first of Verne's important narrative pieces ('Les Premiers Navires de la marine mexicaine' and 'Un voyage en ballon' in 1851, 'Martin Paz' and 'Pierre-Jean' in 1852), the vaudeville establishes itself as a fixture. It will be present not only in further writings for the stage (for example in *Monsieur de Chimpanzé*, an operetta, or 'singerie musicale' ['musical monkey business'] as Verne calls it, written in 1857 in collaboration with Michel Carré and performed in 1858–59), but also in the narrative writings themselves. While the 'serious' Jules Verne will concentrate increasingly on questions of travel, geography or history, the theatrical Verne remains, constantly and overtly reminding us that the textual world he creates is an artificial and unreal one, a playful charade which points an ironic finger at itself despite all its pretences at veracity. The larger-than-life characters such as the madman of 'Un voyage en ballon' owe much to Verne's involvement with the theatre, and their con- trived antics and heady discourses are those of his stage creations. The sheer extravagance and excess of such characters is crucially important in undermining the so-called 'realism' of narrative and in flagging up its literary credentials and its artistic conventions. But Verne will always excel at the depiction of disproportionate, extraordinary characters whose unwieldy appearance or profuse speech make of them a theatrical spectacle and remind us that the writer's fundamental business is that of entertainment.

One of the first and most memorable of these early, 'theatrical' char- acters is Anselme des Tilleuls, the ungainly, eponymous hero of *Le Mariage de M. Anselme des Tilleuls* (1855). As in the vaudeville plots of the same period, this is a story about finding the right marriage alliance, and, like the plays, it ends with the problem having been solved. But Anselme himself is larger than life in every sense, not only physically, but also in terms of his clumsiness, his lack of intelligence and his lack of beauty. He is the target of merciless and high-spirited irony on the part of the author, and despite his eventual success in finding a spouse he remains more in the tradition of Thomas Diafoirus, the hapless doctor's son in Molière's *Le Malade imaginaire*, than in that of the successful suitor (we shall see later in this chapter how readily Verne revives the 'Diafoirus' figure elsewhere in his work). But the entertainment is heightened by the addition of another character, Anselme's Latin teacher Naso Paraclet. Since Anselme wishes to get married in order to ensure the continuation of his line, Paraclet (scarcely the source of consolation or the fount of wisdom that his name evokes)[15] sets about finding him a spouse – though he himself has never known anything remotely akin to conjugal bliss, since his abiding obsession is Latin. In fact all truth and wisdom, for Paraclet, is to be found in the niceties and complexities of Latin grammar. He intersperses all his advice to Anselme with reflections on the subtleties of verbs, gerundives, subjunctives, nominatives, accusatives, ablatives and so on. From the comedy of character, we find ourselves returned to the comedy of language, as Paraclet confuses and conflates conjugation and conjugality, believing implicitly that '[les] principes de toute morale [sont] enfouis dans la grammaire'[16] ['the principles of all morality are hidden within grammar']. Eventually, however, Paraclet is successful on behalf of his protégé, for, in his discussions with local notables, he meets a court registrar (or *greffier*) who is as obsessed with Latin grammar as he is, and who has a daughter. Negotiations and grammatical discussions follow. Anselme, the maladroit youngster, is married off to the equally maladroit Mademoiselle Lafourchette, who matches him in ugliness and lack of grace. Between them they produce a horde of children, 'indistinctement mâles ou femelles' (SC, p. 76) ['indistinctly male or female'], at the rate of one a year.

As in *Les Châteaux en Californie*, Verne indulges his taste for scatological and scabrous word-play in this highly exuberant text. It is littered with innuendoes, many of them referring to the sexuality of the characters themselves. Paraclet, on approaching the first family into which he hopes to marry Anselme, explains to them that the young man is a 'lampe virginale, que j'ai moi-même remplie d'une huile nouvelle, je l'ai montée

---

15 The Greek word *parakletos*, designating the Holy Ghost, has been variously translated as 'advocate', 'intercessor', 'teacher', 'helper' or 'comforter'. It should be added that the name of Anselme himself in this tale is a reminder of Saint Anselm, the eleventh-century ecclesiastical philosopher. In the Augustinian tradition, Saint Anselm believed in the necessity of faith and revelation as the foundations of philosophy and reason. Clearly, in Verne's story, Anselme sees Paraclet as the source of all revealed wisdom.

16 *Le Mariage de M. Anselme des Tilleuls* (1855) in *San Carlos, et autres récits inédits*, édition établie par Jacques Davy, Régis Miannay, Christian Robin, Claudine Sainlot (Paris: Le Cherche Midi, 1993), pp. 49–79 (p. 56). This volume is designated SC hereafter.

avec soin' (SC, p. 61) ['virginal lamp that I myself have filled with new oil, and have mounted with care']. And, in the *dénouement* of the narrative, Verne puns on the meaning of 'Tilleul' ['lime tree'], as we learn that the marriage of the daughter of the magistrate to Anselme will be a case of 'la fille d'un greffier de province se greffant sur un orgueilleux Tilleul' ['the daughter of a provincial court registrar, grafting herself onto a proud Tilleul'], and that they will together be able to 'planter de longues allées de tilleuls' (SC, p. 73, p. 76) ['plant long avenues of lime trees']. Here, once again, we see the young Verne challenging the norms of acceptability in his own social world, through highly colourful and inventive word-play. While commentators such as Soriano have been quick to see some of Verne's double-entendres as signs of repressed homosexual urges,[17] we should not lose sight of the fact that they are first and foremost the signs of a writer and wordsmith. That being so, the question of whether Verne was or was not a closet homosexual seems entirely devoid of interest, and in any case it seeks a yes/no answer where almost certainly none exists. Sexual innuendo allows the author to indulge above all in verbal antics, as comic writers have done through the ages. Though Verne's word-play now passes – in some cases at least – from the characters to the narrator of his fiction, its self-conscious entertainment value remains much the same. Words designate their own ability to make the world 'unreal', to turn it into something larger than life, more absurd and, in the end, irredeemably *verbal*. This, together with the fanciful nature of a plot which involves elaborate and implausible schemes to marry off a young man, and which finally achieves that goal, sets Verne's narrative squarely in the tradition of the vaudeville, in which a problem is unravelled, and a solution found after a series of – often verbal – misadventures.

Throughout the *Voyages extraordinaires* we will find characters who remind us, in one way or another, of those vaudevillesque traditions from which Verne's writing emerges in the important early stages. The hyperbolic, sometimes immoderate, sometimes downright schoolboyish humour will later become a powerful device in maintaining the interest of Verne's youthful target audience (and it is hardly surprising that pedagogues such as Lidenbrock or Palmyrin Rosette – true 'descendants' of Naso Paraclet – are sometimes held up to ridicule). Exaggerated playfulness is one of the constants of Verne's writing, and curiously, it is often

17 For more general comments on Jules Verne's latent homosexuality, see Marc Soriano, *Jules Verne: le cas Verne* (Paris: Julliard, 1978), pp. 72 ff., p. 147 and p. 170. The theory of Verne's homosexuality originated in the important study by Marcel Moré, *Le Très Curieux Jules Verne*.

overlooked in adaptations of his work. The result is that the popular image of Verne in our own time is that of a gung-ho author concerned principally to depict heroic and noble characters pushing back the frontiers of science or exploration.[18] Readers who return to the original texts of Verne's novels are often surprised by the sheer amount of humour in them, and even in his best-known works there are larger-than-life characters whose *tics* of behaviour or language or whose extraordinary appearance puts them firmly back into the theatrical tradition. The loquacious and eccentric Lidenbrock, constantly 'performing' for an imaginary audience in *Voyage au centre de la terre*, is one such character, as is the even more loquacious Calistus Munbar in *L'Ile à hélice*. But we find permutations of this eccentricity in almost every Vernian text, from the misfits of the Gun-Club who at the beginning of *De la terre à la lune* consider how to turn their energies from war-mongering to exploration, as they poke their prosthetic limbs angrily into the fire; to Michel Ardan in the same novel, whose dramatic behaviour is the source of many of its best moments; to the antics of Kéraban-le-têtu, who with his Molièresque fixation is the comic character par excellence; through to the absurd experiments of Doctor Ox. Elsewhere, in the 1887 text *Gil Braltar*,[19] two equally incongruous characters are set alongside one another, and the intrinsically theatrical theme of disguise heightens the comic mix. On the one hand, there is Gil Braltar himself, a madman who wants to recapture Gibraltar from the British, and on the other hand General Mac Kackmale, who is entrusted with the island's defence. Both masquerade as apes – first Gil Braltar, who uses the skin of an ape in order to approach Government House unrecognised, then Mac Kackmale, who captures Gil Braltar and

18 Such a view of Jules Verne was damagingly recycled by I. O. Evans in *Jules Verne and his Work* (London: Arco, 1965), perhaps the least reliable account of the author that has ever been produced in English. Interestingly, however, quite the opposite approach to Verne is in evidence in Frank Coraci's 2004 film *Around the World in Eighty Days*, in which the more serious side of Verne's world-view is almost entirely overlooked. But as an exaggerated send-up of the *Tour du monde* theme (with the expected liberties in relation to the plot of the novel) the film occasionally suggests – for all its obvious failings – the flavour of Verne's work more generally. Fogg, played by Steve Coogan, is an obsessed inventor in the mould of Verne's best scientist-pedants; and Passepartout, played by Jackie Chan, is a clown and a performer. Though we may feel that Verne's story has been reduced to a series of kick-boxing spectacles against various backdrops, something of the exuberance of the original is retained. For all that, the 1956 Michael Todd version of the film starring David Niven undoubtedly remains the cinematographic benchmark.

19 The story is included with a number of other shorter pieces in volume 39 of the Rencontre series, after *L'Agence Thompson and Co*.

takes over his disguise. However, disguise brings not revelation in this case, but confusion. Nobody knows whether the figure going out of the town is Gil Braltar, or the general himself, just as nobody knew whether the figure coming into the town was a monkey or a madman. Apes appear to be men, and men appear to be apes, even as they are pretending to be other men. And later, when the captured Gil Braltar is exhibited in cities throughout the old and new worlds, some claim that it is not the madman, but General Mac Kackmale himself. And both men, in any case, can easily be confused with monkeys (the name Mac Kackmale – or 'macaque mâle' – is a pun on the ape which inhabits the rock to this day). However, it is Mac Kackmale's likeness to a monkey which ensured the safety of the rock, and in the final lines of the tale we encounter its eccentric moral:

> Cette aventure a été une leçon pour le gouvernement de Sa Gracieuse Majesté. Il a compris que si Gibraltar ne pouvait être pris par les hommes, il était à la merci des singes. Aussi, l'Angleterre, très pratique, est-elle décidée à n'y envoyer désormais que les plus laids de ses généraux, afin que les monos puissent s'y tromper encore.
>
> Cette mesure vraisemblablement lui assure à jamais la possession de Gibraltar. (AT, p. 433)

> [This adventure was a lesson for her Gracious Majesty's government, which deduced that, if Gibraltar was not at risk of being taken by men, it was nonetheless at the mercy of the apes. Thus England, that most practical of countries, resolved to send only the ugliest of her generals there, so that the monkeys will continue to be deceived.
>
> It would seem that this measure has ensured her the possession of Gibraltar in perpetuity.]

Thus do we have Verne's take on the old legend that, as long as the apes continue to inhabit the rock, Gibraltar will remain a British possession. But the levity and the verbal inventiveness with which he achieves this are a reminder that this supposedly 'realist' writer remains essentially in the theatrical tradition, with high-spirited humour a dominant and central element.

Disguise, false identity and recognition

Of the many theatrical devices in the *Voyages extraordinaires* that build on the legacy of Verne's early involvement with the theatre, the theme of disguise itself is perhaps the most frequent and the most regularly used. Disguise is everywhere in Verne's writing. True, disguise is a theme we will also find in some of the most popular novels in nineteenth-century France, from Dumas *père*'s *Le Comte de Monte Cristo* to Hugo's *Les Misérables*. But part of the reason for the success of such novels was because their narrative techniques were closely modelled on devices associated with the theatre, among which disguise takes pride of place. Disguise implies, self-evidently, that a character is escaping recognition, and is doing so in order to solve some problem or to bring about a change in circumstances. It is the very stuff of dramatic intrigue. Often in Verne, disguise is used as a means of spying on someone, or at least of participating incognito in a project or a journey. In *Face au drapeau*, the engineer Simon Hart assumes a false identity in order to take on a job as attendant to Thomas Roch, the mad inventor who has devised a powerful new weapon. His aim is to try to wrest the secrets of Roch's device from him. As is so often the case, the initial masquerade here is duplicated by a further one, when the pirate Ker Karraje – also in pursuit of the secret of Roch's weapon – appears as the mysterious but well-connected comte d'Artigas. In theatrical fashion, one disguised character shadow-boxes with another – both of them unwittingly disguised for the same purpose – and many of the developments in the plot are born of this confrontation between false personae. Elsewhere, disguise becomes an integral part of the adventures or mysteries that motivate the journeys in Verne's novels, perhaps most often because of the hangers-on who infiltrate an expedition with dishonourable intentions. In *Les Enfants du capitaine Grant*, the quartermaster Ayrton aboard Glenarvan's yacht turns out to be none other than the feared bandit Ben Joyce. In *Les Frères Kip*, the dastardly Vin Mod conceals his identity in order to spy on the Kip brothers in their hotel room, where he hides an incriminating murder weapon and some money. Here, disguise is linked with classic cloak-and-dagger intrigue. But the assumption of a fake persona will sometimes also have the effect of bringing out more fully the reality of a character. Disguise, if not always directly followed by unmasking, can nonetheless be an inverted form of revelation, for example when the disguised person behaves in a manner that arouses suspicion. Such is the case of Torrès, the passenger taken aboard the river craft in *La Jangada*, whose behaviour is so surly and whose demeanour is so hostile that he alienates every single one of his fellow travellers; or of Negoro, the slave-trader who poses as a member of the ship's crew in *Un capitaine de quinze ans*, but whose evil intentions are revealed by Dingo the dog.

Disguise can also be a prelude to discovery or to self-discovery in Verne, as it so often is in the theatre. In *Voyages et aventures du capitaine Hatteras*, the journey to the Arctic Circle is begun in the apparent absence of the Captain himself, who contrives to send secret instructions about the route to follow. Yet, as it turns out, Hatteras – believed to be absent – is on board the *Forward* all the time, disguised as a ship's hand, and he makes his belated and highly dramatic *entrée en scène* as late as Chapter 12 of the story. But in other instances, the question of disguise and revelation is more intimately linked to the theme of identity. In *Le Chemin de France*, Jean Keller has always assumed that he is German. But this turns out to have been a 'masking' of his real identity from himself, and he learns later that he is in reality French – a discovery that reconciles him to what he is and to how he feels. Revelation about the truth of a character often turns out to be a significant *coup de théâtre* in Verne's novels. The most obvious and spectacular case (echoing in some respects the disguise of Hatteras as a ship's hand in the early novel) is that of the seaman Hunt, taken on board ship by Captain Len Guy in *Le Sphinx des glaces*, as part of the captain's expedition to find the ship that his brother had owned in Poe's *Narrative of Arthur Gordon Pym*. But Hunt turns out, by his own admission at the beginning of Part II of the story, to be none other than Dirk Peters, a fictitious character from Poe's story who had accompanied Pym on his expedition. The revelation here could not be more dramatic – the more so since an invented literary character appears to have come to life – and has been prepared with all the techniques of suspense that one associates with the theatre (such as the 'scenes' in which Hunt is heard uttering the name of Pym in the dead of night). It is the more sensational for the fact that disguise and its unmasking does nothing to clarify the problem this novel poses about the relationship between the fictional world and the real one, even though the abandonment of disguise is a powerful sign that falsehood has at last been replaced by truth. But disguise will sometimes also confirm that an imaginary, adopted persona is in fact the true one, and role-playing unexpectedly produces a more fitting identity than the character's normal persona. When, in *Le Tour du monde en quatre-vingts jours*, Passepartout finds himself performing in a circus as part of a troupe of acrobats with long noses, this quintessentially theatrical figure finds himself back in his element, even if he does end up making the human pyramid collapse when he recognises his master in the audience and leaps out.

Le Tour du monde en quatre-vingts jours is, typically, a novel that is structured around the notion of disguise. Fix, the detective, follows Fogg around the world, all the while disguising his real occupation and intentions – but the mask slips constantly, and he is comically incapable of maintaining his pretence. Meanwhile Fogg, whom Fix suspects of not being the man he is, but rather of being the bank robber described in the British press, remains imperturbably and implacably himself – a depressingly different figure from the 'disguised' one Fix would like to think he is. It is only outsiders who confer an imagined identity upon Fogg, seeing in him another figure, though naturally that travesty of the real man will come to play an important role when Fogg is arrested in the final stages of his journey and fails to make his return to London as planned. Doubles and shadows – Fix 'doubles' Fogg as he follows in his footsteps, and the shadow of the bank robber is ever present – are the natural corollaries of disguise, and they are everywhere in this novel. But the theme of the double will recur throughout the *Voyages extraordinaires*, and nowhere more so than in *Nord contre sud*, the novel about the American Civil War whose plot depends on the presence of identical twins. The Texar brothers, true villains in the cloak-and-dagger tradition, are responsible for a kidnapping. However, when one of them is confronted with the accusation, it appears that he has a perfect alibi, and only later does it emerge that there were two of them, each in different locations at the moment of the crime. Using each other as masks or foils, they create confusion; but, as happens with theatrical disguises, the answer is perfectly simple once the disguise has been revealed. And as so often in the case of plots involving crime and disguise (the same theme will be apparent in *La Jangada* and *Les Frères Kip*) the narrative here revolves around a criminal investigation, whose task it is to uncover the real 'story' of what happened. Though such narratives are clearly also indebted to Poe, and reveal Verne to be one of the many nineteenth-century writers forging a path towards the modern detective story, their theatrical elements are crucial to the mixture.

The theme of disguise is, then, quintessentially dramatic, and it often leads to spectacular developments in the plot, a heightening of tension, or revelations that close off an 'act' and usher in the next phase. In *Un capitaine de quinze ans*, there is a typically dramatic and showy use of disguise, when the party of travellers is diverted by the villain Negoro and taken to Kazonndé in Central Africa. Negoro's intention is to sell the black members of the party as slaves, but one of them, the appropriately named Hercule, manages to escape. Like other Vernian 'giants' (for example the circus acrobat Matifou in *Mathias Sandorf*), Hercule has something of the performer and the entertainer about him, and with it the imagination to stage his own theatrical scenes. Returning to the homestead where two of the travelling party are confined, he disguises himself as a witchdoctor and mesmerises the locals with mumbo-jumbo about stopping the rain. Completely convinced, they are taken in by this 'act', at which point Hercule proceeds to the next stage of his plan. Pointing to Mrs Weldon and her son Jack, he ominously declares that they are the ones whose presence has brought on the curse of the bad weather, and that they will need to be removed if his spell is to work. Gathering them up, he takes them away to a secret place in the forest where they are reunited with other members of their party. The act has succeeded. What is noticeable here is that the scene of disguise is itself a miniature drama within the story, staged by one of its characters, with roles that are duly assigned and performed. Its artificiality is thus underlined, but as in the vaudeville dramas of Verne's youth, artifice and contrivance are themselves the means of unravelling a problem and reaching a satisfactory *dénouement*.

Perhaps the story in the *Voyages extraordinaires* that is most fully based on disguise is *Mathias Sandorf*. But it was primarily a novel, not a drama, that was the inspiration for this story. In his dedication of the text to Dumas *fils* in memory of his father, the author of *Le Comte de Monte Cristo*, Verne writes: 'Je vous dédie ce livre en le dédiant aussi à la mémoire du conteur de génie que fut Alexandre Dumas, votre père. Dans cet ouvrage, j'ai essayé de faire de *Mathias Sandorf* le *Monte Cristo* des *Voyages extraordinaires*. Je vous prie d'en accepter la dédicace comme un témoignage de ma profonde amitié.' ['I dedicate this book to you, just as I dedicate it to the memory of that storyteller of genius, Alexandre Dumas the elder, your own father. I have tried to make of *Mathias Sandorf* the *Monte Cristo* of the *Extraordinary Journeys*.'] The interesting response of Dumas *fils*, recorded alongside Verne's dedication in the 1885 Hetzel edition, underlines the affinities between Verne's style and that of Dumas's father: 'Il y a entre vous et lui une parenté littéraire si évidente que, littérairement parlant, vous êtes plus son fils que moi' ['There is such an obvious literary relationship between the two of you that, from a literary point of view, you are more his son than I am'].

Like Dumas's famous novel, Verne's story is also one of an elaborately constructed — and sometimes unpredictable — revenge, where the wronged character comes back in a new disguise, after an absence of several years during which he is assumed dead. As in *Monte Cristo*, the character is fabulously wealthy, and all the more powerful for his ability to stage events from behind the scenes without being seen or denounced. Sandorf, alias Doctor Antékirtt, is also a man of science and knowledge who, after his escape from the death sentence, has made his second fortune by dispensing cures as he travels. But in the Vernian tradition he is also a polyglot who has learned Arabic and other languages in the course of his peregrinations. He is thus able to assume the 'disguise' not only of a new identity and a new profession, but also of language itself. And although Verne's basic model for Sandorf is the figure of Edmond Dantès — the falsely accused young sailor in *Le Comte de Monte Cristo* who escapes from the island fortress in which he is imprisoned – both Dumas's novel and Verne's own are abundantly, self-consciously and expansively dramatic in scope, style and pace.[20] In both cases, the central character's disguise enables him to manipulate events from a position of invisibility. Sandorf is not only a polymath and a polyglot, he is also an artist who creates and self-consciously plays out a drama in the full knowledge that his invented 'plot', involving his own disguise, will produce the desired result. Drama is, then, not only at the origin of this story, it is also represented within it through the theme of disguise. And disguise, together with the revelations it produces so dramatically, is everywhere. As in other novels in the *Voyages extraordinaires*, one disguise is almost invariably reflected by another, or by several others, creating a hall of mirrors in which truth and falsehood themselves become shifting, problematic concepts. The ultimate disguise, indeed, is taken on by the young man who will end up as Sandorf's son-in-law, Pierre Bathory. He is, like Sandorf himself, assumed to be dead, until one day in a dramatic Lazarus scene he rises up back to life (an act which recalls Sandorf's own motto: 'la mort ne détruit pas, elle ne rend qu'invisible' ['death does not destroy, it merely renders invisible']). Meanwhile, another 'disguise' is confusing matters further, for it appears that the beautiful and admirable Sava is the daughter of the traitor Toronthal. How can it be that such a paragon of virtue and integrity has been sired by a man so clearly at the opposite end of the moral scale? In the end, the revelation comes about that Sava is none other than the long-lost daughter of Sandorf himself, and in almost vaudevillesque fashion, this paves the way for the eventual marriage of Sava and Bathory. The problem is unravelled, the final unmasking of the characters reveals the truth, and everything is put back in place in due and orderly fashion. This is clearly the stuff of theatre, and like a true dramatist, Verne cleverly assembles the pieces but conceals the facts until a solution is in sight.

A number of Verne's stories take the question of disguise one stage further and venture into the terrain of cross-dressing. As in Molière or Marivaux, women dress up as men and gain privileged access to the closed world of male society. In true dramatic tradition, this can also involve sexual confusion, with characters feeling an attraction that they cannot initially comprehend or accept. But the revelation of the disguise resolves the conflict and allows them to give free rein to their instinctive feelings. One such story is *Les Forceurs de blocus*, set against the background of the American Civil War. Jenny Halliburtt and her manservant

---

20 Like Verne, Dumas had also written for the stage before turning his attention to the novel, and had huge success with plays such as *Antony* (1831) and *Kean* (1836).

Crockston infiltrate the crew of the *Delphin*, on its way from Glasgow to Charleston. Jenny's purpose is to rescue her father, a Northerner held in Charleston since the beginning of the war. As the vessel pushes out to sea and Crockston, unmasked as an impostor, is about to receive a lashing, Jenny steps in and asks to speak to the captain. The latter, on observing her more carefully, is struck by 'la figure jeune et douce du novice, sa voix singulièrement sympathique, la finesse et la blancheur de ses mains, à peine dissimulée sous une couche de bistre, ses grands yeux dont l'animation ne pouvait tempérer la douceur' (FB, p. 362) ['the sweet young face of the novice, his peculiarly attractive voice, the delicacy and whiteness of his hands, hardly disguised under a brownish tint, the large eyes, the liveliness of which could not hide their tenderness']. In fact, though this is the point at which the unmasking takes place, it is also the point at which real sexual attraction between Miss Halliburtt and Captain Playfair begins. The revelation itself produces confusion, embarrassment and, eventually, love. Jenny remains aboard, and continues to work her charms on Playfair.

In Verne's world, women naturally have to take on disguise if they are to enter the jealously guarded male preserve that is life aboard an ocean-going vessel. How long the disguise lasts is dictated by the particular requirements of the plot. The theme of the young woman dressed as a man in order to sail the high seas will be used again by Verne in *Le Superbe Orénoque*, where Jeanne de Kermor, travelling from France to South America in search of the father she has never seen, assumes the disguise of a young man and calls herself Jean. Like Jenny Halliburtt, she travels with an 'uncle', whose false credentials and implausible identity soon come to be questioned by other characters in the story. However, the unmasking of the young woman takes a little longer, and there is sexual confusion as one of the Frenchmen involved in this expedition begins to take an increasing interest in 'Jean'. The revelation about Jeanne de Kermor's real identity, withheld for maximum dramatic effect, comes at the end of the first part of the novel. Thereafter, the young couple are free to fall in love and to pursue the quest to find Jeanne's father – who in the event had also assumed a disguise, or at least a new identity, many years earlier when, as Colonel de Kermor, he had wrongly believed that both his wife and his daughter had perished in a shipwreck and had set off to the other side of the world to start a new life. The *dénouement* of the story thus allows for a spectacular reunion of father and daughter, lost to each other for nearly a lifetime, and the marriage of the daughter with her newly found fiancé. Once again, it is a plot in which confusion and disarray are replaced in the final instance by order and completion, as the true identities of the characters are revealed. And once again, this is an abundantly theatrical subject, as the plot proceeds towards a solution in which the loose ends are neatly and self-consciously tied up. Not only does this remind us of the theatrical dimension of Verne's work, it also reinforces that contrived literariness which is his hallmark throughout the *Voyages extraordinaires*.

Love, betrothal, marriage

The question of disguise is almost always linked, at some level in Verne's stories, to the love intrigue. Again and again in the *Voyages extraordinaires*, plots will conclude happily with a marriage or a betrothal, a solution achieved after numerous setbacks and diversions. Recognition and 'unmasking', in every sense, thus mark out the *dénouements*, in which genuine emotions are at last revealed, so that truth and realism can finally triumph over pretence and falsehood. And the lesson about love in the *Voyages extraordinaires* is always very simple. There is no force greater and more wholesome than that of a mutual attraction between two well-suited persons, and no obstacle that it cannot ultimately overcome. We always sense that the plot will therefore work out, even when a couple seem to be irrevocably separated by external circumstances – as is the case, for example, of Grip and Sissy in *P'tit-Bonhomme*, who finally get engaged after being lost to each other and to the central character for years. Closure with marriage or betrothal is, then, the contrived and staged ending to many of Verne's stories. The playful final flourish of *Clovis Dardentor*, *Les Indes noires*, *L'Etoile du sud*, *Kéraban-le-têtu*, *La Jangada* (which ends on a double marriage) – to name but a few of the most obvious examples – acts as a gentle reminder to the reader that the world of make-believe and of spectacle ends at this point. The conventional nature of the ending is ironically emphasised, providing at once the necessary 'feelgood factor' and the wake-up call that is required for the final curtain.

The happy solutions of Verne's plots are a reminder not just that he writes in a theatrical tradition, but also that he models his storylines on those of the traditional fairy tale. Handsome princes, damsels in distress, and evil wrongdoers who imprison them or send them off on false quests, are never far away (La Stilla, of *Le Château des Carpathes*, is the ultimate sleeping beauty – but her awakening by the handsome prince will be an artificial one). Verne's literary credentials are always multiple, always complex, since he draws on so many sources and traditions at once. But one of the reasons why it is important to insist in particular on the theatricality of his *dénouements* is because they also produce a self-conscious fore-grounding of the medium itself. Verne uses the techniques and traditions of the stage precisely to designate his fiction as a pretence, an entertainment, an artifice which must achieve closure. Often the characters will be brought on stage in a rousing finale, as is the case for example in *Les Forceurs de blocus* or *Le Rayon vert*, which both end with a wedding scene. In such stories, each of the major characters is able to come back on stage and take their final bow before the curtain goes down, and the fiction ends with the clear recognition that this was a constructed, make-believe world. The reader is implicitly invited to be aware of this artifice rather than to suspend disbelief completely.

Yet, in the very best theatrical tradition, Verne often makes it look as though his couples have insurmountable obstacles in their way. Disguise may be only one of many barriers, which can include the Romeo-and-Juliet theme of warring families, the Molieresque presence of pig-headed and wrong-thinking fathers, or occasionally the simple failure of the lovers themselves to recognise their affinities. Dramatic conflicts and misadventures ensue. False problems are sometimes put in the lovers' way in order to make the eventual solution seem more spectacular, more improbably prised from the jaws of impossibility itself. The meanderings, surprises and about-faces of the drama, as it proceeds towards its conclusion, can seem almost unbelievably tortuous. The vaudeville tradition achieves an unlikely balance between, on the one hand, the setting of obstacles that seem to militate increasingly against any chance of a solution, and on the other hand, the contrivance of that happy ending that we always knew to be inevitable. Part of the pleasure that such plots generate is that they force us constantly to guess at how the irreconcilable will be reconciled. They present logical puzzles, which they then artfully solve for us. Much of this is also about the art of concealment, since the solution must be left to the last possible moment, and to the point at which it seems most unlikely. In the *Voyages extraordinaires*, we find precisely this coexistence of apparent impossibility and ultimate inevitability, together with the art of concealment. In *Kéraban-le-têtu*, for example, everything in the plot seems to take the young couple farther away from their longed-for marriage, as the larger-than-life central character literally sends the entire cast off on a massive detour. Naturally, we know that the story will end happily, but the whole point of it is that this conclusion should appear invisible, impossible, implausible, and that for much of the story it should be seen as an ever-receding goal. The complications that are thus produced, with lovers being separated and ultimately reunited against all the odds (a plot structure that replicates the highly successful dramatic mix of *Michel Strogoff*), are in inverse proportion to the simplicity of the story's finale.

A similar process will be apparent in *La Chasse au météore*, the novel about a comet full of gold which is observed by two amateur astronomers as it approaches Earth. Since the two astronomers are in dispute about who first sighted the comet, it seems more and more unlikely that their respective offspring will be able to go ahead with the marriage that has been planned for them. The difficulties are increased when an international commission gets involved in the quest for the comet, and its 'ownership' becomes a political matter. Yet the problem is spectacularly solved when the comet itself disintegrates on landing and there is nothing left to fight over. The warring families are reconciled, having recognised that the quest for wealth or fame was a false one (a moral which recalls that of *Les Châteaux en Californie*), and the young lovers are free to go ahead and marry. And as so often happens in theatre too, the main marriage plot here is echoed in minor but exuberant mode by the presence of two highly eccentric characters, Seth Forsyth and Acadia Walker. The couple arrive at the beginning of the story in Whaston [sic], Virginia, where in a typically Vernian 'scene' they are married on horseback. They later divorce, but finally remarry at the end of the story when they discover, on board the vessel making its way to the comet's landing place, that their relationship is after all alive and well – like the two warring but seasick astronomers, who are finally 'réunis dans l'abominable communauté des haut-le-cœur' (CM, p. 203) ['united in the abominable togetherness of retching']. Thus their double marriage frames the tale and provides one of its humorous dimensions, while mirroring in ironic yet theatrical mode the ups and downs of the lovers' predicament. A similar framing structure had been used in *Claudius Bombarnac*, where two equally eccentric characters – Fulk Ephrinell, a denture salesman, and Horatia Bluett, an employee of the London firm Holmes-Home travelling to China in order to negotiate a supply of human hair for the manufacture of wigs – decide to marry on board the train in which they are travelling, then later divorce as they are incapable of reconciling their business interests. Such improbable characters, with such implausible occupations and interests, would almost be worthy of Ionesco. Above all, their antics show that Verne has an unfailing eye for the theatrical.

Where there are stories of love, marriage and betrothal, there will always too be third parties – unwanted suitors who are put in the way of true love for the sake of family interests, or interferers who wish to alter the course of events in pursuit of their own goals. Often, in the latter case, these interests will include the hope of acquiring an inheritance. Such is the case in *L'Archipel en feu*, where the dishonourable Starkos, who has compromised the banker Elizundo in affairs of human traffic during the Greek wars of independence, demands the hand of the banker's daughter. The daughter, Hadjine, was engaged to the French officer Henry d'Albaret. In a classic good-versus-evil struggle, d'Albaret eventually sees off his rival in dramatic circumstances when he bids a higher price than him for the girl in a slave market – another of those key Vernian scenes on which everything turns. Starkos, who turns out to be none other than the redoubted pirate Sacratif (the theme of disguise returns once again) is killed, and the courageous and eminently well-suited young couple are free to marry and live happily ever after. The evil and inappropriate suitor can be found on many other occasions in the *Voyages extraordinaires*. In the early story *Un hivernage dans les glaces*, the unwanted André Vasling boards the ship on which the story's leading lady, Marie, travels in search of her lost fiancé, with dangerous and unpleasant consequences. In *La Jangada*, Torrès tries to blackmail Joam Garral for the hand of his daughter. In a Gothic permutation of the theme in *Le Château des Carpathes*, the Baron de Gortz competes with Franz de Telek for the soul of the dead La Stilla. And in the posthumous *Le Secret de Wilhelm Storitz*, the eponymous hero, refused the hand of Myra, goes to ultimate lengths to prevent her union with the chosen suitor, Marc Vidal, by making her invisible. Evil wrongdoers and interferers abound in the *Voyages extraordinaires*, and they heighten the drama by providing the crucial element of suspense. Almost always, they are not so much fully-fledged characters as simple dramatic devices, overtly used as such, to heighten tension and increase the possibilities of surprise or sudden *coups de théâtre*.

There are, too, unwanted suitors who come purely from the comic tradition and who, like Molière's Thomas Diafoirus, are the laughing stock of one and all, incapable of commanding any respect. We have already noted that Verne revives the Diafoirus type in the figure of Anselme des Tilleuls – though with the difference that Anselme does at least succeed in finding his match – but there are other notable cases of such characters in the *Voyages extraordinaires* who seem to have been taken directly from the comic stage tradition. One is Aristobulus Ursiclos in *Le Rayon vert*, the cousin and official fiancé of Helena Campbell at the beginning of the story. However, Ursiclos arouses not a jot of interest or passion in his fiancée. Like Molière's Diafoirus, this hapless suitor is ridiculed first and foremost through his name, as well as being a victim of knowledge for its own sake and of the pedantry that so often goes with it. Garrulous, pompous, self-important and completely out of touch with his own feelings (in so far as he has any) or the feelings of others, he launches into laborious monologues at every opportunity and bores everyone around him. Invited by Helena's two uncles to play a game of croquet with them, he explains the technicalities of the game and the laws of physics to Miss Campbell, but clearly cannot match theory with practice, since he shows himself to be clumsy, ungainly and lacking in coordination. Later, Miss Campbell hears him give a definition of the sea — that element that she considers to be the wildest and most romantic of all — which she finds extraordinary in its literal-mindedness: 'La mer!... Une combinaison chimique d'hydrogène et d'oxygène, avec deux et demi pour cent de chlorure de sodium! Rien de beau, en effet, comme les fureurs du chlorure de sodium!' (RV, p. 133) ['The sea! A chemical combination of hydrogen and oxygen, with two and a half per cent of sodium chloride! And there is really nothing as beautiful as the fury of sodium chloride!'] Described on the same page as 'l'importun' ['the intruder'], Ursiclos will clearly not stay the course as a suitor, notwithstanding the official backing that he has received. However, in the best comic tradition, he remains entirely unaware of his ill fortune and remains unchanged to the last, explaining human emotions to the betrothed couple in exactly the same manner as he had defined the sea. Tears, he says, are 'un composé de chlorure de sodium, de phosphate de chaux et de chlorate de soude' (RV, p. 227) ['a composite of sodium chloride, lime phosphate and sodium chlorate']. Ridiculous yet theatrical, Ursiclos will be matched by another official suitor in the *Voyages extraordinaires*, this time one who shows himself up through clumsiness and stupidity rather than through pedantry. He is Agathocle, the young man described at the beginning of *Clovis Dardentor* as 'la nullité dans la bêtise, la bêtise dans la nullité' (CD, p. 7) ['worthlessness in stupidity, and stupidity in worthlessness']. Incapable of having an opinion or of articulating an intelligent thought about anything, Agathocle has nonetheless been chosen as the improbable fiancé for the stylish and beautiful Louise Elissane. That he is no match for her becomes painfully and increasingly obvious, and the relationship — or rather the non-relationship — between these two youngsters follows much the same pattern as that of *Le Rayon vert* when a more appropriate suitor turns up. Verne's *mise en scène* of such characters takes us right back to the climate of his early writings for the theatre, reminding us once again both of the importance of the theatrical tradition in the *Voyages extraordinaires*, and of the self-conscious undermining of narrative realism that is achieved through it.

Theatrical characters and roles

The colourful situations that Verne creates between his leading ladies and their unwanted suitors are matched, in the *Voyages extraordinaires*, by other patterns of relationship that seem to have emerged straight from the theatre. One of the most striking of these is the relationship between masters and servants. Traditionally, in the theatre, comedy arises from servants outwitting their masters – a theme that is refined by Molière, then taken to its conclusion by Beaumarchais. In Verne's novels, it is not so much that the servants are smarter, but rather that the roles of each are exaggerated to the maximum and, occasionally, inverted. In *Le Tour du monde en quatre-vingts jours*, it is often Passepartout who manages to get Fogg out of trouble by his decisive and imaginative interventions, and it is he who talks to Aouda and perhaps gives her the best account of his master's feelings. The oddly motionless and emotionless Fogg relies almost totally throughout the story on his enterprising, energetic and expansive manservant. On his arrival in Suez, Fogg even delegates the business of sightseeing to Passepartout, 'étant de cette race d'Anglais qui font visiter par leur domestique les pays qu'ils traversent' (TDM, p. 47) ['being the type of Englishman who order their servants to visit the countries they pass through']. But the pairing of master and servant here in a theatrical duo is a crucial factor in making the novel so entertaining, and they are such complete opposites that they become absolutely necessary to each other. A similar and equally theatrical pairing is evident in *Vingt mille lieues sous les mers*, with the characters of Conseil and Aronnax. Here, the role of the servant shows Verne at his dramatic best. Conseil, an almost perfect stage creation, comes alive because of what is most mechanical about him, namely his impeccable and unfailing politeness to his master Aronnax. He is hugely funny, but the comic effect depends on his remaining unfathomably serious and maintaining that role to the very last. Addressing Aronnax in the third person even in the most extreme and dire circumstances, he never once fails him, but by the same token nor does he ever fail his 'audience', the reader. Conseil maintains unswerving commitment to the role that has been assigned to him. Verne's emphasis on Conseil's speech singles him out as a quintessentially theatrical creation. He is immediately recognisable by a style of language which leads him on many occasions into absurdity – such as when on one occasion he points out to the distracted Aronnax who is reading his own book: 'C'est le livre de monsieur que lit monsieur!' (VML II, p. 516) ['It is Sir's own book that Sir is reading!']

Yet the exaggerated and faultless good manners of Conseil are as nothing compared to the impeccable credentials of the manservant Patrice in *Clovis Dardentor*. Here, once again, we have an inversion of roles, for it is the master who has a tendency to be crude and vulgar, whereas the manservant always maintains the very highest standards. As it happens, though, this suits them both perfectly, for we read: 'Au fond, si Patrice était marri d'être au service d'un maître si peu gentleman, Clovis Dardentor était fier d'avoir un serviteur si distingué' (CD, p. 58) ['In the end, if Patrice was sorry to be in the service of such an ungentlemanly master, Clovis Dardentor was proud to have such a distinguished servant']. Like Conseil, Patrice never fails to address his master in the third person, but unlike Conseil, it will sometimes be to chide his master for his lack of good manners. Distinguished, well mannered, and utterly snobbish, Patrice is the perfect foil to the expansive and sometimes coarse Dardentor, whom he regularly calls to order. Patrice is quick to point out the slightest sign of any slippage of standards to Dardentor, but this leads him into the most difficult of verbal contortions, as here: 'Je préfère ne pas entendre monsieur, lorsque monsieur exprime sa pensée fort désobligeante en de pareils termes. En outre, je ferai observer à monsieur que le béret dont il a cru devoir se coiffer ne me paraît pas convenable pour un passager de première classe.' ['I prefer not to listen to Sir, when Sir expresses his unpleasant thoughts in such terms. Furthermore, I would like to point out to Sir that the beret which he has seen fit to place on his head seems to me to be unsuitable for a first-class passenger.'] There is mischievous irony in the 'cru devoir' of this sentence, which enables Patrice to be quite as forthright, even as offensive as his master, but in exquisitely elegant terms. And, as if to confirm that Patrice has some justice on his side, the narrator steps in and – a little apologetically, for he too is inclined on occasions to assume a theatrical pose – points out of Dardentor's headgear: 'en effet, le béret, posé en arrière sur la nuque de Clovis Dardentor, manquait de distinction' (CD, p. 59) ['it is true that the beret, which Clovis Dardentor was wearing over the back of his neck, was lacking in distinction']. Though Patrice fantasises about leaving his master and finding someone more suitable, these characters are naturally an inseparable combination, necessary to each other not only because of their psychological co-dependency, but also and most importantly as a theatrical pair whose presence heightens the sheer entertainment value of the text. And while Patrice gets increasingly flustered and bothered about his master's behaviour, his master finds himself having to watch his own speech and his manners ever more carefully. In one of the funniest developments of this theme, the narrator himself even gets caught up in the sense of guilt that should be Dardentor's when, in the final chapter, he writes: 'Avec M. Dardentor, les choses ne "traînaient pas" – qu'il soit permis d'employer cette locution assez vulgaire, dût Patrice s'en offusquer' (CD, p. 206) ['With Mr Dardentor things rarely "sat around" – if I may be permitted to use this somewhat vulgar expression, at the risk of offending Patrice']. Thus does Verne squeeze the final drop of humour out of this entertaining master–servant duo.

In earlier comments about disguise, I noted the frequency of doubles or complementary characters in Verne. What also needs to be stressed is that these duos often function exactly like the master–servant combination, heightening the entertainment value and the extravagant theatricality of the text by their similarities and their differences. Verne stages dramatic confrontations or oppositions throughout the *Voyages extraordinaires*, starting with Fergusson and Kennedy in *Cinq semaines en ballon*, those two friends who are so different in their attitude and behaviour, but who are so necessary to each other. A similar oppositional structure will be apparent in the passionate Lidenbrock and his diffident nephew Axel in *Voyage au centre de la terre*; and again between Nicholl and Barbicane in *De la terre à la lune*, so completely opposed in their theories about what will happen on this expedition that it ultimately becomes necessary for them to travel together in the company of Ardan. Since they have had a bet about whether the *Columbiad* will make it into space, Verne indulges us with a scene of high comedy in the early stages of the sequel novel, *Autour de la lune*. As the craft makes its way into space, Nicholl admits that he has lost the bet, hands over nine thousand dollars to his rival, and – absurdly – asks him for a receipt. No less absurdly, Barbicane obliges: 'Et sérieusement, flegmatiquement, comme s'il eût été à sa caisse, le président Barbicane tira son carnet, en détacha une page blanche, libella au crayon un reçu en règle, le data, le signa, le parapha, et le remit au capitaine qui l'enferma soigneusement dans son portefeuille' (AL, p. 280) ['And seriously, phlegmatically, as if he were at his cash register, President Barbicane took out his notebook, tore out a blank page, wrote out a proper receipt, dated, signed and initialled it, and handed it over to the captain, who placed it carefully in his wallet']. The unlikely pairing of these characters enables the novelist to dwell on scenes in which they interact, and to draw maximum comic effect from them. It is an old theatrical trick, in which the incongruous opposition of characteristics is pushed to the point of caricature and leads either to scenes of prolonged misunderstanding and argument, or to exaggerated reconciliations of differing interests. Where it is not verbal – as in the speech patterns of Conseil or Patrice – Verne's comedy is character-based or visual, often concentrating on the utterly absurd but totally complementary gestures of characters such as Nicholl and Barbicane.

Occasionally, too, Verne turns the trick around and, passing over what may be extreme differences between two characters, he emphasises their similarities (which in the end amounts to much the same thing). In *Le Rayon vert*, the two uncles – whose common identity is suggested in the title of the first chapter of the story, 'Le frère Sam et le frère Sib' ['Brother Sam and Brother Sib'] – are almost indistinguishable. Though physically not identical twins, as are the Texar brothers in *Nord contre sud*, they are nonetheless complementary in almost everything they say and do. As the guardians of Helena Campbell, they have committed themselves totally to her and to each other: 'Unis dans la même tendresse, ils ne vécurent, ne pensèrent, ne rêvèrent […] que pour elle' (RV, p. 3) ['United by the same tender sentiment, they lived, thought and dreamed for her alone']. True, we read that one is like a mother, the other like a father to the orphaned girl, but these spurious 'differences' serve only to reinforce their ultimate similarity. Their tenderness for their niece is compared by the author to the kindness and affection of the Cheeryble brothers in Dickens's *Nicholas Nickleby* (another of those literary allusions which Verne sprinkles so generously throughout his writing).[21] But, as ever when he sets up complementary characters, Verne exploits the theatrical possibilities of the duo. In this case, he uses his characters to create a comic dimension which provides relief from the story's more serious elements. A similar lightheartedness will be introduced into a more sombre narrative in the case of the two acrobats of *Mathias Sandorf*, whose very names confer on them a kind of geographical complementarity: Cap Matifou and Pointe Pescade. Physical opposites, these two men are nonetheless emotional doubles. Matifou is a giant of a man whose physical strength is exceptional; Pescade is small and can therefore hide in confined spaces or pass through small entrances. Between them, they form a unit which would be entirely dysfunctional without one of its halves, but they recognise their interdependence and thrive on it. The fact that they are circus entertainers means also that their actions are by definition 'spectacular' – a kind of staged entertainment within the broader compass of the novel. We see them perform in a series of 'scenes', such as the one in which they are first introduced into the story, when Matifou prevents a newly built launch from heading prematurely down

---

21 In Dickens's novel, the twin brothers Charles and Edwin Cheeryble are business partners and genial philanthropists who befriend Nicholas Nickleby.

its slipway. Such scenes stress and underline these characters' roles as performing artists. And they perform not only in the supposedly 'real' world that this fiction represents, but also within the fiction itself, where they provide scenes of comic relief. Their performances are a form of *mise en abyme*, though less of the novel itself than of theatre and the stage.

Theatrical performances abound throughout the *Voyages extraordinaires*, where there are constant references – either implicit or explicit – to the stage and its associated institutions: public oratory, pedagogical performance, opera and music, or, as in the case of Matifou and Pescade, the circus. *De la terre à la lune* is only one of many novels in which oratory is central. The speeches made by Barbicane and Ardan (the latter with a considerable degree of audience participation) seem to return us directly to the theatre. In both cases, the dramatic, clinching phrase or affirmation (for example, Ardan's stupendously disarming 'Je ne reviendrai pas' (TL, p. 184) ['I shall not return'] when asked how he plans to get back from the moon) is key to the unfolding of the plot. Speeches, tirades and brilliant exchanges are everywhere in this novel, and they are represented in all their theatrical extravagance. Elsewhere in the *Voyages extraordinaires*, Verne's eccentric pedagogues provide wonderful set pieces of oratorical brilliance. These monologues in the midst of a rich dramatic extravaganza are exemplified in the passionate, almost frenzied speech by Lidenbrock, who 'rehearses' his future performance at the Johannæum, 's'adressant à un auditoire imaginaire' (VCT, p. 327) ['addressing an imaginary audience'], when the underground travellers have discovered a human body from the quaternary period. Axel symbolises in his solitary presence the admiring throng of future students: 'Le professeur se tut, et j'éclatai en applaudissements unanimes' (VCT, p. 332) ['The professor fell silent, and I burst into unanimous applause']. Elsewhere, the audience may not be the imaginary one of a classroom or amphitheatre, but the extemporised one of fellow travellers. Paganel, in *Les Enfants du capitaine Grant*, frequently launches into rich rhetorical set pieces for the benefit of his travelling companions, and is happy to play to whatever audience he finds before him. So, too, is Palmyrin Rosette, the astronomer-mathematician in *Hector Servadac*, as he buttonholes his fellow travellers and forces them to participate (usually by their ignorance) in his fantastically complex, but truly stellar demonstrations. And, should they wish to pause for breath, he is there to remind them with a spectacular put-down that breathing itself is a luxury: 'On ne respire pas en mathématiques, monsieur, on ne respire pas!' (HS, p. 346) ['You do not breathe in mathematics, sir, you do not breathe!'] This recalls Ardan's riposte that, once on the moon, he will try to save what little oxygen there is by breathing only on important occasions (TL, p. 181). Verne's most theatrical creations are also, in addition to their oratorical talents, capable of wonderful one-liners such as these.

Alongside the orators and the pedagogues, we also find characters who are either directly borrowed from the theatre, or explicitly recall the institutions of stage and performance. Opera and music are frequently referred to in Verne's stories, most memorably in *Le Château des Carpathes* where the diva, La Stilla, dies on stage as the memory of her music lives on in the minds and the hearts of the other protagonists. Here, by a trick of technology (a combination of mirrors and a phonograph), the singer gives a performance from beyond the grave, watched by the solitary grievers who cannot live without her memory. She will remain forever in their minds as a stage figure, caught and frozen in that final, fatal performance. And elsewhere, we find musicians performing in, for example, *L'Ile à hélice*, where the whole question of 'live' performance (as opposed to virtual performance) is debated in a more lighthearted manner. In *La Jangada*, both opera and stage are recalled in yet a different form, through the character of the barber Fragoso, who is explicitly compared to Beaumarchais's and Mozart's Figaro. Fragoso becomes famous as a 'performing barber', bringing in a huge clientele from the Upper Amazon basin. Like so many of Verne's extrovert eccentrics, Fragoso is a dramatic 'type', extravagantly generous with his words and his gestures, a focus of entertainment who is recognised as such by the other characters. He is a representative of the theatre and of theatricality in all its guises within the novel itself.

Finally, one of the most interesting cases of the overlap between the novel and theatre in Verne's work comes with the character of Miss Waston [sic] in *P'tit-Bonhomme*. A famous actress, she charitably takes P'tit-Bonhomme into her care after he is rescued from a fire. However, her dramatic career spills over into her very identity as a person, and even into the role she plays within the story itself. The boundaries between fiction and theatre are blurred in various ways. Verne makes it immediately apparent that the 'stage' has come alive within the text of his novel when, on the first appearance of Miss Waston, he describes her as 'cette femme charitable, qui venait d'entrer en scène de cette façon quelque peu mélodramatique' (PB, p. 54) ['this charitable woman who had just come onto the scene in a somewhat melodramatic fashion']. Her fictional actions are themselves stagey and dramatic. But the confusion becomes even greater in the following chapter when Miss Waston has the idea of teaching her new ward how to act for the stage. At that moment she is rehearsing for a play entitled *Les Remords d'une mère*, and it so happens that this coincides with questions to her from P'tit-Bonhomme about his own mother. Miss Waston replies that P'tit-Bonhomme's mother, wherever she is, must be a great woman – for that would fit the plot of the play in which she is acting. Clearly, her counsels to P'tit-Bonhomme are always framed in terms of the plays she is working on and, despite the young boy's seriousness of mind, he becomes increasingly perplexed about this apparent overlap between the real and the stage worlds. But this is more than a simple matter of confusion in one character's mind, for the narrator himself gets caught up in the process, forgetting to distinguish between P'tit-Bonhomme the fictional character, and his theatrical counterpart Sib, the character of the young boy Miss Waston is making him rehearse. Thus we read of this irredeemably histrionic woman: 'Tantôt elle saisissait Sib, l'embrassait, le secouait avec une violence nerveuse, tantôt sa présence l'agaçait, elle le renvoyait, et il n'y comprenait rien' (PB, p. 170) ['Sometimes she would seize hold of Sib, kiss him and shake him with a nervous violence; but sometimes his presence would irritate her, so she would send him away, and he could not understand why']. However, the confusion does not stop there. The role of Sib, rehearsed by P'tit-Bonhomme, is that of a young orphan – a status exactly similar to P'tit-Bonhomme's own. The young boy, required to act out a role that he takes to be 'real', has to put on rags. Perplexed and frightened by the condition he finds himself in, P'tit-Bonhomme is also convinced that the Miss Waston he sees on stage is the very same woman as the real person who took him under her wing – after all, she herself has encouraged the illusion – so he addresses her on stage, on the opening night of the play, by her real name. The 'drama' ends as a disaster. Miss Waston flees, and P'tit-Bonhomme once again finds himself on his own. The 'play' within the fiction ends up having depressingly real consequences, despite the fact that it had all the hallmarks of artifice, and that its leading lady was the most contrived and artificial of characters.

The confusion between drama and reality in P'tit-Bonhomme's story is a reminder that the artificial, make-believe world of the stage can spill over into real life, just as in fiction the presence of theatrical scenes, performances and artificial representations can cross into the narrative itself. There is no dividing line between fiction and theatre. Fiction is a theatre, just as the theatre is a fiction, and Miss Waston's appearance and disappearance in *P'tit-Bonhomme* is an illustration of the fact that Verne's narrative style relies on theatre and theatricality in many ways. The stage not only influences the style and the scope of Verne's novels – which are structured dramatically, are based on theatrical devices such as disguise and complementary characters, and make extensive use of dialogue and performance – but it frequently reappears within them. Theatre is also an entertainment within the entertainment, a play within the 'play' of fiction, the ultimate scene of drama, tension, confrontation, surprise, and their *dénouements*. In the *Voyages extraordinaires*, the novel thus echoes and re-uses dramatic traditions and styles, and in so doing it exposes its own artificiality. Verne's early apprenticeship in the theatre remains a crucial factor in his later writing style, and accounts for much of its playful self-consciousness.

Chapter 5

Self-Consciousness: The Journey of Language and Narrative

We saw earlier how Jules Verne repeatedly and ostentatiously recycles written documents in his work. Text, in all its forms, proliferates and multiplies through the pages of the *Voyages extraordinaires*, like that self-perpetuating swarm of locusts in *Aventures de trois Russes et de trois Anglais dans l'Afrique australe*, whose sheer number 'défiait toutes [les] causes de destruction' (A3, p. 143)[1] ['defied all attempts to destroy them']. Placing his citational mode of narrative on open display, Verne reinforces the point that no text can ever stand alone, that every script depends for its existence on innumerable others which nourish it and which may in their turn consume it. Within this context of flamboyant textuality, we saw also that Verne refers frequently and specifically to literature as a field of endeavour and a body of work, by way of situating his own writing clearly within it and reinforcing his claim to be a literary figure. In this process of highlighting the literary credentials of the *Voyages extraordinaires*, the use of the theatre occupies a particular place, for it emphasises the extravagant playfulness and the self-conscious, contrived artificiality of narrative. The *Voyages extraordinaires* are anything but a mere objective, realistic account of travel and technology in the nineteenth century (though it is certainly possible to read them on that level as well); rather, they are an intensely self-conscious experiment with the very tools of the writer's craft, narrative and language, which they place on almost permanent display.

The present chapter will focus on the self-consciousness of Verne's approach to writing. More than drawing our attention specifically to the corpus that writing produces, or even to its relationship to other texts, self-consciousness is the act of gazing inwards, the glimpse we get behind the scenes into the processes and the creation of narrative, the awareness of what narratologists call 'the narrative situation'. It is the moment or the state in which the writer appears to stand back from his or her own act of composition, even as that composition is unfolding, and to exploit the creative possibilities of his or her own detachment. Self-consciousness

---

1 See above, p. 25.

can be a literal process of stepping out of the diegesis and witnessing its unfolding (or frustrating that process, as Sterne does in *Tristram Shandy* or Diderot does in *Jacques le fataliste*); or it can involve a symbolic evocation of the craft and the business of writing, as when a narrative contains stories which mirror or interfere with the main diegesis; or it can take the form of a contrived manipulation of narrative and fictional conventions, when their artifices are placed on open display. In many of these cases – even in the *roman personnel* – self-consciousness is accompanied at some level by a move towards a heterodiegetic, outside voice which comments either explicitly or implicitly on the narrative unfolding before our eyes. Often, too, this will involve some form of dialogue with an implied reader.

Now let it be emphasised that Verne is far from being the first or the only writer to stand back from his own storytelling framework and offer us this external, or pseudo-external, perspective on it. He joins a long and illustrious tradition which extends from Cervantes and Rabelais through to Proust, Gide, Borges, Calvino and a host of other writers. The heterodiegetic voice itself – self-conscious or not – is also the stock-in-trade of most nineteenth-century realist writers, perhaps first and foremost of Balzac, who is intensely aware of the rhetorical advantages to be gained by addressing his implied reader or commenting on the features of his own narrative (as he does memorably, for example, in the early pages of *Le Père Goriot*). More than Balzac, Stendhal (whose self-mocking narrator is in some respects close to Verne's) will problematise the narrative voice and feign to step outside the diegesis in order to reflect ironically on the actions of his characters or the progress of his story.[2] While understandably we will find less of this in authors such as Flaubert or Zola, in whose work the narrative focus purports to be impersonal (falsely, of course, since this too is a rhetorical strategy), the point to be underlined is that Verne's approach is typical of that of many authors of the same period. It would be foolish to claim for him some kind of originality in this respect, for it is nothing of the sort. Where Verne's approach differs is not in essence, but in degree. The self-conscious pointing up (sometimes hamming up) of his own narrative devices or options, or the playful and

2   An obvious and well-known example of this latter process in Stendhal is when, some pages after the beginning of *La Chartreuse de Parme*, the narrator suddenly pauses to reflect (for the reader's benefit) that he has yet to introduce his hero: 'Nous avouerons que, suivant l'exemple de beaucoup de graves auteurs, nous avons commencé l'histoire de notre héros une année avant sa naissance' (Stendhal, *Romans et nouvelles*, ed. Henri Martineau (Paris: Gallimard, Bibliothèque de la Pléiade, 1948), vol. II, p. 33) ['We shall admit that, following the example of many serious authors, we have begun our hero's story a year before his birth'].

showy manipulation of his own materials as a novelist, is present everywhere in his writing and comes as a constant and deliberate interruption
of the narrative flow. More, perhaps, than any other novelist in nineteenth-century France, Verne appears to open up the secrets of his craft,
drawing attention to the tools of his trade, playing ostentatiously with the
very conventions of narrative. Whether this be in explicit interventions
as a heterodiegetic narrator commenting on the contents of his stories, or
in contrived manipulations of the basic materials of fiction – character,
plot construction, description – Verne appears to beckon the reader
behind the scenes of his writing, inviting close observation of the decisions and processes of the novelist's work. Now this is not necessarily to
say that we gain a 'real' insight into the nuts and bolts of Verne's own
working methods by reading the *Voyages extraordinaires*, for naturally the
self-conscious invitation to come behind the scenes is *itself* a fiction.
There may, and probably will, be a considerable degree of overlap
between the implied or inscribed novelist and the real one, but its precise
extent and nature will always be a matter of speculation. What is beyond
doubt, however, is that Verne systematically builds a self-conscious gaze
into the fictional process. And what is perpetually fascinating in his writing is that such a high degree of self-consciousness accompanies a storytelling mode premised on the novel's ability to evoke an objective, factual
reality that is 'out there', beyond the realm of words themselves. While
the *Voyages extraordinaires* manifestly encourage our belief in a world that
is scientifically verifiable and factually stable, they constantly appear to
undercut that belief by returning us to the awareness that everything
depends on how we view, recreate and *narrate* our reality. At every level,
Verne's self-consciousness will be a reminder that our reality is made up
of words and narratives. By his apparent interference in the framework
and the progress of his stories, Verne never allows us to forget for long that
the reality of his textual representations is heavily mediated.

The heterodiegetic voice

As a writer steeped in the tradition of the theatre Verne is naturally aware
of the wonderful possibilities that exaggerated and showily contrived plot
structures and characters can offer. But theatre is based on 'showing', and
narrative introduces another dimension, that of 'telling'. The habit of
stepping back from the narrative to reflect on its possibilities and on its
fictional content, and of appearing to share those reflections with the
reader, is one that Verne acquires early in his writing career. In the unfin-

ished *Un prêtre en 1839* written in the 1840s, we find the narrator intervening to reflect on the beauty of a young woman, then going on to the
wider question of the links between novels and the so-called 'real' world.
Of his lovestruck hero, he writes:

> Jules Deguay avait été frappé de la beauté de la jeune fille, et c'était à bon
> droit. Ce n'est pas que dans un roman il soit nécessaire que les jeunes filles
> soient belles. Aucunement. Ce serait même peu galant, car on en viendrait à
> dire peut-être que le sexe n'est beau que dans les romans, que la copie flatte
> l'original. Néanmoins, la jeune fille était belle, et [...] nous convenons de sa
> beauté. (P39, p. 33)

> [Jules Deguay had been struck by the girl's beauty, and with good reason.
> This is not to say that girls necessarily have to be beautiful in novels. Not at
> all, and it would even be ungenerous to maintain such a thing, for it would
> perhaps lead to the claim that the fair sex is fair only in novels, and that the
> copy flatters the original. Nonetheless, the girl was beautiful, and we
> acknowledge her beauty.]

The self-mocking tone, invoking a 'fake' distinction between the world of
fiction and that of reality in order to enlist the reader's belief more fully,
is a standard narrative device. Verne uses it to increase the awareness that
fiction is indeed a pretence which requires a willing suspension of disbelief. Rather than hide from the processes that lead to this narrative con-
tract, he chooses to focus openly on them. He will do so again a little later
in the same story when, faced with a decision about which line of the narrative he will follow, he places his cards face up on the table, in a style
highly reminiscent of Sterne and Diderot: 'Si le lecteur veut bien le per-
mettre, et s'il ne craint pas de trop se fatiguer, nous allons courir après le
fiacre mystérieux; je crois que nous le rattraperons aisément.' (P39, p. 41)
['If the reader will permit us to do so, and is not afraid of growing weary,
we shall run after this mysterious cab, which I think we shall catch
easily.'] Far from concealing that he must make choices about which sub-
plot to focus on – always a problem in narratives that involve travel and
movement, and in which by definition different plot strands tend to separate into different locations – Verne makes a virtue of necessity and
revels in the fact that writing so obviously requires these kinds of decisions.[3] He never allows us to overlook the fact that this is a contrived and
artificial world, a puppet show that the narrator himself ultimately con-

---

3 For an excellent discussion from a novelist's point of view of the question of choices
   between multiple narrative possibilities, and the techniques that may be required to
   navigate between them, see Michel Butor, 'Le Roman comme recherche', in *Répertoire*
   (Paris: Editions de Minuit, 1960), pp. 7–11.

trols. Yet he senses, even in this difficult early novel abandoned at a point where the plot disintegrates into several different strands, that a significant part of the pleasure and the instructive value of writing comes from the obvious artificiality of the medium. Subsequently, Verne will retain the habit of intervening to remind his reader that the story before his or her eyes is an invention, a creation in which nothing occurs automatically and of necessity. In the posthumously published *La Chasse au météore* we find exactly the same technique, which remained a constant throughout Verne's career as a novelist. As he introduces the two young lovers, Francis Gordon and Jenny Hudelson, the narrator feigns to hold back from his wish to describe the latter: 'Mais c'est trop tôt appeler l'attention sur cette jeune personne. Le moment n'est pas venu où elle doit entrer en scène, et il convient de ne la présenter qu'au milieu de sa famille. Cela ne saurait tarder. D'ailleurs, on ne saurait apporter assez de méthode dans le développement de cette histoire, qui exige une extrême précision.' (CM, p. 26) ['But it is too soon to draw attention to this young person. The moment has not yet arrived for her entrance, and she should only be introduced surrounded by her family. That will happen soon enough. Besides, one cannot be too careful over the development of this story, which demands extreme precision.'] Let it be underlined once more that the indecision or the mock anxiety the novelist appears to express here, on realising that he may be introducing a character too early, is fictional in every sense. This is not the 'real' Jules Verne playing out real hesitations, but a personified narrator feigning them in order to be able to pursue a reflection about fiction, its conventions, its structures and its techniques. In so doing, he reminds the reader that this is an unreal world governed by a strictly narrative order. One consequence is that the reader becomes more attuned to the storytelling devices deployed by the author, and more sensitive to the fact that the content of the story is dependent on its verbal mediation. This is not the art that conceals itself, but art that makes itself conspicuous and draws attention to its own contrivances. Like Stendhal in his famous (and deeply problematic) reflections about the novel as a mirror, or about the place of politics in the novel,[4] Verne too

---

4 See for example Stendhal, *Le Rouge et le noir*, in *Romans et nouvelles*, vol. I, p. 557: 'Eh, monsieur, un roman est un miroir qui se promène sur une grande route. Tantôt il reflète à vos yeux l'azur des cieux, tantôt la fange des bourbiers de la route' ['Well, sir, a novel is a mirror that you take out along the highway. Sometimes it reflects the blue of the sky, sometimes the filth of the mud patches in the road']. See also *La Chartreuse de Parme*, in *Romans et nouvelles*, vol. II, p. 405: 'La politique dans une œuvre littéraire, c'est un coup de pistolet au milieu d'un concert' ['Politics in a literary work are like a pistol shot in the middle of a concert'].

stands back and reflects on his medium, even as he pushes his story forward to the next stage. Again and again the narrator will adopt a voiceover mode to remind us, even in the briefest of asides, that the story before our eyes is indeed a story. Within the fiction, there is a constant, murmuring discourse about fiction itself, a metalanguage which discusses and displays the medium.

This may often occur in simple, deft asides, which themselves are unproblematic in narrative terms. In *P'tit-Bonhomme*, at the outset of the story, the narrator will find himself pointing out that this *is* a story, when for example he tells us: 'C'est à Westport que nous allons trouver P'tit-Bonhomme au début de son histoire' (PB, p. 2) ['It is in Westport that we shall find P'tit-Bonhomme, at the beginning of his story']. A little later, when the hero has made his first appearance, he adds: 'Telle fut l'entrée en scène de P'tit-Bonhomme, le héros de cette histoire' (PB, p. 19) ['Such was the arrival on stage of P'tit-Bonhomme, the hero of this story']. In this latter example, the theatrical expression 'entrée en scène' doubles up with the reference to the hero of the story to reinforce the reminder that this is a created, narrated environment. Yet the use of such metanarrative tags by Verne, by way of marking out the fictional and sometimes dramatic texture of his world, also helps him to move the story forward. While the process of stepping outside the diegesis, however momentarily, might be expected to herald a pause in the momentum, on the contrary it usually enables the narrator to shift the focus and to move on with gathering speed. More generally, we find throughout Verne's work an interesting and perhaps surprising coexistence of fast-moving narrative and the ironic, self-conscious or even self-deflating narrative gaze. The proliferation of such interventions as the above therefore does nothing to puncture the forward flow of narrative. What is noticeable, however, is the sheer extent to which a heterodiegetic narrator draws our attention to the components of the narratives that unfold in the *Voyages extraordinaires*. We never escape for long from the awareness of the textual, narrative, or literary quality of the novelist's representations.

The habit of ironic self-reference is perhaps nowhere more pronounced than in some of those chapter titles where Verne flags up the contents of his story – a clear pastiche of the eighteenth-century convention in which a (sometimes not so brief) summary of a chapter or a part of a novel is offered in advance.[5] While the purpose of the technique was

---

5 Fielding's *The History of Tom Jones* (1749) offers a typical example of the use of this technique, and we find chapter headings of the following kind: 'A short description of Squire Allworthy, and a fuller account of Miss Bridget Allworthy, his sister' (Part

originally either to whet the appetite, or to focus the act of reading – especially in those cases where texts were being read aloud – in the *Voyages extraordinaires* this often becomes an opportunity to comment ironically on the processes of narrative or to subvert them. The title of the first chapter of *Clovis Dardentor* ('Dans lequel le principal personnage de cette histoire n'est pas présenté au lecteur' ['In which the main character of this story is not introduced to the reader']) provides a striking example of this in its undermining of our expectation that the main character will be introduced. Verne here makes an ironic use of the negative – a technique that, as we shall see, he deploys to great effect in other contexts too – in a situation where the reader traditionally expects to be given positive information. Yet, despite appearing to tell us only what is absent from his chapter, Verne is nonetheless conforming to tradition in another way, for long novels do often begin obliquely, even without their main character, who may be introduced into the narrative a little later. Verne thus comments on a tradition in the novel even as he appears to break with it. The following chapter title ('Dans lequel le principal personnage de cette histoire est décidément présenté au lecteur' ['In which the main character of this story is most definitely introduced to the reader']) reassures us that the story will continue in the manner we might expect. Yet elsewhere he uses wonderfully bathetic chapter titles which undermine the convention entirely. Chapter 11, we are told in its title, 'n'est qu'un chapitre préparatoire au chapitre suivant' ['is merely a chapter of preparation for the next one']. If so, we might wonder what the point of the title is, until we reflect that its point is precisely to be pointless, to play on its own futile 'respect' for the convention.

One novel that is particularly effective in its use of chapter titles is *Le Tour du monde en quatre-vingts jours*. Underlining their status as a framework device, the chapter titles frequently parody the narrative genre from within – either because they suggest the pointlessness of summarising contents, or because they tease the reader to guess at what they cannot reveal, or because they are able to offer an ironic advance comment. The title to Chapter 17 ('Où il est question de choses et d'autres pendant la traversée de Singapore à Hong-Kong' ['Which deals with various different

---

I, Chapter 2). Since Fielding is also one of the formative influences of that ironically self-conscious tradition in which Verne writes, we should not be surprised either to find that his chapter titles often explicitly evoke the question of authorship and of reading, as in the title to Part I, Chapter 7: 'Containing such grave matter, that the reader cannot laugh once through the whole chapter, unless peradventure he should laugh at the author'.

things during the crossing from Singapore to Hong Kong']) is a playful and amusing way of saying nothing whatsoever while feigning respect for the convention. The supremely vague 'de choses et d'autres' is a deliberately weak choice of words which teasingly pretends to let us down. A similar effect is achieved in the following chapter title ('Dans lequel Phileas Fogg, Passepartout, Fix, chacun de son côté, va à ses affaires' ['In which Phileas Fogg, Passepartout and Fix each go separately about their own business']), where the bathos of the closing words suggests that we will glean almost nothing from our reading of this chapter and that it marks dead time in the narrative. Nothing could be further from the truth, but the metatextual commentary here is added to by the contrast between the title and the contents of the chapter. On other occasions, verbal riddles or other conundrums are set up, as in the title to Chapter 27 ('Dans lequel Passepartout suit, avec une vitesse de vingt milles à l'heure, un cours d'histoire mormone' ['In which Passepartout follows a course in Mormon history at a speed of twenty miles an hour']), where it turns out that the speed referred to is not that of the rate of delivery of the lecture, still less of Passepartout's learning ability, but of the train in which Fogg and his companions are travelling. And finally, there may also be a suggestion that the contents of a chapter provide a narrative opportunity, as for example in Chapter 27 ('Qui procure à Passepartout l'occasion de faire un jeu de mots atroce, mais peut-être inédit' ['Which gives Passepartout an opportunity to make a dreadful, but perhaps unpublished pun']). The reference here is to Passepartout's description of the punch that Fogg lands on Fix, after his needless incarceration in Liverpool, as 'une belle application de poings [homonym of 'points'] d'Angleterre' (TDM, p. 312) ['a fine application of English fists/English needlework']. The suggestion is that the pun, never printed before, now finds its way for the very first time into a book – and since the book is the one that the reader has in his or her hands, the self-reference is evident.

The self-conscious humour of these and other chapter titles in *Le Tour du monde* plays a very significant role in establishing the tone of the text as a whole. By playing off the descriptive title against the actual contents of the narrative, Verne offers an ongoing, if tongue-in-cheek, commentary on his text. He uses this technique widely and to great effect in the *Voyages extraordinaires*, often in those stories that have a strongly humorous dimension (*Clovis Dardentor*, *Hector Servadac*, *L'Ecole des Robinsons*, and others). As the examples from *Le Tour du monde* suggest, he creates a wide variety of effects around the technique, and uses it above all for its entertainment value. Nor is he averse to creating rhythmic, alliterative chapter titles which please and which draw attention to their own linguistic

quality through poetic or semi-poetic effects, as in one noteworthy example from *Kéraban-le-têtu*, where Chapter 3 bears the title: 'Dans lequel le
seigneur Kéraban, encore plus entêté que jamais, tient tête aux autorités
ottomanes' ['In which Keraban, pigheaded as ever, pigheadedly opposes
the Ottoman powers']. The alliteration increases and the rhythm gathers
pace as the sentence proceeds. Prosodic analysis will show that of the
three word-clusters in this sentence, the second and the third are deca-
syllables (while the first falls one syllable short). The contrived sounds
and rhythms have the effect of a hint coming from the author, reminding
us to seek out the pleasures of the text – even as he suggests that his central character undergoes no significant evolution in this chapter.

While Verne's use of chapter titles appears to fulfil the function of
framing the narrative within the broader conventions of storytelling, or
of subverting that process and emphasising its artificiality, in some cases
it also provides a springboard for metatextual commentary within the
narrative itself. Such is the case on a number of occasions in *Le Sphinx des
glaces*, where the chosen title of a chapter is the subject of a series of
reflections by the narrator. In the second part of the novel, Chapter 6 carries the simple title: 'Terre?...' ['Land?...'] But the narrator immediately
reminds us in a direct intervention that this is an echo of Poe: 'Tel est l'u-
nique mot qui se trouve en tête du chapitre XVII dans le livre d'Edgar Poe.
J'ai cru bon, – en le faisant suivre d'un point d'interrogation, – de le
placer en tête de ce chapitre VI de mon récit' (SG, p. 294). ['This one word
forms the title of chapter XVII in Edgar Poe's book. I deemed it appropriate, with the addition of a question mark, to place it as the title of this, the
sixth chapter of my story.'] By his reprise of Poe's chapter title – with the
addition of the question mark, on which he comments, but also of three
suspension points which he refuses to gloss – the narrator is here able to
discuss both Poe's text and his own, and implicitly to draw attention to
the similarities and the differences between them. He raises the whole
complex question of intertextuality and the relationship between different stories. Is this a copy, a reworking, or a continuation? Is the originality of the present story compromised or reduced by the presence within
it, like a palimpsest, of an 'original' document? Or is the value of the 'original' in some way enhanced by the presence of the copy? By their nature
these are intensely self-conscious questions. This may not be obvious
material for high adventure, or for narratives of exploration and the unexpected, yet that is precisely what it becomes in Verne's story. By constantly interrupting the linear flow of a so-called 'adventure' narrative,
and focusing on the very techniques and conventions through which the
adventure is mediated, he succeeds in heightening, not reducing, the sus-

pense and the interest of his tale. Another example of precisely the same technique – though this time without the implicit discussion of textual parallels – occurs at the beginning of Chapter 14 ('Onze ans en quelques pages' ['Eleven years in a few pages']) of the second part of the novel. In the opening sentence, the narrator once again comments on his chapter title: 'Le titre donné à ce chapitre indique que les aventures de William Guy et de ses compagnons après la destruction de la goélette anglaise, les détails de leur existence sur l'île Tsalal depuis le départ d'Arthur Pym et de Dirk Peters, vont être très succinctement racontés' (SG, p. 400) ['The title given to this chapter suggests that the adventures of William Guy and his companions after the destruction of the English schooner, and the details of their existence on Tsalal island following the departure of Arthur Pym and Dirk Peters, will be very succinctly recounted']. While this seems at first glance to be no more than an analytical elaboration of the chapter title itself, it allows the narrator to refocus his story and to encompass a broader sweep of time. It is a classic storytelling device, designed to place the reader at a new vantage point, and the moment's pause that it allows, brief as it is, enables the novelist to change gear and bring his story rapidly up to date. Self-consciousness is thus one of the very techniques by which the narrative is able to proceed. If Jules Verne constantly reminds us that his world is a narrated one, the reminder is far from being gratuitous, since it is retrieved and returned to the narrative process, becoming part of its onward movement.

Intratextuality

Throughout the *Voyages extraordinaires* Verne uses the technique of glossing his own words, as he does with the chapter titles in *Le Sphinx des glaces*. But the process of self-reference, or of cross-reference, goes much further than this. As his years of literary production accumulate and the corpus of novels grows, Verne also indulges in reprises or in echoes of other texts by his own hand. For this particular form of intertextuality I shall use the term *intratextuality*, implying a network of references within a given corpus of texts rather than beyond it.[6] Though essentially the

---

6 On intratextuality in Verne, see also Compère, *Jules Verne écrivain*, pp. 108–21. Compère establishes several categories of this process in the *Voyages extraordinaires*, the most important of them being explicit self-reference, self-parody, and variation. Compère affirms that, through such processes, Verne 'pose sans cesse le problème de la vraisemblance dans la fiction, des limites de la création littéraire' (p. 119) ['constantly raises the question of plausibility in fiction, and of the limits of the

process here is just the same as with intertextuality, which affirms the interdependence of several or of many texts, it often has the added practical benefit of providing a plug for an author's own writings, by raising awareness of them or by implicitly stressing their importance and value. It also increases the sense that the text which makes the intratextual references finds a natural place within an already existing corpus, and this puts its status beyond dispute. There is an excellent example of this technique in *Le Sphinx des glaces*, where at the end of Chapter 10, Part II, the author appends a long footnote, signed 'J.V.' In it he points out that on 21 March 1868, 28 years after Jeorling and his fellow explorers found themselves marooned on an iceberg drifting through the Antarctic ocean, another explorer succeeded in passing through the ice-floes and reaching the ninetieth degree of latitude: 'Et, à l'instant où l'horizon, juste au nord, coupait en deux parties égales le disque solaire, il prenait possession de ce continent en son nom personnel et déployait un pavillon à l'étamine brodée d'un N d'or. Au large flottait un bateau sous-marin qui s'appelait *Nautilus* et dont le capitaine s'appelait le capitaine Nemo.' (SG, p. 360) ['And just as the horizon, a little to the North, was bisecting the solar disk, he claimed this continent in his own name and unfurled a muslin flag embroidered with a golden "N". At sea floated a submarine called the *Nautilus*, whose captain was named Nemo.'] There is no attempt here to present this as a 'mere' fiction. On the contrary, Verne recalls this adventure as if it were recorded history. Whether there is an element of tongue-in-cheek mischief here is hard to assess, especially in a text in which the imagined veracity of a previous fiction (Poe's *Arthur Gordon Pym*) is one of the mainstays of the narrative. However, it is clear that the effect of this reference is to remind the reader of a previous novel in the *Voyages extraordinaires* and to evoke it as a classic that is assumed to be part of everyone's culture. But, by the same token, the reference places *Le Sphinx des glaces* effortlessly in the company of the previous novel, and underlines its claim to become a similar classic. And, it is implied, if Nemo's story can now be relayed as though it were part of the agreed history of polar exploration, then so too will Jeorling's story come to have the same status.

I have already referred to Verne's play *Voyage à travers l'impossible*, performed at the Théâtre de la Porte Saint-Martin in 1882–83, which is

---

literary']. However, he points out that Hetzel appears to have discouraged and disliked these references by Verne to his own novels. In support of this he cites a letter by Verne to Hetzel *fils* in which the author feels it necessary to justify why he adopts this tactic in *Sans dessus dessous*, where borrowings from and references to the previous lunar novels are inevitable (p. 110).

based on a reprise of a number of different texts in the *Voyages extraordinaires*.[7] However, this is clearly a case of a text which is a commercial spin-off, relying on the enormous success of the fiction in order to generate comparable success in the theatre. The line between self-conscious intratextuality, which makes important points about the nature of text itself, and the rehashing of earlier themes and ideas will always be problematic. Just as Verne's uses and occasional abuses of other authors' texts have come under close scrutiny, so too the recycling of his own material will sometimes – almost inevitably – lead him into facileness and repetition. But this crossing of the line is one of the dangers that arise in the case of an author who so consistently stresses the interdependence of texts, and who so conspicuously builds his own fiction out of that process. Some years prior to the theatrical success of *Voyage à travers l'impossible*, Verne had already written to Hetzel on 4 August 1875 of his idea to write a book which would be 'le résumé des *Voyages extraordinaires*' ['a compendium of the *Extraordinary Journeys*'], in which 'j'embarquerais dans un appareil *plus lourd que l'air* tous nos bonshommes, Fergusson, Aronnax, Fogg, Clawbonny, etc. et que je les ferais naviguer au-dessus de tout notre monde'[8] ['I would send out in a heavier-than-air machine all of our men – Fergusson, Aronnax, Fogg, Clawbonny etc. – and would make them travel above our whole world']. Fortunately, perhaps, this project never saw the light of day, and, in any case, one of its ironies is that Verne felt moved to record his idea because he had become aware of a rival's novel written in apparent imitation of the *Voyages extraordinaires* and embodying a similar project.[9] However, that same year saw the appearance of one of the key novels of the *Voyages extraordinaires* – *L'Ile mystérieuse* – in which the process of self-reference is used with all the complexity and the ambivalence that we will later find in *Le Sphinx des glaces*. Apart from its obvious echoes of earlier texts – for example of *Cinq semaines en ballon*, since the castaways are deposited on their island by a balloon which comes to ground – *L'Ile mystérieuse* contains two extended and important reprises of other novels from the *Voyages extraordinaires*.

7 See above, p. 98.
8 See Dumas, Gondolo della Riva and Dehs (eds.), *Correspondance inédite*, vol. II, p. 52.
9 The novel was Alphonse Brown's *La Conquête de l'air. Quarante jours de navigation aérienne* (Paris: Glady, 1875). It was reviewed on 3 August 1875 in *Le Petit Journal* and judged by the editor of that publication to be an 'imitation…parfaitement licite' ['perfectly legitimate imitation'] of Jules Verne rather than a 'contrefaçon' ['forgery'] (see Dumas, Gondolo della Riva and Dehs (eds.), *Correspondance inédite*, vol. II, p. 52, n. 1).

The first of these episodes is a recapitulation of the plot of *Les Enfants du capitaine Grant*, and particularly of the episode that had led to the exile of Ayrton on a desert island – a punishment that he had received as a traitor and a criminal. Discovered by the inhabitants of Lincoln Island, Ayrton is 'rescued' and a process of re-education, or re-civilisation, begins. *L'Ile mystérieuse* offers both a continuation of the plot of the previous novel, and an inversion of it. Where at the end of *Capitaine Grant* Ayrton had gone down in the scale of human depravity, and was found by the characters of the later novel in a condition like that of a wild animal, the process in *L'Ile mystérieuse* is precisely the reverse. Ayrton is subjected to civilising influences once more and reacquires the skills and the sense of morality that, it is implied, are the unfailing corollary of good company and respectable society. With both its recapitulation of the plot of the previous novel, and its continuation of it in inverted form, *L'Ile mystérieuse* thus makes the point that the text itself – like the individual, who is dependent on society – requires the presence and the company of other texts to nourish its existence and ensure its positive evolution. The inverted mirror image of the previous text is neither a degraded copy nor a cheap attempt to capitalise on a previous success, but a comment on the nature of text itself. And this is also the case with the second of the episodes of *L'Ile mystérieuse* that builds upon a previous text. With the reappearance at the end of the novel of Captain Nemo from *Vingt mille lieues sous les mers*, Verne has the chance of adding a conclusion to his previous story, while taking it in an unexpected direction. Nemo, formerly of unspecified nationality, now acquires a much clearer identity as Prince Dakkar, who had financed the Cipayes uprising in 1857 and lost his wife and children in the revolt. Nemo, alias Dakkar, here appears as an old man, and several dimensions are added to the previous representation of him, not least his status as an anti-Christ figure in his final descent into the depths of the ocean as he dies alone in the *Nautilus*. The reference to, and re-use of, the previous text thus enables Verne to present a far more complex image of his character. Grafting one text onto another, he plays on the echoes of the established narrative as a means of adding resonance to the new one, while throwing retrospective light on the earlier story. In so doing, he implicitly makes the point that all text is necessarily derivative, but perhaps also that originality must be found in the recognition of this. Writing thus establishes an inherent critical distance from itself and its techniques, by exploring the gaps and inconsistencies between itself and its models. Verne exploits this area of similarity and difference between two texts to find his own unique literary voice.

There are several novels in the *Voyages extraordinaires* which, like *L'Ile mystérieuse*, operate as echo chambers for other texts in the series. As Compère points out,[10] the work which evokes the largest number of Verne's own novels is *Sans dessus dessous*. Naturally, echoes and reprises of earlier texts in the corpus will by definition be found more often in later works, but we should distinguish between two forms of the process. The first is the deliberate grafting of one story onto another, or onto a previous group of stories – as is the case with *Sans dessus dessous*, which completes the so-called Gun-Club trilogy, or (in its latter stages) with *L'Ile mystérieuse* as we have just seen. The second is the apparently opportunistic referencing of previous tales – as in the example I quoted of the reference to Nemo in *Le Sphinx des glaces*, which provides the novelist with the chance to present his previous story as 'history'. More often than not, however, these opportunistic evocations of previous stories are ludic or humorous, or even extend to self-parody by the novelist. In *Hector Servadac*, as the inhabitants of the comet find themselves approaching Earth once more, they work out that the best way to leave the comet and return to their original domain is by balloon. But Servadac is not happy about this: 'Un ballon! s'écria le capitaine Servadac. Mais c'est bien usé, votre ballon! Même dans les romans, on n'ose plus s'en servir!' (HS, p. 497) ['"A balloon?" cried Captain Servadac. "But your balloon is such an old idea. They don't even dare to use that in novels these days!"'] The reference to *Cinq semaines en ballon*, and to the phenomenal success of that earlier novel, is obvious – but, implies Verne's character, such was the impact of the previous text that the theme must now be considered worn out and unusable. However, the fact that the present novel now also uses the balloon theme is an ironic comment on the recycling of an earlier fictional success. The issue is, let it be said, less the recycling itself than the obvious irony with which it is done. Verne gets away with using the balloon theme precisely *because* he flags it up as the stuff of fiction, scarcely credible as a device even in that context. Through the reference to an earlier novel in the *Voyages extraordinaires*, he once again draws our attention to the processes and the techniques of fiction, creating – if only momentarily and in ludic mode – that space in which a critical gaze at fiction from within fiction is integrated into the onward-moving story.

Much the same effect will be achieved in *Claudius Bombarnac*, where the miserably corpulent (and improbably named) Baron Weissschnitzerdörfer is attempting to complete a circuit of the world in 39 days, vying with the much more modest record set by the American journalist

---

10 *Jules Verne écrivain*, pp. 108–109.

Nellie Bly two years before the novel was published.[11] The reference to *Le Tour du monde en quatre-vingts jours* is clear, the more so since Verne's novel had been the acknowledged inspiration for so many real attempts at reducing the time of a global circuit, including those of Nellie Bly herself. However, the theme here becomes open self-parody. A hopeless and hapless caricature of Fogg, the constantly out-of-breath baron is always running out of time and running after trains. He misses every opportunity to get ahead, yet finds no means of compensating for his setbacks. At the end of the story we learn that, having missed two ships across the Pacific, and after getting shipwrecked on a third, he finally completes his circuit in no less than 187 days. The outcome, for poor Weissschnitzerdörfer, is nothing short of a spectacular failure. There is open self-parody by the novelist here, but since *Bombarnac* is also more generally about the business of writing itself, the sub-plot involving the rotund and perspiring baron serves as a constant reminder that we are never far from the institutions of fiction.

There are many similar instances of self-parody in the pages of the *Voyages extraordinaires*.[12] One of the most extended self-parodies of all, however, is *L'Ecole des Robinsons*, in which Verne takes a favourite theme – that of the character or group of characters who find themselves shipwrecked on a desert island – and makes a mockery of it. Although we find too a more general parody of the *robinsonnade* theme here – the dancemaster Tartelett often evokes Robinson literature by way of comprehending the situation that he and Godfrey find themselves in – the entire novel is a reflection on the question of civilisation versus the natural world and on the 'colonisation' of nature that is at the centre of all of Verne's castaway novels. More particularly, and as Jean-Michel Racault has convincingly argued, this novel also involves a parody of *L'Ile mystérieuse*.[13] Insisting heavily and ironically on the clichéd nature of the Robinson theme, Verne inverts the processes of his earlier text. This island, while appearing to be 'mysterious', is in fact nothing of the kind, since it had been bought by Godfrey's uncle and the whole adventure staged. This is not nature, but nurture; not an untamed wilderness, but an illusion

---

11 Starting out from New York, Nellie Bly completed a circuit of the globe in 72 days in 1889–90 – though a few years later, challenging a new record of 70 days set by George Francis Train (also mentioned in *Claudius Bombarnac*), she managed the journey in 66 days, even finding the time during her circuit to visit Jules Verne himself in Amiens.

12 For some other notable examples, see Compère, *Jules Verne écrivain*, pp. 110–13.

13 Jean-Michel Racault, 'Le détournement d'un mythe littéraire: la réécriture parodique de la robinsonnade dans *L'Ecole des Robinsons*', in *Jules Verne 8: Humour, ironie, fantaisie*, pp. 111–37.

produced by human artifice. The process of education and of the colonisation of nature – central to *L'Ile mystérieuse* – turns out to be a non-
process, for Godfrey's apparent 'apprenticeship' through his ordeal with
nature is in fact nothing of the sort. Rather, it is a controlled experiment,
a situation which is contrived by a man with all the wealth and credentials that come from an economically advanced society. In this situation
too we find a parodic echo of *L'Ile mystérieuse*, where the mysterious presence on the island turns out, in the end, to be none other than Captain
Nemo. However, whereas in *L'Ile mystérieuse* the presence of the secret,
controlling force is taken seriously – for Nemo is a godlike figure and an
outcast who has rejected Imperial civilisation – in *L'Ecole des Robinsons* it
degenerates into absurdity and exaggerated game-playing. Even the wild
animals are false, and the Man Friday figure, who appears to be such a
recalcitrant apprentice of English, in the end reveals himself to be a perfect speaker of the language. Absolutely everything is shown, in the end,
to have been an illusion and a contrivance – a trick and a fake at the level
of the story's contents, and an elaborate game at the level of writing, in
which the author plays his composition against his own previous writings
on the same theme, and more generally indulges in a send-up of Robinson
literature. This is perhaps not the most successful or important of Verne's
novels, but it reveals another aspect of his self-conscious approach to the
question of writing, and his willingness to use literature itself (including
his own work) as a subject for his stories.

Stories and their telling

The telling or the writing of stories is, then, among the most widespread
and variously exploited themes in the *Voyages extraordinaires*. But perhaps the most sustained example in the entire corpus of a ludic and self-
mocking manipulation of the conventions of storytelling, indeed of the
construction of a story out of self-reference, is to be found in *Claudius
Bombarnac*. This is a story about the creation of a story, the diary of a
writer who is desperately on the lookout for a plot, an adventure, a subject for his own texts. The theme is worked through with great brio and
gusto by Verne, who handsomely succeeds in making his hero's failure to
find and to tell a story into the lively and dramatic subject of his own
novel. Bombarnac's 'non-story' turns into a dazzling and virtuoso display
of Verne's own writing talents.

Claudius Bombarnac is the story of a Parisian journalist who, at the
behest of the newspaper he works for, undertakes a journey from the

Caspian Sea through to Peking on the Great Trans-Asiatic railway. As the journey gets under way, he is on the lookout for matters of interest, in accordance with instructions given by his editors. After all, he says, in a *clin d'œil* that already implicates his author, 'je suis de ceux qui pensent qu'ici-bas tout est matière à chronique, que la terre, la lune, le ciel, l'univers, ne sont faits que pour fournir des articles de journaux, et ma plume ne chômera pas en route' (CB, p. 8) ['I am one of those who consider that everything in this world is a potential source of copy – that the earth, the moon, the sky and the universe were made only to provide newspaper articles – and my pen will not be idle during the journey']. His constant hope is that something dramatic will spring into his field of vision and take over the course of his writing. But, in the event, his writing follows the meandering and apparently shapeless movement of the very journey that is being undertaken. Nonetheless, structure is created out of the perceived absence of structure, and a 'story' – the one we read – is wrested from the non-story that the hero-narrator experiences. As in *Le Tour du monde* and many other novels, we see a mapping of the plot in terms of geographical trajectory, but here with an added degree of self-consciousness.

Optimistically, Bombarnac gives each of the train passengers a number, feigning the hope that particular characters will take on dramatic identity and that he, the journalist, will be up to the task of giving them literary shape and of writing them into his plot.[14] Finding a Romanian stowaway in a crate, the eleventh character he has come across, Bombarnac excitedly proclaims that this must at last be his hero, the subject on whom he can exercise his true literary skills: 'Aussi, ce brave numéro onze, avec les amplifications, antonymies, diaphores, épitases, tropes, métaphores et autres figures de cette sorte, je le parerai, je le grandirai, je le développerai' (CB, p. 81) ['And so, as for this fine number eleven, with a few amplifications, antonymies, diaphors, epitases, tropes, metaphors

---

14 This idea anticipates the situation in Michel Butor's *La Modification* (1957), in which the central character of the story travels on a train from London to Rome and gives provisional identities to each of the characters in his compartment, constructing stories and scenarios about them and their lives. As his journey progresses, his thoughts and imaginings become the substance of his own story, and perhaps too of the novel that he later decides he must write. The parallel underlines just how close Verne sometimes is to certain more recent traditions in the French novel. Butor's own reading of Verne is frequently evoked in the course of his work. In an interview for a special Jules Verne issue of *Le Monde des livres* (18 March 2005), Butor describes Verne's work as one of those 'sites privilégiés, qui me permettent de mieux voir et comprendre où je suis dans cette espèce de dérive où nous sommes tous emportés' (p. 3) ['privileged sites that better enable me to see and to understand where I am in this torrent that carries us all away'].

and similar figures of speech, I shall adorn him, I shall make him larger than life, I shall develop him']. But, naturally, the suspense of the story depends to a large extent on the narrator *not* knowing until near the end who his hero really is, or was, or will be, so Bombarnac dwells repeatedly on the apparent absence of a hero by way of prolonging his specular reflections and of maintaining uncertainty: 'Il me faudrait un héros, et jusqu'à présent ses pas ne se sont point fait entendre dans la coulisse' (CB, p. 181) ['I need a hero, and until now his steps have not been heard in the wings']. The author-in-search-of-a-character theme is thus played out with all its resonances in Verne's story, and the irony is that, while the first-person narrator laments the absence of real drama around him, his account of events unwittingly builds up into a fully fledged adventure story in the classic tradition. As the narrative gaze that observes everything but its own narrative performance, he is the only one who cannot see this. This is no mean technical feat by Verne the writer, who thus succeeds in using a self-deprecating hero, unaware of the fictional implications of what he observes around him, to create a story that is full of suspense, reversals, ironies and, of course, reflections on the nature of storytelling itself. It also shows that Verne is perfectly comfortable in the use and exploitation of a first-person narrator whose understanding of events must be seen to be limited. While there are a number of other significant uses of first-person narrative in the *Voyages extraordinaires* (notably in *Voyage au centre de la terre* and *Vingt mille lieues*) this one differs in that it exposes its narrator ironically throughout the story. Through self-conscious narrative, Verne nonetheless creates high drama, proving that reflexivity and pacy, racy narrative are by no means incompatible.

While *Claudius Bombarnac* is explicitly constructed around the theme of writing and storytelling, there are other moments in the *Voyages extraordinaires* at which the subject of stories and their telling comes more briefly into the foreground. In fact, the pages of Verne's novels abound with storytellers eager to turn their lived experience into fictionalised accounts, and their presence is a symbolic reminder of the novelist's own activity, a *mise en abyme* of the narrative process. Characters such as Joe, Fergusson's manservant in *Cinq semaines en ballon*, or Ned Land, the Canadian harpoonist in *Vingt mille lieues sous les mers*, are revealed to have natural storytelling gifts that are tellingly profiled within the narrative. Ned Land, though naturally 'peu communicatif' ['not very communicative'], exploits 'cette vieille langue de Rabelais qui est encore en usage dans quelques provinces canadiennes' ['the old language of Rabelais that is still used in a few Canadian provinces'] and gives colourful accounts of his adventures and travels in the polar seas. He turns out to be a fine storyteller, attuned by instinct to the techniques of epic poetry, as Aronnax observes: 'Il racontait ses pêches et ses combats avec une grande poésie naturelle. Son récit prenait une forme épique, et je croyais écouter quelque Homère canadien, chantant *L'Iliade* des régions hyperboréennes.' (VML, pp. 30–31) ['He told of his fishing expeditions and his battles, with a great natural sense of poetry. His accounts took on an epic form, and it seemed to me that I was listening to some Canadian Homer, declaiming the *Iliad* of the polar regions.'] Apart from allowing the novelist to plot his own story in relation to a classical literary landmark, this is also an echo of (and perhaps an implicit tribute to) the epic mode of Melville's narrative in *Moby-Dick*. But the point is that Verne here directs us to the question of the creation of fiction, and in so doing encourages us to reflect on the way his own narrative is shaping up. The reader thus becomes more alert to the processes and the techniques of fictionalisation, a consequence that was even more obvious in the case of Verne's treatment of Joe in the earlier *Cinq semaines*.

Like Ned Land, Joe is a natural storyteller and warms at an early stage to his task. While Fergusson recounts his expeditions to the officers in the wardroom of the *Resolute* as it heads to Zanzibar, Joe discovers his talent for spinning a yarn as he whiles away time in the company of the deck hands. Like Ned Land, he too, despite his lack of education, reveals an instinctive grasp of techniques tried and tested through the ages. We are told that 'Joe trônait sur le gaillard d'avant, et faisait de l'histoire à sa manière, procédé suivi d'ailleurs par les plus grands historiens de tous les temps' ['Joe reigned supreme on the fo'c's'le, and created history in his own manner, a procedure which after all has been followed by the greatest historians of the ages']. Interestingly, though, Joe's tales at this point are projections into the future, rather than tales of the past. Once he has managed to get the sailors to accept the incredible idea of a balloon journey across Africa – a move which has the implicit purpose, too, of persuading the reader of the credibility of the framework narrative in *Cinq semaines* – his imagination knows no bounds: 'L'éblouissant conteur persuadait à son auditoire qu'après ce voyage-là on en ferait bien d'autres. Ce n'était que le commencement d'une longue série d'entreprises surhumaines.' (5S, p. 57) ['The stunning storyteller persuaded his audience that, after this journey, many others would be undertaken. It was just the beginning of a long series of superhuman enterprises.'] If ever there were a case of a novelist setting out his own future programme of work through one of his characters, then surely this is it. In Joe's moment of triumphant storytelling, as he dreams of journeys and explorations that man will undertake, we find the *Voyages extraordinaires* in embryo, even the prospect of the lunar novels. But, in his reference to the idea of a journey to the moon, Joe uses a technique that he will also deploy at the end of this narrative, and which distinguishes him as a *raconteur* from Ned Land. He deliberately plays down the whole idea ('Ma foi, c'est trop commun! tout le monde y va, dans la lune' ['Ah me, that is far too common – everybody goes to the moon!']), suggests that it is utterly banal, and adopts the role of the blasé narrator. Clearly, though, he sees the advantages of this tactic, for it increases the sense of amazement among his listeners, and he is therefore able to hold them more effectively in thrall. Is this the novelist himself revealing his hand? While understatement or affected indifference is not Verne's most frequently used rhetorical strategy, it is certainly one of the devices available to him as a storyteller, and Joe's own reliance on it is flagged up as one of the standard techniques of the narrator's art. This attitude will again be apparent at the end of the story, when the explorers return to London and are able to 'cash in' on their adventures. While Fergusson once again gives the official version, this time at the Royal Geographical Society, Joe gives his own more colourful version of events. He succeeds in heightening the impact of his story through his insistence that it was really nothing much at all. But, as he does this, the novelist himself naturally 'piggy-backs' on this understatement, which contrasts so ostentatiously with the story that has just come to a conclusion, and makes an implicit comment on its action-packed, racy quality. Although Joe's talents as a storyteller function generally as a symbolic parallel to those of the novelist himself, perhaps as a device to heighten our awareness of the techniques and the action of storytelling, here they impact directly on the conclusion of the novel and enable us to stand back and view the story as the artifice that it is, or was.

There are other instances in the *Voyages extraordinaires* when stories told by Verne's fictional characters have a direct and performative impact on the unfolding of the framework narrative. At this level, the story within the story is much more than a symbolic reflection of it, for it demonstrates how the telling of stories can itself be an 'event' with wide-ranging consequences for the plot. The technique of *mise en abyme* is a classic sign of self-conscious narrative that turns its gaze inwards, but in Verne the inward gaze, far from being the moment of stasis that one might expect, becomes the means to move the story forwards. Such is the case in *La Jangada*, Part I, Chapter 19, significantly entitled 'Histoire ancienne' ['Old Story'/'Ancient History']. Here, the criminal Torrès, taken on board the river craft constructed by Joam Garral, tells a story of a murder that took place in Brazil back in 1826 (the actual narrative of *La Jangada* is set in 1852). The story is that of a certain Dacosta, a security guard in the diamond trade who gave away the secret of a convoy's movements, committed a murder, was imprisoned and condemned to death, then at the eleventh hour escaped and left Brazil, never to be heard of again. As Joam Garral knows, this is a version of his own story, and we will learn that Torrès has come to seek him out because he wants to blackmail him into giving him his daughter in marriage. But the 'story' with which Garral is now confronted, and which induces such a sense of great foreboding in all those who listen to it, differs from the real story of his past in a number of important respects. While it is true that Garral had been condemned to death in Brazil in 1826, and had then fled and begun a new life, Torrès's version of events assumes that Garral was the guilty criminal. But Garral is innocent and one of his motives for returning now to Brazil is to clear his name. Faced with his 'story', albeit in a distorted form, Garral must act to put matters right. The plot of Verne's novel will thus depend on the confrontation of different tellings of the same story, and their resolution. Implicit to the whole unfolding of the novel is the question of how these different versions can be reconciled, and how the true account of Garral's past can emerge and be accepted. Stories, as much as events, dictate the flow of the narrative, and underline just how much the business of storytelling is itself an action or an event.

The relaying of stories within the diegesis is therefore rarely innocent or straightforward. Even where stories appear to be quite remote from the actual plot of a novel, they may turn out to have an impact at some level. In *L'Etoile du sud*, at a dinner held by her father to celebrate and display the diamond that has apparently been 'manufactured' by Cyprien Méré, Alice Watkins tells the story of a fabulous diamond that had belonged to a nobleman at the court of Henri III. The nobleman in question, M. de Sancy, had offered the diamond as security to the royal treasury, and had used a manservant to transport it on his behalf. Although the manservant failed to arrive at his destination, Sancy never doubted his loyalty, and it was later discovered that he had been killed by enemy troops. However, in order to safeguard the diamond, he had swallowed it, and it was later found in his stomach. Though in some ways this story is outside the unfolding of the plot in Verne's own novel – it does not have the same performative impact as Torrès's story in *La Jangada* – two crucial clues from it will remain to help us solve the hermeneutic puzzle of the main narrative. The first is that the servant, despite doubts, remains loyal, as will also be the case with Matakit in the framework story. The second is that the diamond is swallowed, as will also happen in the main story, although in this case it is not by the servant, but by Alice Watkins's pet ostrich. The parallels – which become apparent retrospectively – are a teasing link between inner and outer story, a clue that the relationship between the framework and the embedded narrative is not likely to be a simple one. Alice Watkins's story about a disappearing diamond is, of course, heavily laden with implications even on a first reading. But it also serves to direct our attention to the telling of stories in a more general sense. As is so often the case with Verne, the plot of a novel is based not only on the representation of events 'out there' in a supposedly real, non-narrated world, but also, and perhaps more importantly, on the relaying and retelling of stories themselves. Narrative is not only about the mediation of its own narrated contents: it is about the ubiquitous presence of narrative itself.

Sometimes, too, we will find that characters in Verne look ahead to the conclusion of the very story in which they figure, trying to foretell, forestall, or at least foresee its ending. The quest for closure is a fundamental human drive, and through it Verne reminds us of the extent to which the events of our lives require and impose a narrative. In *Le Superbe Orénoque*, one of the two young Frenchmen on the expedition has fallen in love with Jeanne de Kermor, who is travelling in search of her long-lost father. Yet the situation, requiring that they travel in different directions and live out different 'stories', seems impossible. Discussing his feelings with his fellow traveller, the lovestruck Frenchman asks: 'Comment cela finira-t-il?' ['How will it finish?'] Whereupon his companion gives the sanguine response: 'Bien! Et il ne crut pas devoir rien ajouter à ce mot.' (SO, p. 431) [' "Well!" And he did not feel it necessary to add another word to this.'] So Verne gives us an obvious hint as to how the intrigue will eventually unfold, through his own characters who, by their beliefs, their decisions and their own conviction about what should happen, will ensure that the narrative will somehow proceed in the right direction. For a brief moment, they have stepped outside their own narrative, viewed it as a complete entity, and looked ahead to its point of closure. The habit of stepping outside of the narrative in this manner in order to foresee its ending is one that Sébastien Zorn, one of the musicians in *L'Ile à hélice*, indulges in rather more frequently and more comically. His constant refrain, throughout the story and in contrast to the beliefs of his fellow musicians, is that their story will end badly. And indeed, Zorn (whose name means 'anger' in German) is proved right, so his repeated grumblings in defiance of the apparent progress of the narrative in a different direction are in the end justified. Though Verne makes of him a caricature, he has a crucial function in the unfolding of the story, for he provides clues that we are eventually no longer able to overlook. The momentum of Zorn's forebodings is in inverse proportion to his significance as a character in almost every other respect. Yet it is precisely because he is treated with such levity that Zorn can more easily be the vehicle of a hermeneutic clue.

Critics have often been struck by the ludic features of Verne's narrative style. These range from the contrived construction of plot in terms of rituals and games to the telling of stories in ways that mockingly invite complicity on the part of the reader.[15] As we have seen, the conventions of the storyteller's art are themselves a constant focus in Verne, and they are highlighted with a playful humour that heightens awareness of the contrived nature of narrative. A feature worthy of particular attention here is Verne's use of the rhetorical device known as apophasis (which asserts something by seeming to pass over or deny it), and the closely related one of praeteritio (which mentions something while stating that it will not be mentioned). This rhetoric of denial, negation or absence – the focus on what is not, or what cannot be – is frequently a pretext to enter into detailed descriptions and digressions, and sometimes the Vernian narrator deploys seemingly disproportionate effort in signalling what he claims to be unable to include in his story. Just like the amorous sonneteer in the *précieux* tradition who, for the first thirteen lines of his piece, enumerates what are not the reasons for his love before concluding with a positive flourish, Verne similarly uses negatives as a means of creating cumulative and ironic effect. The telling of stories at such points depends on the telling of what is manifestly *not* the story. What is not seen and not observed by his characters can turn out to have as much weight in the narrative as what is actually experienced. Verne's narrator plays mockingly on the novelist's urge to offer background information, even where that may not be relevant. We have seen that *Claudius Bombarnac* is based essentially on the formula of telling a story by default, in the apparent absence of that elusive story. But Verne extracts varied effects from this principle in the course of his narrative. Descriptions and digressions occur as counterpoints to the main narrative precisely because, we are told, this is not what the narrative is about. When at the outset Bombarnac receives a telegram instructing him to abandon his project of visiting the Caucasus and to travel to Peking instead, he rues the fact that he will be unable to send back studiously prepared reports about the region he is now in. In so doing, he nonetheless succeeds in providing some of the details that would have figured in the reports, thus gaining a small

---

15 For an example of a study which emphasises the first aspect, see Marie-Hélène Huet, 'L'exploration du jeu', in *Jules Verne 1: 'Le Tour du monde'*, pp. 95–108; for an example of the second, see Compère, *Jules Verne écrivain*, Chapter 5, 'Le Ludotexte', pp. 89–121.

narrative victory despite his feigned disappointment. Against the odds, it seems, he manages to work in what he professes to be unable to write about:

> J'étais studieusement préparé, pourtant, largement approvisionné de documents géographiques et ethnologiques, relatifs à la région transcaucasienne. Donnez-vous donc la peine d'apprendre que le bonnet de fourrure en forme de turban, dont se coiffent les montagnards et les Cosaques, s'appelle 'papakha', que la redingote froncée à la taille où s'accrochent les cartouchières latérales, est nommée 'tcherkeska' par les uns et 'bechmet' par les autres! (CB, pp. 2–3)

> [I was studiously prepared, however, and had a substantial stock of geographical and ethnological documents relating to the Trans-Caucasian region. Try giving yourself the trouble to learn that the turban-shaped fur hat worn by mountain dwellers and Cossacks is called a 'papakha', or that the overcoat with folds at the waist where cartridge belts are fastened is called by some the 'tcherkeska' and by others the 'bechmet'!]

There is something of the affected and self-mocking pedantry of Mérimée's narrators here, as when in *La Vénus d'Ille* the reader is frustrated by the insertion of pompous digressions, or when at the end of *Carmen* we are given a linguistic disquisition instead of closure. The inclusion of detail appears as a distraction from the narrative, yet the narrator's pedantry is itself part of a tongue-in-cheek plan to frustrate and to tease. The introductory chapter of *Claudius Bombarnac* exploits this seam, accumulating facts and details that Bombarnac claims he will have to pass over. The narrator thus does what he says he cannot do. Many of his subsequent descriptions are constructed in a similar way, working in details and facts by default, as though he is stepping in, despite the momentum of his 'real' story, to write the story that he had really wanted to write. As an educator, Verne is also aware of the advantages of enumerating what he claims his reader does not need to know, for he thus appears to dissociate himself from the knowledge that he imparts, and sides complicitly with the 'pupil' against the 'teacher'. Providing copious material about the towns and regions his hero passes through, he therefore plays conspicuously on its irrelevance as the very means of justifying its inclusion.

That instructive function of the novelist's art will further be exploited with the introduction into the story of the character of Major Noltitz. Fabulously knowledgeable about everything, it seems, this crashing bore gives pedantic accounts about many of the cities on the travellers' route, and Bombarnac in his turn feels obliged (in case they turn out somehow to contain a clue to his own story) to relay these masses of detail to the

reader. Meanwhile, as Noltitz describes in the fullest detail the cities and
regions that Bombarnac himself does not have the leisure to visit, Bombarnac evokes with feigned ruefulness those places and curiosities that he
claims he would have liked to include. Superfluous fact is integrated into
the ongoing narrative with a tongue-in-cheek lament that it *cannot* figure.
The pretexts for such lists can be ironically contrived, but that, of course,
is the point. The presence of fog on one section of the journey will be just
such a pretext, leading Bombarnac to lament: 'Je n'ai *rien* vu des gorges et
ravins, à travers lesquels circule le Grand-Transasiatique, *rien* de la vallée
de Lou-Ngan, où nous stationnons à onze heures, *rien* des deux cent trente
kilomètres que nous avons franchis sous les volutes d'une sorte de buée
jaunâtre' (CB, p. 246, my italics) ['I saw nothing of the gorges and ravines
through which the Grand Trans-Asiatic passes, nothing of the valley of
Lou-Ngan where we stopped at eleven o' clock, and nothing of the two
hundred and thirty kilometres that we covered beneath the swirls of a
kind of yellowish haze']. Here Verne combines the device of apophasis
with another ancient rhetorical strategy, anaphora, in which the repetition of a word – often at the beginning of a phrase as here – gives added
emphasis to the claim being made. Yet the repetition of 'rien' is also a
decoy, allowing the narrator to include in its wake what it appears to
forbid or exclude. What Verne knows and teasingly exploits is the fact
that, whether preceded by a negation or not, details that are itemised in a
list have a positive presence.

The same technique had also been used with considerable success in
the earlier *Le Tour du monde en quatre-vingts jours*, another of those texts
whose hero is a limited reflector and register of human experience, and
whose adventures therefore require ironic 'completion' by the narrator.
Fogg himself is evoked at the outset in almost entirely negative terms.
What is *not* known about him, suggests the tongue-in-cheek narrator,
clearly amounts to much more than what *is* known about him. As he sets
the opening scenes of his novel in London, Verne contrives to evoke many
of the institutions of that city on the slenderest of pretexts – that of mentioning that Fogg had never been seen in any of them. The emphatic list
of negatives builds upon the extended repetition of 'ni', which occurs no
less than 22 times in the course of a single paragraph. To this is added the
reinforcement of terms such as 'aucun' and 'jamais', until a formidable
non-picture emerges:

> On ne l'avait jamais vu ni à la Bourse, ni à la Banque, ni dans aucun des
> comptoirs de la Cité. Ni les bassins ni les docks de Londres n'avaient jamais
> reçu un navire ayant pour armateur Phileas Fogg. Ce gentleman ne figurait
> dans aucun comité d'administration. Son nom n'avait jamais retenti dans un

collège d'avocats, ni au Temple, ni à Lincoln's-inn, ni à Gray's-inn. Jamais il
ne plaida à la Cour du chancelier, ni au Banc de la Reine, ni à l'Echiquier, ni
en cour ecclésiastique. Il n'était ni industriel, ni négociant, ni marchand, ni
agriculteur. Il ne faisait partie ni de l'*Institution royale de la Grande-Bretagne*,
ni de l'*Institution de Londres*, ni de l'*Institution des Artisans*, ni de l'*Institution Russell*, ni de l'*Institution littéraire de l'Ouest*, ni de l'*Institution du Droit*,
ni de cette *Institution des Arts et des Sciences réunis*, qui est placée sous le
patronage direct de Sa Gracieuse Majesté. Il n'appartenait enfin à aucune des
nombreuses sociétés qui pullulent dans la capitale de l'Angleterre, depuis la
Société de l'Armonica jusqu'à la *Société entomologique*, fondée principalement
dans le but de détruire les insectes nuisibles. (TDM, p. 1 and p. 3)

[He had never been seen either at the Stock Exchange or at the Bank of England or at the trading posts of the City. The basins and docks of London had
never welcomed a ship commissioned by Phileas Fogg. This gentleman
belonged to no board of directors. His name had never been mentioned in
any barristers' chambers, neither the Temple, nor Lincoln's Inn, nor Gray's
Inn. Never had he defended an action, not at the Courts of Chancery, nor the
Queen's Bench, nor the Exchequer, nor the Ecclesiastical Court. He was neither an industrialist nor a businessman, nor a merchant, nor an agricultural-
ist. He belonged neither to the Royal Institution of Great Britain, nor to the
London Institution, nor to the Institution of Artisans, nor to the Russell
Institution, nor to the Western Literary Institution, nor to the Law Society,
nor to the Royal Society for the Arts, Manufacture and Commerce which
enjoys the direct patronage of Her Majesty the Queen. In sum, he belonged
to none of those numerous societies that throng together in the capital of
England, ranging from the Harmonica Society to the Society of Entomolo-
gists – the latter founded principally with the aim of destroying harmful
insects.]

While this passage creates a remarkably detailed picture of what Fogg is
not – ironically implying in the process that much must be known for such
affirmations to be made with certainty – it succeeds too in offering generous amounts of local colour. But the idea of local colour itself must be
taken with a pinch of salt. It is the stock-in-trade of fiction set in communities or regions with which the intended reader is unfamiliar, and Verne
is playing upon and parading this convention with humorous intent. That
much of the detail is superfluous – and intentionally so – becomes fully
apparent in that final sentence of the paragraph, where the enumeration
of Fogg's non-credentials degenerates into discussion of trivia. Fogg
emerges as a negative image, a space to be filled in, a series of gaps that are
themselves perhaps as eloquent as any real information we might glean
about him. And from this it is clear that the story that is *not* told can be
every bit as forceful and as dramatic as the story that *is* told. In a novel

which plots out an adventure as action-packed and as eventful as a circuit of the globe, Verne's occasional insistence on the absent components of the story comes as an ironic and very modern comment on the nature and the characteristics of narrative. The telling of the story is also the telling of the non-story, the profiling of what is absent and of what would ideally be required to complete it.

But the story itself is amusingly developed out of the non-person and non-event that Fogg so often seems to be. Since Fogg is so often oblivious to the outside world, taking refuge in his eternal games of whist, the narrator makes it clear that he must step in and speak 'over the character's head' if the story is to progress at all. In a further use of apophasis in his description of Bombay, the narrator tells us about everything that Fogg in his absence of curiosity *fails* to see. And once again, the emphasis on the negative is provided by Verne's anaphoric use of 'ni', echoing that earlier introductory discussion of Fogg in London: 'Ainsi donc, des merveilles de Bombay, il ne songeait à rien voir, ni l'hôtel de ville, ni la magnifique bibliothèque, ni les forts, ni les docks, ni le marché au coton, ni les bazars, ni les mosquées, ni les synagogues, ni les églises arméniennes, ni la splendide pagode de Malebar-Hill, ornée de deux tours polygones' (TDM, p. 64) ['And so, of all the marvels of Bombay, he sought out not a single one, neither the City Hall, nor the magnificent library, nor the forts, nor the docks, nor the cotton market, nor the bazaars, nor the mosques, nor the synagogues, nor the Armenian churches, nor the splendid pagoda on Malabar Hill, decorated with two polygon-shaped towers']. If Fogg is so inept as a tourist, it is implied, then the narrator will simply have to do the job for him. Naturally, the latter warms to his task with somewhat more than the requisite amount of enthusiasm, allowing himself to be carried away with the detail that Fogg does not observe, and displaying his own narrative credentials for the reader's benefit. In this way, Verne succeeds magnificently in maintaining a focus on the question of narrative itself and of how stories are, or are not, told. In this tale of high adventure, the question of storytelling itself remains as one of the major components. Just as the narrative describes the progression of Phileas Fogg's journey around the globe, so too the journey of narrative itself is never lost from view.

The storyteller's materials

As much as the techniques of narrative, the actual materials that the storyteller uses –in particular the essential building blocks of words and language – are exuberantly and extravagantly showcased in various ways throughout the *Voyages extraordinaires*. We have already seen in our reading of the early theatrical works that word games, puns, verbal *tics* and linguistic riddles abound from the outset in Verne's writing. And while the later novelist so often highlights the spellbinding alterity of words in those sumptuous lists of scientific or exotic terminology, so too his characters frequently reveal the mysterious potency of language to suggest unexpected links, to offer surprising revelations, or simply to puzzle by its density or opacity. Words are a permanent fascination, and the novelist works to display them. The fantastically contrived names of so many of Verne's characters – Blockhead, Clou-de-Girofle, Frycollin, Hurliguerly, Sir James Jejeebhoy, Orfanik, Pigassof, Scorbitt, Tartelett, Urrican, Ursiclos, Ygène, Zinca Klork, to name but a very few – are themselves a reminder of the strangeness, the phonetic richness, or sometimes the almost absurdly suggestive resonances of words, and they offer a constant humorous challenge to the reader. And while some of Verne's names yield their symbolism easily (Nemo, Speedy, P'tit-Bonhomme, Parazard, Passepartout, Playfair) others remain almost literally impenetrable, yet no less fascinating for it. 'Fogg' may suggest the *brouillard* that was a constant feature of nineteenth-century London (and to the modern reader may even denote a contrast to the *débrouillard* ['resourceful'] character of Passepartout), but the doubling of the 'g', while mysteriously appropriate, cannot easily be explained; and the combination of the surname with a forename as unusual as Phileas (which happens also to have been the name of an ancient Greek geographer) in the end makes for a sonority which itself transcends symbolism.[16] The name of Phileas Fogg, like so many others in the *Voyages extraordinaires*, resonates through the pages of the novel with an almost talismanic force. This is just one way in which our attention is drawn to words as sites of curiosity in themselves, supremely worthy of the text-traveller's attention.

In some instances, extended word-play involving names can operate as a leitmotif, as in *La Jangada*. Early in the story, the barber Fragoso is rescued by a young woman called Lina when, after an uncharacteristic fit of despair, he attempts to commit suicide by hanging himself in the rainforest. He falls in love with Lina, and the memory of the creeper (*liane*)

---

16 In the previously quoted interview with R. H. Sherard, 'Jules Verne Revisited', Verne has this to say about names in his novels and his choice of a name for the hero of *Le Tour du monde*: 'I do attach certain importance to them,' he said, 'and when I found "Fogg" I was very pleased and proud. And it was very popular. It was considered a real *trouvaille*. And yet Fogg – Fogg – that means nothing but *brouillard*. But it was especially Phileas that gave such value to the creation. Yes, there is importance in names. Look at the wonderful creations of Balzac.'

that had led her to him is like a bond (*lien*) between them. For Fragoso, everything in his existence will now revolve around these three minimally differentiated words: *Lina, liane, lien*. He perpetuates the imagined confusion by giving the nickname 'Liane' to Lina herself, reinforcing this sense of a bond, or *lien*, between them and between the words that have played such a crucial role in his story. In this sense, Fragoso himself recognises that his story is not only dictated *by* language and words, it is also literally *about* them. The impact and the effect of words on the way that he makes sense of and narrates his own existence is shown to be fundamental.

Language more generally is also placed on display in the *Voyages extraordinaires* as an almost edible substance – so abundant, so varied and so positively delicious, that we should not be surprised to find an ever-present parallel between the delights of the lexicon and the *délices* of the table. Since numerous critics have drawn attention to this idea of language in the *Voyages extraordinaires* as a store of appetising food to be tasted, consumed and digested, let us stick to a few brief remarks here.[17] The first point is that Verne conspicuously focuses on the savour, the flavour and the texture of language. The enumerations of deep-sea fish and plants in *Vingt mille lieues sous les mers* are often accompanied by remarks about their taste, as though a parallel is being established between, on the one hand, the feel of the words themselves on the tongue and the palate, and, on the other hand, the culinary properties of the creature or plant that they designate. Through the metaphor of consumption and nutrition, language is represented as a flavoursome and deliciously varied medium. We are seldom far in Verne's writing from this sense of the taste of words themselves, as they roll over the tongue and through the mouth, or perhaps get hastily swallowed. Language is an object to be relished and enjoyed (though sometimes, too, Verne shows that words can stick in the throat or prove indigestible) rather than being a mere instrument of description and denotation. The tone is set and the metaphor established in the early novel, *Un Prêtre en 1839*, where the witch Abraxa one day explains to the hero that she had been faced with a choice between

---

17 On the subject of food in Verne, see the helpful introductory discussion by Andrew Martin in *The Knowledge of Ignorance*, pp. 123–28. The subject is treated more extensively in Christian Chelebourg, *Jules Verne: L'Œil et le ventre, une poétique du sujet* (Paris: Minard, 1999). A comparison of food themes in Verne and Flaubert can be found in my own study entitled 'Eat My Words: Verne and Flaubert, or the Anxiety of the Culinary', in John West-Sooby (ed.), *Consuming Culture: The Arts of the French Table* (Newark: University of Delaware Press, Monash Romance Studies, 2004), pp. 118–29.

innumerable cabalistic sciences before she finally decided on her own speciality:

> J'avais à choisir entre l'aéromancie, [...] la capnomancie, la chiromancie, la cartomancie, la nécromancie, l'aratomancie, l'axinomancie, l'alphatomancie, l'alomancie, l'arithmomancie, l'astragalomancie. En prononçant tous ces noms de la science cabalistique, la vieille se complaisait intérieurement comme une reine qui domine un peuple nombreux ou un homme affamé en présence de mets sans nombre. (P39, pp. 170–71)

> ['I had to choose between aeromancy, capnomancy, chiromancy, cartomancy, necromancy, aratomancy, axinomancy, alphatomancy, alomancy, arithmomancy, and astragalomancy.' As she pronounced all these terms of cabalistic science, the old woman took inner pleasure at them, like a queen who dominates a large populace, or a starving man in the presence of innumerable dishes of food.]

The words here acquire a cumulative, incantatory effect that is especially suited to the theme of the passage. But while Verne uses two metaphors to evoke the substantial quality of language – power and food – it is the second that will have the longer career in the *Voyages extraordinaires*, perhaps because it conveys the oral and sensory nature of words so well. Language, in Verne, teases the taste buds, lingers on the tongue, gets gobbled up with obvious pleasure and, just occasionally, spat out with distaste.[18] It is never itself a neutral instrument with which to look at the world and to represent it objectively. On the contrary, it is very much a part of that sensual and linguistic reality that Verne's characters have themselves to come to terms with. In order to tell the story of their world, they must also feel the texture of the words that they use, and must taste them in their mouth. In *Cinq semaines en ballon*, as the balloon flight begins and the travellers see Zanzibar beneath them, we learn that Joe 'fit à lui seul une terrible consommation d'onomatopées. Les oh! les ah! les hein! éclataient entre ses lèvres.' (5S, p, 80) ['Joe managed on his own to devour a host of onomatopoeic words. The "Ohs" and the "Ahs" exploded between his lips.'] While he does this, his companions take in the experience in other ways, the contrast reinforcing, as is so often the case in Verne, the characters' different modes of perception. Fergusson observes and takes notes, Kennedy (who is all eyes) simply looks, but Joe – whose translation of everything into words is a visceral, primal activity – must

---

18 Naturally, this intensely oral quality of language has led certain critics to suggest that Verne's writing style can and should in part be explained by the presence of an oral fixation. On this subject, see especially Chelebourg, *Jules Verne: L'Œil et le ventre*, 'Nourritures de poète', pp. 181–92.

experience the scene through language, almost literally feeling the taste of it 'exploding' in his mouth through those onomatopoeic interjections. A similarly oral mode of experience will return with Ned Land of *Vingt mille lieues*, whose primary impulse is to taste and to eat the sea creatures he observes.

The parallel between the act of description and the processes of consumption is a constant reminder in Verne that language cannot be neatly separated from some natural, non-linguistic world that is simply there to be represented in words. The telling of stories is also the story of language and its place in man's world, and the parallel with an image of man as a hunter-gatherer in an untamed wilderness is always implicit. While nature in Verne's stories produces immeasurable provisions of food, so too language is a self-perpetuating storehouse of consumable produce, an object to be plundered, tasted, digested, and cultivated. Reading, too, prolongs the metaphor of consumption, and in *L'Ile à hélice* we learn that certain printed items on the millionaires' island, designed as ephemeral publications, are produced in edible form: 'Elles n'ont d'autre but que de distraire un instant, en s'adressant à l'esprit... et même à l'estomac. Oui! quelques-unes sont imprimées sur pâte comestible à l'encre de chocolat. Lorsqu'on les a lues, on les mange au premier déjeuner.' ['Their aim is merely to provide temporary distraction for the mind... and indeed for the stomach. Yes! Some of them are printed on edible paste with chocolate ink. When you have read them, you simply eat them at the next meal.'] The parallel between food on the one hand, and reading or literature on the other, is further reinforced by the ironic reactions of two of the characters. Yvernès responds with: 'Voilà des lectures d'une digestion facile!' ['That is easily digested reading material!'] while Pinchinat adds: 'Et d'une littérature nourrissante' (IH, p. 83) ['And good literary nourishment']. The texts that human language produces are, then, themselves seen as consumable and digestible, perhaps nothing more than food for thought. Through the extended metaphoric display of his own narrative material as food, Verne reminds us of the relative status of language and of writing.

But if language itself is placed on display in various ways in the *Voyages extraordinaires*, so too are languages generally – foreign languages or professional and scientific discourses – in all their miraculous diversity. All the tongues in the world, implies Verne, are not enough to describe the fabulous Babel of its riches. If his main characters are so eager to learn foreign languages, and usually so effective at it, it is not merely because Verne wishes to provide a salutary example to the youthful reader about the benefits of intercultural competence. Rather, he is making a more fundamental point about the varied linguistic nature of the world in which we live. Language does not merely designate reality, he implies, it is reality itself, in all its cornucopian diversity. The learning of tongues is a means of seizing the world more fully, of engaging with it more comprehensively, indeed of 'travelling' more completely through it. Words, in whatever language, are the 'open sesame' to the secrets of the universe. Since the infinite variety of nature has its precise parallel in the endless inventiveness of human languages, the task of the novelist, as much as for the explorer or scientist, is to link the two – to find words that match the objects, and objects that match the words. So words, in all their abundance and in whatever language, are the cornerstone both of the writer's art and of the nineteenth-century explorer's attitude. Wherever the words may come from, it is implied, they must be found if the untold mysteries of creation are to be unlocked, transformed into an orderly series of narratives, and properly opened up to human scrutiny. In a tone of linguistic self-consciousness that anticipates Rimbaud, Axel will exclaim in *Voyage au centre de la terre* as he contemplates in awe the marvels of the subterranean world: 'A des sensations nouvelles, il fallait des mots nouveaux' (VCT, p. 250) ['For new sensations, new words had to be found']. In this *prise de conscience*, Axel senses that the experience of new places and discoveries must find its own idioms and terminologies if it is to have meaning. Whatever language or languages are available, they must be fully exploited. Yet if Axel himself feels linguistically challenged ('les paroles me manquaient' ['words failed me'], he says) his uncle Lidenbrock is the most voluble and articulate of speakers – in almost any language. Like the novelist engaging through language with the immense multiplicity of the world, Lidenbrock has grasped the essential principle that mastery of the lexicon, or of a range of lexicons in a range of different languages and idioms, is the best means of matching up to the fabulous abundance of Nature. At home in Icelandic, German, French and Italian, Lidenbrock also speaks Latin, the language of the nineteenth-century scientist.

In all of this, though, he is merely typical. Many of Verne's heroes gain huge advantages by their serendipitous knowledge of languages at key moments of their story, not only because they are thus able to engage with reality and verbalise their experiences in the languages available to them, but also because they are able to interpret and understand what is happening to them in the first place. Language allows its speaker not only to decipher and to decode, but also to relay and re-narrate. In *Cinq semaines en ballon*, when the travellers have landed among a potentially hostile tribe, Fergusson addresses a chieftain in Arabic (5S, p. 112) and is able to gain precious time when he realises that the locals think the balloon is the moon (though all the languages in the world will not save him when, later in the same chapter, the real moon emerges from behind the clouds and the trick is exposed). In *Mathias Sandorf*, Sandorf/Antékirtt is another of those great Vernian polyglots who has learned his languages by travelling widely. This enables him to listen in on conversations that would otherwise be closed books to him, as he does notably one day when one of his betrayers is speaking in Arabic: 'Sarcany et l'étrangère, par cela seul qu'ils employaient la langue arabe, devaient se croire assurés que personne ne pourrait les comprendre en cet endroit. Ils se trompaient, puisque le docteur était là. Familier avec tous les idiomes de l'Orient et de l'Afrique, il n'allait pas perdre un seul mot de cet entretien.' (MS, I, p. 305) ['Sarcany and the unknown woman must have believed that, by dint of speaking Arabic, they were not at risk of anyone listening in on their conversation here. They were wrong, for the doctor was present. Familiar with all the languages of the Orient and of Africa, he was not going to lose a single word of this exchange.'] Antékirtt is able to hear and to make sense of a part of the story of his betrayal, and his understanding of another tongue is the key with which he is able to unlock his own past and reflect on his way forward. Language, like knowledge itself, is power. The world is word.

So Verne gives a conspicuous role to the learning of languages, by way of profiling more generally the importance of language in our negotiation of the world. The heterogeneous terminology that is such an important feature of Verne's own descriptions in the *Voyages extraordinaires* is mirrored by the heteroglossic quality of his characters' speech. In *En Magellanie*, the Kaw-djer will effortlessly move from one language to another (M, p. 84), while in *Le Secret de Wilhelm Storitz* the Vidal brothers speak French, German and Hungarian and indulge in conversations which sometimes mingle the three languages into a new and more powerful hybrid (WS, p. 64). This mastery of languages is usually a sign of a character's openness and willingness to engage with all manner of difficulties or obstacles, and is rarely a skill acquired by the less admirable figures in the *Voyages extraordinaires*. Implicitly, too, the Vernian polyglot, using his knowledge of languages as a means both of 'reading' his world and of re-narrating it, is likened to the figure of the novelist. The major Vernian heroes add the learning of languages effortlessly, it seems, to their arsenal of weapons, scientific instruments or travelling provisions. Sometimes, perhaps, this seems almost too effortless for plausibility. In *Seconde patrie*, the Zermatt family start learning English on the arrival on their island of Jenny, a young Englishwoman who has been shipwrecked, while she learns German. Within a few weeks, we are told, Fritz speaks English fluently – but perhaps he has been inspired by something other than the mere love of language: 'Comment n'eût-il pas fait des progrès rapides avec un professeur dont les leçons lui étaient si agréables?' (SP, p. 71) ['How could he have failed to make rapid progress when the lessons of his teacher gave him such pleasure?'] Be that as it may, the essential point is that for Verne foreign languages and scientific terminologies, like cryptograms, are a means of reading the world and of understanding it, yet they offer the speaker a further and more active resource, which is the option to reclassify and restructure the world with the new lexicons that have become available. Like the numerous textual documents that the writer echoes in the composition of his novels, languages and discourses reappear and resonate endlessly in the Vernian characters' adventures.

Conversely, it becomes apparent in the *Voyages extraordinaires* that when a character fails to understand foreign tongues, or fails to be understood in them, the world becomes incomprehensible and impenetrable, almost literally a closed book. Such is the case for the hostages aboard the *Nautilus*, before the first appearance of Nemo, when they attempt to interpret the speech of their captors. Aronnax is nonplussed by the 'idiome singulier et absolument incompréhensible' ['strange and absolutely incomprehensible language'] used by the first man he speaks to, yet he clearly senses from this man's appearance, gestures and behaviour that there are meanings to be deduced, and that there is a necessary link between his physical behaviour and his actual speech. Aronnax observes: 'Diderot a très justement observé que le geste de l'homme est métaphorique, et ce petit homme en était certainement la preuve vivante. On sentait que dans son langage habituel, il devait prodiguer les prosopopées, les métonymies et les hypallages.' (VML, I, pp. 73–74) ['Diderot was right to observe that human gestures are metaphorical, and this little man was certainly living proof of it. One sensed that, in his normal language, he must make frequent use of prosopopoeia, metonymy and hypallage.'] Aronnax then directs several fruitless attempts to communicate with the men of the *Nautilus*. First he speaks to them simply and slowly in French, but to no avail. Then he asks Ned Land to tell their story in English, but with a similarly negative result. Thereafter Conseil gives the third account in German, once more without success. Aronnax is reduced to speaking in Latin, eliciting no more response than a few words exchanged between the men in their 'incompréhensible langage' (VML, p. 78) ['incomprehensible language']. The experience is a complete failure. Language here, far from uniting and including, divides and excludes. It is like the cryptogram that cannot be read, the storybook that refuses to open. Conseil, in a remark that is typically utopian, suggests that this is the problem in a world where humanity does not possess a single, universal language,[19] but Ned Land deduces that these men speak an invented language that is deliberately exclusive. Language has shown itself here to be as much an obstacle and a hindrance as a facilitating device. Nonetheless, the point is made that words, in whatever language or idiom, are crucial to human interaction with the world, and that they impose their necessity on almost every situation, even negatively. The novelist, himself so obviously interested in the question of language, thus puts linguistic matters centre-stage in his own narrative, using his characters' failure to comprehend as a means to build up suspense.

Just as the obstacle raised by the failure of understanding reveals the crucial importance of language in stories such as *Vingt mille lieues*, so too the obstacles or quirks that are so often a part of normal human speech are a further reminder in the *Voyages extraordinaires* of the treacherous and complex linguistic path that characters must plot through their lives. Speech impediments or *tics* are such a common feature in Verne that they invariably focus our attention on the choices and combinations of vocabulary, the style, the mannerisms or simply the sounds of characters' words. Language with all its quirks and its oddities is placed at the forefront of the reading experience. We are never allowed to forget for long that Verne's fictional characters are living in and through a verbally created medium, or that their adventures are dependent on words and made up of language. And sometimes it seems that those characters who are the most fluent and articulate are also those whose speech is destined to encounter the most obstacles. Lidenbrock in *Voyage au centre de la terre* is one such example. Magically talented and knowledgeable, he is a master of scientific terminology and deploys his skills to dazzling effect in his classes on mineralogy at the Johannæum. However, Lidenbrock 'ne jouissait pas d'une extrême facilité de prononciation' (VCT, p. 5) ['did not enjoy great facility of pronunciation']. He stutters, especially in public, and since 'il y a en minéralogie bien des dénominations semi-grecques, semi-latines, difficiles à prononcer, de ces rudes appellations qui écorcheraient les lèvres d'un poète' ['there are, in mineralogy, numerous half-Greek, half-Latin terms that are tricky to pronounce, difficult words which would scorch the lips of a poet'], the obstacles before him can be immense. But as Axel is implicitly able to remind us, the obstacle here is itself a sign of the richness of terminology, the phonetic resonance of words, and the

19 We should remember, too, that shortly before his death Jules Verne became deeply interested in the question of Esperanto. For more on this see Gilles de Robien, *Jules Verne: Le Rêveur incompris* (Paris: Michel Lafon, 2000), pp. 7–11.

sheer strangeness or otherness of their appearance. Language, it is suggested, is a difficult yet truly wondrous terrain: 'Lorsqu'on se trouve en présence des cristallisations rhomboédriques, des résines rétinasphaltes, des ghélénites, des fangasites, des molybdates de plomb, des tungstates de manganèse et des titaniates de zircone, il est permis à la langue la plus adroite de fourcher' (VCT, pp. 5–6) ['When you are dealing with rhombohedral crystallisations, retinasphalt resins, ghelenites, fangasites, molybdates of lead, manganese tungstates and zircon titanites, even the most skilful tongue might be expected to slip']. For anyone who attempts to read this sentence aloud, the final statement is likely to be self-fulfilling. The words are almost impossible to pronounce correctly and perfectly at the first attempt. The sentence, an exemplary demonstration of the very point that it makes, thus turns in on itself and its own material. Here too is another case of Verne bringing lists into his narrative by default, on a tongue-in-cheek pretext, though this time it is to highlight the qualities and characteristics of words themselves rather than simply to display knowledge or to provide pedagogical guidance. By giving us a list of those terms that Lidenbrock is *not* able to pronounce, Verne cleverly exploits a negative statement and builds his own sentence out of it. Thus does language spring up even where it should not, like the exotic flora described in many a Vernian text, demonstrating their irrepressible presence and energy.

The passage referred to earlier describing the initial linguistic difficulties encountered by Aronnax and his fellow hostages reminds us that for Verne language, with its codes and secrets, can become an issue and a problem in any circumstances. But the Vernian explorer or traveller must constantly decipher all manner of languages: body language and physiognomy, cryptograms, the language of natural phenomena, and even the language of silence itself. Verne is perhaps not noted for minimalism, and the use of silence is a device we might be more likely to associate with a writer such as Samuel Beckett. However, characters such as Hans in *Voyage au centre de la terre* are important illustrations of the expressiveness of brevity or silence. There is one occasion in the *Voyages extraordinaires* when silence becomes the most expressive of all languages, and that is in the story of the seaman Hunt in *Le Sphinx des glaces*. If he barely speaks a word, Hunt is supremely eloquent through his appearance, his gestures and his work. In many respects, he *is* the problem that Verne's story has to solve in its middle stages, a kind of fictional puzzle that must be deciphered. Hunt's silence here is to be understood not merely as a psychological trait, but as a narrative device by an author who must withhold information in order to increase the sense of mystery. Everything about

Hunt is a statement, a 'language' that delivers a symbolic comment on the progression and the telling of the story in which he figures, or delays the solution of the problem. And like Lidenbrock, Hunt is also afflicted by a problem with speech, in this case a difficulty in putting together his sentences coherently and fluently. 'L'hésitation de Hunt', says the narrator, 'ne venait point de ce qu'il ne savait que répondre, mais, ainsi qu'on va le voir, d'une certaine difficulté à exprimer ses idées. Elles étaient très nettes cependant, bien que sa phrase fût entrecoupée, ses mots à peine reliés entre eux.' (SG, p. 234) ['Hunt's hesitation came not from the fact that he did not know what to say, but, as we shall see, from a certain difficulty in expressing his ideas. And yet these were very clear, even if his sentences were halting and his words scarcely linked together.'] So, through his fragmented speech, Hunt delivers only partial clues about who he is and where the story is going. The absence of clear explanations and comprehensive statements does, however, serve the novelist's own purposes admirably, for he is able thereby to intensify the sense of mystery that surrounds Hunt. The first words that Hunt speaks in the story are perhaps his most eloquent in their minimalism. In a dream, he is heard to utter over and over again: 'Pym… Pym… le pauvre Pym!' (SG, p. 199) ['Pym… Pym… Poor Pym!'] Thus he draws attention to the fact that he appears to possess some important knowledge, while revealing nothing whatsoever. Hunt's own language, his near silence, is here a fictional correlative of the novelist's art and his or her aim of maintaining suspense. Once again, then, we see that a character's particular idiom or mode of speech is placed in a position of symbolic prominence in the Vernian narrative.

On other occasions, the idiosyncrasies of a character's speech are treated in a more light-hearted vein, but are no less important in drawing our attention to the question of language. Alongside the expansive and voluble characters of the *Voyages extraordinaires* (Paganel, Ardan, Calistus Munbar and others), whose uses of language are the embodiment of their own exuberance, there are many whose articulations are hesitant, repetitive, embarrassed, clumsy or simply lacking in spontaneity. In *Kéraban-le-têtu*, the servant Nizib has the regrettable *tic* of repeating, in a servile and totally wonderstruck way, the end of his master's sentences, thus prolonging Kéraban's words in an admiring echo. In *Vingt mille lieues*, Conseil's speech – like his character – is precisely at the opposite end of the spectrum to Ned Land's. Where Ned waxes lyrical, Conseil is measured, precise and impeccably 'neat' in his speech, which becomes the living embodiment of the scientific impulse to classify and to order. Unable to recognise any of the creatures and species whose names are so familiar to him, Conseil is nonetheless able to produce entire lists of related names once his skills of verbal recall have been triggered. Yet for all his mastery of the scientific lexicon, his use of language will remain constrained and strangely unreal. As we saw in our discussion of theatricality in the *Voyages extraordinaires*, Conseil never gives up his use of the third person in his conversations with Aronnax, which he takes on occasions to absurd extremes. This is also true of the manservant Patrice in *Clovis Dardentor*, whom I discussed in the previous chapter. Through his exaggerated and imposing politeness, and particularly through his attention to language, Patrice seems to remind us that Dardentor's 'story' is capable of being reworded in a completely different manner. The ongoing 'war of words' between Patrice and Dardentor is a prominent feature of this lively and intensely comic story, where language itself is a source of dramatic conflict.

The writing of character

It was Henry James who, in a celebrated discussion of Flaubert, maintained that the creation of such limited reflectors and registers of human experience as Emma Bovary or Frédéric Moreau must surely be the sign of a defective imagination.[20] The depiction of fine characters as the mark of a rich novelistic sensibility was, for that generation of normative literary critics to which James belonged, an axiomatic requirement of 'good' narrative. What James appears to have underestimated in Flaubert is the importance of irony, which works with exquisite complexity and awareness around the very literary stereotypes that appear to shape and inspire his characterisation. The apparent mediocrity of his fictional beings is in many respects an ironic response to literary representations of heroism, tragedy and emotion. Yet if Flaubert's characters have increasingly been accepted as products of a literature that exposes and subverts its own literary origins, that debate appears scarcely to have begun in the case of Verne.[21] While critics have rightly focused on the stylistic and intertextual qualities of Verne's writing, or on its deeper mythical structures and origins, or on its uses of scientific discourses, the question of characterisation *per se* is rarely problematised to the same extent.

20 See Henry James, 'Gustave Flaubert', in *Literary Criticism*, vol. II: *European Writers* (New York: Penguin, 1984), pp. 314–46.
21 My own analysis of characterisation in *Le Tour du monde en quatre-vingts jours* (*Verne: 'Le Tour du monde en quatre-vingts jours'*, Chapter 4, 'Making Character Readable', pp. 65–77) is an attempt to sketch out an alternative way of approaching 'characterisation' in Verne, using the example of a single text.

My evocation of Flaubert in this context is therefore pointed and deliberate. Flaubert is the supreme example of an author who exploits the literary resonances of 'character'. Perhaps we need to recognise that Verne too plays knowingly and ironically against stereotypes and conventions, and that he uses the very notion of character as a literary category to be profiled, displayed, subverted or distorted for narrative effect. If we look to his novels with Jamesian eyes, in search of deep, subtle and complex figures who will challenge our sensibilities and extend our awareness of the intricacies of human emotion, we are sure to be disappointed. Yet by the same token, if we reduce our appreciation of his characters to a focus on some modern version of heroism – seeking inspiration in those *Boys' Own Paper* qualities of courage, determination and leadership – it is obvious that we will very soon find ourselves in a dreary dead end of over-simplification.[22] Marie-Hélène Huet proposes one possible way out of this impasse. She suggests that the accusation of weakness of psychology in Verne's novels can be countered with the argument that he deliberately sets out to create characters whose actions are governed by an idea or a principle.[23] But while the argument is obviously valid, it might seem that an unnecessary concession is being made here. Why should Verne have to answer accusations of weakness of psychology, any more than Flaubert? If we adopt a course which looks at the *uses* that Verne makes of his characters, rather than remaining fixed on their 'qualities' as supposed exemplars of human behaviour, we will find much of the subtlety that his detractors claim he lacks. As with his uses and dramatisations of language, Verne puts the conventions of characterisation on show at the heart of the literary text. In this, he reminds us that character is a constructed literary category, an artifice and a fictional device, and he offers an implicit challenge to the very novelistic conventions within which he writes.

Now we should also accept that this will not always be the case, and that, in some instances at least, Verne tries to give 'genuine' and meaningful depictions of character. Nemo is probably the most complex and the most interesting of all the characters in the *Voyages extraordinaires*, but serious and developed representations of character are also a notable feature of novels such as *Mathias Sandorf*, *Le Chancellor* or *En Magellanie*.

22 I. O. Evans wrote himself precisely into this corner in his suggestion that we should enjoy in Verne's novels 'one of the great themes of literature, the story of strong, adventurous and self-disciplined heroes and heroines, displaying a dogged determination and stalwart courage in facing hardship and peril for the sake of a worthy ideal' (*Jules Verne and his Work*, p. 9).
23 *L'Histoire des Voyages extraordinaires*, pp. 33–40.

Elsewhere there are some serious but perhaps uninspired representations of love intrigues, and several well-intentioned but unsuccessful depictions of female characters. Figures such as the heroine of *Mistress Branican* come across as real if unconvincing attempts by the novelist to create psychological and emotional empathy, and there is certainly no suggestion of irony or send-up here. More often than not, though, Verne uses his apprenticeship in the theatre of the vaudeville to exaggerate or to simplify, and specifically to place the emphasis on dramatic or fictional roles rather than on psychological characteristics. He concentrates on making character readable and entertaining, and he does this in various ways. In some cases he playfully strips characters of their complexity and turns them into caricatures, just as Flaubert does with characters such as Homais, or Bouvard and Pécuchet. In other cases he endows them to excess with a single quality (heroism, devotion or sensitivity on the one hand, selfishness, aggression or greed on the other – even pigheadedness in one case that we are about to discuss) and turns them ostentatiously into a narrative function or role. In still other cases, he places characters into those theatrical pairings that emphasise and exaggerate their complementarity or their differences.

This artificial sharing out or division of supposedly psychological characteristics turns our attention away from character itself, and towards questions of narrative economy and balance. Verne thereby also blocks any attempt we may make to enter into psychological empathy with the characters. As in Bergson's famous formula, Verne applies 'du mécanique sur du vivant'[24] ['the mechanical upon the living']. Yet the reduction of characters to single characteristics or mechanical gestures is not without its risks. Novelists who resist empathy with their characters will frequently pay the price with their critics, as the legacy of Flaubert has shown. A number of characters in the *Voyages extraordinaires* come perilously close to alienating the reader, perhaps most obviously Kéraban-letêtu. While Verne here succeeds admirably in extracting a gamut of comic effects from the notion of pigheadedness, he also perpetually runs the risk of forcing his reader to draw the conclusion that Kéraban is a deeply unattractive and uninteresting character, unworthy of the novelist's interest or the reader's attention. Kéraban so often imposes unreasonable demands on his entourage, and so signally fails to respond to the needs and feelings of

---

24 Henri Bergson, *Le Rire* (Paris: PUF, 1978 [1900]), p. 29. Elsewhere, Bergson effectively makes the point that comic treatment of character precludes empathy and requires psychological detachment. As he puts it, 'le rire n'a pas de plus grand ennemi que l'émotion' (p. 3) ['laughter has no greater enemy than emotion'].

others, that he cannot be seen as anything other than a man who has lost his humanity and who is trapped in a prison of his own making. The challenge to Verne the novelist is to turn such blatantly unappealing material into credible fictional entertainment and to make the reader want to enter that uncomfortable space of imagined closeness to the character. In order to do so, he must not only exaggerate the comic qualities of Kéraban – which he does magnificently – but also contrive to make him likeable, at least at some level. That task is more difficult, since by definition the character's stubbornness slams the door on psychological empathy. However, Verne resolves the contradiction by stressing Kéraban's good and humane qualities, even when we may be disinclined to believe that they are genuine. The obvious admiration and esteem in which he is held by his servant Nizib and his friend Van Mitten (who nonetheless suffer greatly at his hands) also acts as a corrective and just rescues Kéraban from total unlikeability. Yet this seems almost like a concession, a necessary pay-off by the novelist who, in the face of the literary problem of constructing a novel around a single, extreme characteristic, compromises and undermines the very principle he sets out with. In order to work as a narrative function, Kéraban has to be implausibly schematic and single-minded. In order to remain readable, he has to shed some of that single-mindedness and become less mechanical. The novel becomes a balancing act between rescuing its central character as a human being, and using him as a focus for the plot. In the end, this is something of a tour de force by Verne, but it illustrates one of the difficulties faced by a novelist exploiting and exaggerating the notion of character itself.

Verne does not always get himself into such deep water when exploiting the mechanical, emotionless qualities of his characters in order to achieve literary effect. Phileas Fogg is an outstandingly successful example of the creation of a character who is 'characterless', but whose apparent absence of character is exploited as a structuring principle throughout the novel. This man who is such a closed book remains intensely readable from the beginning to the end, precisely because Verne makes of him such a paradox. From the start, Phileas Fogg is placed on display as a character about whom nothing is known, whose feelings are impenetrable and whose motives are inscrutable. He is an automaton, filling out the ledger of his arrivals and departures with punctilious precision, and filling in the empty hours of travel with his mind-numbing games of whist. Nor does he appear to evolve in any meaningful sense. Even as he is on the point of having his most significant conversation with Aouda, we read: 'Son visage ne reflétait aucune émotion. Le Fogg du retour était exactement le Fogg du départ. Même calme, même impassibilité.' (TDM, p. 318) ['His face showed no emotion. The Fogg who had returned was precisely the same as the Fogg who had set out. The same calm, the same impassivity.'] Yet, for all that, Fogg wins his bet, displays heroism and courage, gets the girl and, we must presume, lives happily ever after – the better for his past experiences. If he is in one sense an empty vessel who simply puzzles us by the absence of feelings, thoughts and emotions with which we can identify, he conforms closely in another sense to the conventions of character, and his personal story reaches a fully satisfactory conclusion. What are we to make of this? While it would surely be unsatisfactory to try to read Fogg as a fully-fledged literary hero displaying qualities that we can empathise with, we are nonetheless permanently – and, it seems, deliberately – frustrated if we attempt to understand Fogg as a man. Verne emphasises his mechanical qualities so strongly, while placing him in a conventionally heroic framework, that we are in the end obliged to see Fogg as a deeply ironic creation, the sign of a highly self-conscious approach to character by the novelist.

The apparent reduction of human character to mechanised and ritualised behaviour is a common tactic throughout the *Voyages extraordinaires*, and is often reserved for the Anglo-Saxon figures. While the device may sometimes appear to be overworked by Verne, it nonetheless acts as a regular reminder that character in a novel is nothing other than a pure illusion. Verne's refusal in such cases to vouchsafe any more than the most basic behaviourist information is a clear challenge to the convention of character, as well as being an obvious comic device. Colonel Everest, in *Aventures de trois Russes et de trois Anglais*, is a Fogg lookalike, a man whose existence is entirely regulated, measured and mathematical: 'Cet astronome, âgé de cinquante ans, homme froid et méthodique, avait une existence mathématiquement déterminée heure par heure' (A3, p. 18) ['This fifty-year-old astronomer, a cold and methodical man, led a life that was mathematically determined hour by hour']. In *Hector Servadac*, the English army officers, Brigadier Murphy and Major Oliphant, are similarly imperturbable, inexplicable in anything but the most rudimentary terms. They do nothing other than play chess, with the same single-mindedness that characterises Fogg's playing of whist. They wait patiently and passively on the comet that has whisked them into interplanetary orbit, in the absolute and hopelessly deluded expectation that Her Majesty will one day contrive to send a rescue party out to them. Never for a moment do they engage with the other characters, and their fate at the end of the story is to remain on the comet playing chess while Servadac and his group have managed to escape and return to earth. 'Character' here is created from non-character, out of a few gestures and mannerisms. If Hunt in

Le Sphinx des glaces is an example of minimalism of language and speech, the British officers are a parallel example of minimalism in their behaviour. And just as the absence of articulate language in Hunt places the whole question of language centre-stage, so too the absence of coherent or developed character in cases such as this draw our attention to the whole novelistic category of 'character'. Verne subverts, distorts and undermines, with great ironic and humorous effect. While his formulae tend, perhaps inevitably, to be repetitive, his mocking use of this classic ingredient of narrative emerges as a crucially important feature.

To reinforce the point that character is a created and artificial construct, Verne often shifts human characteristics onto nature or machines, and vice versa. As Andrew Martin has persuasively argued, there is a process of transfer and exchange here.[25] While some characters in Verne live through their adventures with an almost unnerving calm, the outside world conversely displays the explosive temperament and qualities of a human being. Yet on other occasions individuals, like volcanoes, tend to be explosive (Lidenbrock is an obvious example), and characters can be like machines which blow up or break down (as when Fogg finally loses his temper and hits Fix). We end up wondering where human temperament or psychology is located, where indeed the 'humours' of the human organism are. In *Voyage au centre de la terre*, nature seems to have all the functions of a human body, swallowing up the travellers and finally expelling them. Elsewhere the elements rise up to challenge man: oceans, ice, air, earth and fire all display their anger and their aggression. It is as though there is a deliberate and contrived exchange, as man is dispersed in nature and in objects, and nature in its turn is endowed with human force. This sometimes acquires a powerfully sexual dimension too, as when in *Le Rayon vert* Olivier Sinclair rescues Helena Campbell from Fingal's Cave in a scene whose descriptions of natural forces can only be described as climactic. Perhaps in this case, it is partly a conventional, nineteenth-century approach to the question of sexual desire, which is connoted rather than described, through the use of the pathetic fallacy. But if nature here becomes a metaphor of desire and its fulfilment, the persistence of the transfer between human and nature in the *Voyages extraordinaires* is a constant reminder that Verne appears to be challenging the boundaries between human feeling and the outside, apparently objective world.

This experiment with the boundaries between character and nature had, it is true, been carried out by many writers earlier in the nineteenth

25 See *The Knowledge of Ignorance*, pp. 167–77.

century, but in Verne it assumes ludic and self-parodying proportions. At the end of *Le Volcan d'or*, Ben Raddle – who has returned home empty-handed after his quest to find gold in the volcano – becomes ill-tempered. His cousin remarks that he has acquired some of the characteristics of the volcano and that they have remained within him. The novel ends with the line: 'Après tout, quand on a eu un volcan dans sa vie, il vous en reste quelque chose!' (VO, p. 508) ['After all, when you have had a volcano in your life, something of it remains with you!'] It is a fitting final example of the way in which Verne sends up the whole notion of character, questions its reality as a construct, and displays its fictional artifices even as he exploits them. Constructing character in the same way that he constructs his plots or develops his descriptions, he shows that the very materials of his own narrative are products of convention and artifice. But that very gaze inwards, which tends to fragment the story that is being told, is part of the creative process. Self-conscious through and through, Verne exposes the traditions on which his approach as a novelist is based, and creatively exploits the detachment that self-consciousness allows. Far from smoothing over the textures of narrative to make them appear seamless, he leaves them conspicuously rough and unfinished. We shall find this unfinished effect once again in the interpolations, lists and scientific disquisitions which are such an important feature of the *Voyages extraordinaires*, and to which we shall now turn our attention.

Chapter 6

Writing and Rewriting

Originality and the literary writer

Towards the end of Flaubert's unfinished *Bouvard et Pécuchet* the two clerks, having run the gamut of knowledge and signally failed to stamp their imprint on any field of human endeavour, return to their erstwhile occupation. As copyists once more, they will mechanically transfer in their own hand what they find in the writings of others. Precisely what the clerks are to copy out has remained a matter of scholarly argument, but one thing is clear: that their decision is something of a defeat, even an act of desperation. It represents a final quest for certainty – however small – in a world in which the proliferation of texts makes absolute knowledge impossible and originality unthinkable. Everything has already been said, everything already written. There remain only two options: to repeat, and to accumulate. Like the parrot in that other famous Flaubertian text, *Un cœur simple*, the two clerks will endlessly echo the sayings of others, hoping that in this act of appropriation and transmission they will find some credible voice of their own.

The problem of the already spoken or the already written, central to the preoccupations of so many key figures in the nineteenth century, is also at the heart of Verne's undertaking. What is 'originality'? At what point does writing become rewriting? If every text is by definition an intertext, when does it cease to resonate with the sound of an individual author's voice, and turn into the mere echo of what is heard through and beyond it? Can there be such a thing as individuality or uniqueness in a century in which, as Musset famously put it in a somewhat different context in his narrative poem *Rolla*, 'Je suis venu trop tard dans un monde trop vieux'[1] ['I came too late into a world too old']? Is the author's recognition that he or she must follow in the footsteps of others enough to guarantee freedom and detachment from them? Is there some way in

---

1 Alfred de Musset, *Rolla*, in *Poésies complètes*, ed. Maurice Allem (Paris: Gallimard, Bibliothèque de la Pléiade, 1957), pp. 273–92 (p. 274).

which the knowledge of sameness, the awareness that the beaten path is the only route, can be exploited? This last question comes to have added significance in the case of Verne, where the subject of journeys into unknown places is also the central metaphor of the writer's own approach. Where is that demarcation line between old and new terrains, between old and new texts? Since Verne's travellers must so often venture into virgin territories or seas with documents in hand, the quest for unknown domains is in many cases demonstrably subordinate to what is already known. The unknown, being unscripted and unscriptable, is to all intents and purposes non-existent. While it is occasionally glimpsed in the pages of the *Voyages extraordinaires*, it is almost always crowded out or surrounded by those seemingly endless rehearsals of what was previously known and has circulated in the texts that went before.

The question of 'originality' – if such a thing exists – is answered by authors such as Baudelaire and Flaubert through complex uses of irony, in which the writer's own claims to be advancing the frontiers of art are continuously deconstructed. In a poem entitled 'L'Héautontimorouménos', Baudelaire evokes the almost exquisite difficulties of irony, which divides the poet from himself and gives him a paradoxical, painful, but hard-won detachment.[2] Irony distances such writers progressively from the clichés, the banality or the sameness that they recognise themselves and their characters to be enmeshed in. There is always the sense in their writing that novelty can be achieved through the recognition of the derivative nature of the very idea of novelty itself.[3] An anguished, intensely modern

---

2 See Baudelaire, *Les Fleurs du Mal*, in *Œuvres complètes*, ed. Claude Pichois, vol. I (Paris: Gallimard, Bibliothèque de la Pléiade, 1975), p. 78:

> Ne suis-je pas un faux accord
> Dans la divine symphonie
> Grâce à la vorace Ironie
> Qui me secoue et qui me mord?
> [Am I not a false chord
> In the divine symphony
> Thanks to voracious Irony
> Which shakes and eats me?]

3 While Baudelaire may dream at the end of *Le Voyage* of plunging 'Au fond de l'Inconnu pour trouver du *nouveau*' (*Œuvres complètes*, p. 134) ['into the depths of the unknown in order to find something *new*'], this is a final act of despair, born of a sense of failure. The quest to find novelty in sameness and banality, rather than in the unknown, is at the heart of the poetic project in *Les Fleurs du Mal*. For a fascinating discussion of the question of 'novelty' as a value in the mid-nineteenth century, see Antoine Compagnon, *Cinq Paradoxes sur la modernité* (Paris: Seuil, 1990). In the opening chapter of his study (pp. 7–13) Compagnon stresses the paradoxical 'novelty'

concept of art emerges, shot through with the self-doubt that defines it. Despite the impression we may have that Verne's writing is almost entirely devoid of similar anguish, it nonetheless raises similar problems about its status and its claim to originality. Beyond the Rabelaisian exuberance, there is a more modern, inward gaze that questions the nature of the author's creativity, puts into doubt the possibility of novelty, and speculates on the function and validity of the novel as an art form. While few would be likely to maintain that Verne deploys irony with the extraordinary subtlety and deftness shown by Baudelaire and Flaubert, the irony is there, as we shall see later in this chapter. It is surely beyond doubt that Verne's style challenges and subverts notions of originality, and that it does so in part by proclaiming its derivative qualities. While Verne may come across to some as a plagiarist and a recycler, there is often a surprising boldness and openness about his re-use and reworking of other texts. This alerts us to the presence of something more complex and more interesting in his approach than a mere slavish following of the already written. Yet, as with so many other aspects of his writing, the process is not uniform, and we need to recognise from the outset that while on some occasions his style ironically exploits its own sources and implicitly comments on them, on other occasions they are used less critically. As always with Verne, there is unevenness, though the unevenness itself is one of the abiding fascinations of his approach.

What, then, are we to make of those 'excrescences' – encyclopaedic digressions, lists, descriptions and borrowings of all kinds – that so frequently appear to halt the flow of the narrative and turn it temporarily into a non-fictional text, whose origins and substance are elsewhere? Why does Verne import so much detail, so many accounts that can be found in other texts, so many discourses of dubious identity? Why do we have the sense that the Vernian text gets so ostentatiously invaded by other texts, or by the echo of other texts? While these imported passages have often been held as the signs of a patchwork approach in which the constraints of storytelling give way to those of pedagogy, it is surely the juxtaposition of different styles that is of interest here. Verne attempts (with varying degrees of success) to combine and to reconcile opposing discourses, or at the very least to make them jostle along together. This combination is

---

of the idea of novelty and underlines that 'la tradition moderne commença avec la naissance du nouveau comme valeur, puisqu'il n'a pas toujours été une valeur' (p. 9) ['the modern tradition began with the emergence of novelty as a value, for it has not always been considered valuable']. He also points to the key role of both Baudelaire and Flaubert in the establishment of this tradition.

especially unusual and – dare one say it? – original in the mid-nineteenth century when literary and scientific discourses were still regarded as almost polar opposites. Whereas literary discourse works, often self-referentially, on language itself, exploring the connotations and multivalent possibilities of word combinations, scientific discourse does precisely the opposite by attempting to use language as an objective denotation, devoid as far as possible of ambiguity.[4] The fact that Verne's novels bring these different registers into the same space invariably results in some of the characteristics of each being transferred onto the other. While scientific language comes on occasions to assume connotative, poetic richness even in its most simple forms, fictional discourse is also able to present itself as objective, reported fact. But the transitions between the two registers are also highly significant, for that moment of joining together is also an attempt to find a new terrain, a hybrid discourse – more effective because more complete – which recalls the mixture of languages spoken by the Vidal brothers in *Wilhelm Storitz*.[5] And the fact that Verne's digressions so often proclaim their dependence on external sources, to which they give both an unusually high level of visibility and sometimes almost overwhelming proportions in relation to the diegesis, is surely no accident. It is because the author operates in between and across different forms of language, often in citational and deliberately parasitical mode, that he challenges the conventional boundaries. By doing so, he discovers new ground in the traces of the old. Verne the writer operates in a manner parallel to that of his explorers.

Questions about whether Verne's encyclopaedic interpolations are optional supporting material – 'ballast' that can be offloaded by the reader-traveller in a hurry – or material that is in some way deeply connected to the hermeneutics of the texts themselves must also, and inevitably, affect our experience of reading the *Voyages extraordinaires*. Putting aside the question of what the writer may or may not have 'intended', the actual experience of processing such passages remains deeply problematic from the reader's point of view. On the one hand, they look dispensable, and naturally they are the first passages to be excised in abridged editions. On the other hand, they are such a hallmark feature of Verne's style that they seem to point to something essential, and to give us

---

4 For an important discussion of this, see Arthur B. Evans, 'Functions of Science in French Fiction', *Studies in the Literary Imagination*, 22 (1989), pp. 79–100, and in particular the theoretical distinctions that are drawn between scientific and literary discourses in the nineteenth century (p. 80).

5 See above, p. 164.

the sense that fundamental clues are being displaced onto areas of the text that are normally considered backwaters in the narrative journey. For many, it is true, these passages are ultimately the sign of a fault or a defect in the writing, and one which can be variously analysed. Sartre, discussing the influence on his own early writing efforts of Jules Verne and Louis Boussenard, amusingly comments on this problem in *Les Mots*, and indicates clearly that he is a believer in the dispensability of Vernian encyclopaedism rather than in its hermeneutical necessity. Interestingly, he suggests that these learned digressions have a radically different status for the reader and for the writer. For the first, they are a problem (though one that is easily solved, as we shall see); for the second, they are a solution:

> Boussenard et Jules Verne ne perdent pas une occasion d'instruire: aux instants les plus critiques, ils coupent le fil du récit pour se lancer dans la description d'une plante vénéneuse, d'un habitat indigène. Lecteur, je sautais ces passages didactiques; auteur, j'en bourrai mes romans; je prétendis enseigner à mes contemporains tout ce que j'ignorais: les mœurs des Fuégiens, la flore africaine, le climat du désert. Séparés par un coup du sort puis embarqués sans le savoir sur le même navire et victimes du même naufrage, le collectionneur de papillons et sa fille s'accrochaient à la même bouée, levaient la tête, chacun jetait un cri: 'Daisy!', 'Papa!' Hélas, un squale rôdait en quête de chair fraîche, il s'approchait, son ventre brillait entre les vagues. Les malheureux échapperaient-ils à la mort? J'allais chercher le tome 'Pr–Z' du *Grand Larousse*, je le portais péniblement jusqu'à mon pupitre, l'ouvrais à la bonne page et copiais mot pour mot en passant à la ligne: 'Les requins sont communs dans l'Atlantique tropical. Ces grands poissons de mer très voraces atteignent jusqu'à treize mètres de long et pèsent jusqu'à huit tonnes...' Je prenais tout mon temps pour transcrire l'article: je me sentais délicieusement ennuyeux...[6]

[Boussenard and Jules Verne do not lose an opportunity to offer instruction. At critical moments, they interrupt the story to digress with a description of a poisonous plant or an indigenous habitat. As a reader, I used to skip these didactic passages. As an author, I stuffed my novels full of them. I claimed to teach everything I myself did not know to my contemporaries: the customs of the Fuegians, the African flora, the climate of the desert. Separated by an act of destiny, picked up by the same ship without knowing it, then victims of the same shipwreck, the butterfly collector and his daughter were clinging to the same buoy. They raised their heads, and each uttered a cry: 'Daisy!' 'Father!' Alas, a shark was prowling in search of fresh meat, and, as it approached, its belly gleamed between the waves. Would these unfortunate people escape death? I went off to fetch volume 'Pr–Z' of the *Grand Larousse*,

---

6   Jean-Paul Sartre, *Les Mots* (Paris: Gallimard, 1964), pp. 118–19.

took it back to my desk, opened it up at the right page and copied out word for word in a new paragraph: 'Sharks are found all round the tropical Atlantic. These large, extremely aggressive sea fish can reach a length of thirteen metres and weigh up to eight tonnes...' I took my time transcribing the article, and felt deliciously boring.]

So, as an actual reader of the *Voyages extraordinaires*, the young Sartre finds the didactic passages eminently skippable, and has no qualms whatsoever about passing over them swiftly. However, as an apprentice writer, following in the footsteps of Verne and Bousssenard, he recognises that there is a certain necessity about the narrative pauses they create. He implicitly confesses to finding solace in being able to escape momentarily from the difficulty of taking the plot forward, by borrowing texts from elsewhere and turning himself temporarily into a pedagogue. Not only does this have the advantage of giving him added authority and credibility as a narrator, it also enables him to keep his implied reader in suspense (though probably not the real one who, if he is like Sartre himself, does not play the game). Boredom, it seems, is the price that the implied reader must occasionally pay for the author's control of his fiction.

For all his humour here, Sartre is naturally suggesting that there is something deceitful about such a method, in which the writer's difficulties are given the trappings of pedagogical worthiness. Yet, dismissive as he appears to be about these 'digressions', his identification of them as essential markers of the style of authors such as Verne and Boussenard points to their niggling centrality. Sartre thus signals the inherently problematic issue of boundaries and transitions – boundaries between the author's own work and that of others, or boundaries between different types of discourses, and transitions between different textual modes and different states or stages of narrative. As he implicitly concedes, writing cannot do without such frontiers, which have their importance not only because the changes of rhythm that they represent are necessary, but also because they expose the essential fragmentedness and dependency of all text. The act of suspending the diegesis and intercalating lengthy descriptions or digressions openly draws attention to the fact that writing is constituted of different forms of discourse. Yet the fact that Verne does this so openly and so conspicuously suggests that he is giving away, by exaggerating it, one of the secrets of the writer's trade. In this respect, far from being a deceitful tactic as Sartre implies, still less a strategy designed to bore the reader, it is a candid comment on the nature of writing and of text. We skip these intercalated passages at our peril, for not only do they tell us about the composite, documented quality of Verne's world, they also tell us about the constraints and the problems faced more generally by the writer of fiction. Furthermore, they reveal the author's own experiment at working through a combination of discourses. Fiction itself is being stretched to the limits by the insertion of new and apparently alien terminologies, just as science is being fictionalised. Playing with the conventions of storytelling, and sometimes exaggerating them to the point of maximum stress, Verne thereby indulges in a reflexive gesture that is also ironic. In this, he finds his true voice as a novelist, a point that Daniel Compère, almost single-handedly among critics of Verne, has recognised and has rightly stressed throughout his work on the author of the *Voyages extraordinaires*. Compère rightly argues that the patchwork quality, far from detracting from the uniqueness and the originality of Verne's writing, in fact gives it greater resonance and depth: 'C'est sans doute un paradoxe, mais la présence des voix des autres donne au texte vernien une richesse et une puissance bien plus grandes qu'à celui qui n'est composé que d'une voix isolée'[7] ['It is doubtless a paradox, but the presence of other voices gives the Vernian text a richness and power far greater than if it were constituted by a single isolated voice']. To Compère's argument we might wish to add that the multivocal, polyphonic quality of Verne's writing can also – and perhaps inevitably – be uneven in its effects and its results. Yet it remains one of the most dominant and striking features of Verne's style, as much for its intrinsic originality as for the flaws and defects that it produces.

Borrowing, recycling, plagiarism

The idea that Verne is a profoundly 'intertextual' writer who achieves originality through his combinations of different discourses and voices is one that the present study endorses, though with some important nuances. Verne's ways of dealing with problems of unity and coherence are varied, and lead to a range of results. On the one hand, the composite nature of his texts can subject them to stresses and strains that lead towards fragmentation rather than to that symphonic wholeness of which Compère speaks. On the other hand, the opposite can also happen, when Verne synthesises his source texts into a single, cohesive account heavily inflected by the voice of a heterodiegetic narrator. This is appropriation rather than dispersal, unity rather than multiplicity, though the material is self-evidently borrowed and re-used. It is on such occasions that the pedagogic voice comes across most strongly, but with pedagogy comes

7 Compère, *Parcours d'une œuvre*, p. 62.

authority, and the implication is that the account being relayed is shared by numerous other authoritative sources. There is no question here of suggesting that the text is venturing onto new territory. Quite the contrary: it explicitly revisits known terrains for the implicit benefit of the reader, indicating that this is a shared, common language rather than a unique one. The incorporation of extraneous discourses in such instances allows a fictional narrator to impose his presence as master of ceremonies in the Balzacian manner. In this way, borrowed and appropriated material goes through the first stages of 'narrativisation'. We find the technique over and over again in the *Voyages extraordinaires*, in those apparent 'pauses' in the story that may take in anything from the techniques of coal-mining to developments in the American Civil War, through to the manufacture of weapons or the construction of ships.

Accounts of explorers and discoveries, in which the facts are rehearsed and relayed in a manner highlighting their status as common knowledge, are especially frequent. In a typical lengthy passage at the beginning of the second part of *Les Frères Kip*, the narrator suddenly appears to stand a long way back from the action of the novel. In doing so, he not only makes it clear that he is calling upon acknowledged and available sources to nourish his own text. He also asserts his own credentials as a narrator and implicitly signals that he is about to take the story forward in new directions: 'La Tasmanie, découverte en 1642 par le Hollandais Abel Tasman, souillée du sang du Français Manon en 1772, visitée par Cook en 1784 et par d'Entrecasteaux en 1793, fut enfin reconnue être une île par M. Bass, chirurgien de la colonie australienne' (FK, pp. 391–92) ['Tasmania, discovered by the Dutchman Abel Tasman in 1642, stained with the blood of the Frenchman Manon in 1772, visited by Cook in 1784 and by d'Entrecasteaux in 1793, was finally recognised as an island by Mr Bass, a surgeon in the Australian colony']. Continuing his account of Tasmania and its explorers for two and a half pages, the narrator indulges his pedagogical prerogative at the same time as he uses it to create one of those breaks in momentum that are so essential to narrative. The technique had already been widely used by Balzac and others, but Verne gives it an interesting new development, since he is able to reconcile the didactic and the narrative imperatives through it. This is one way in which those borrowed and recycled texts that reappear in the *Voyages extraordinaires* (and there can be no doubt that this one belongs in such a category, even if Verne's precise sources remain unknown) are integrated into a new narrative framework, and it shows that the warring discourses of science (or geography, or history) and fiction do not always remain separate. We shall need to bear this point in mind over the pages that follow, for it gives an indication that 'rewriting' (for example, of history or geography books) can itself become a genuine act of 'writing', as the manuals get translated and transmuted into a new discourse, and revalorised by their appearance in a new framework. Novelty and originality are to be found, not necessarily in new territories and invented discourses, but on the well-trodden paths of previous textual journeys. A new narrative register emerges – not always with equal effectiveness, but it is clearly there in this fusion of styles.

That Verne does commandeer massive amounts of material, and that he recycles it within his own fiction, is naturally beyond question. Judgments about whether such a procedure is legitimate and compatible with the aims of narrative will inevitably vary. It should, however, be stressed that Verne uses his interpolations in various ways and at various levels, and of course with variable consequences. Whereas in some instances he might arguably be branded a lazy writer who fills out large swathes of his own novels with unacknowledged borrowings, on other occasions he can be seen to rework his sources intensively, or to range critically between several sources and to balance different accounts. On other occasions still – perhaps his most frequent approach – he quotes his own sources openly, often to assess or judge them by way of distancing himself from the material he nonetheless exploits.[8] Through the pages of the *Voyages extraordinaires*, we come across a roll-call of famous names that include not only scientists and explorers (Cuvier, Darwin, Agassiz, Arago, Figuier, Flammarion and many others) but also philosophers and thinkers (Comte, Saint-Simon, Fourier, Lassalle, Marx, Guesde and so on). But where Verne does not name his sources, we should not necessarily assume this to mean that he is simply trying to pass off chunks of other texts as his own material. Stylistic markers signal the transitions into 'borrowed' discourse, as in the example from *Les Frères Kip* given above, and Verne appears to stake his narrative authority on the reader's ability to recognise these as imports. Often we do not know where such passages come from (though

8 An interesting case of this technique occurs with Verne's use of source material for his description of three Australian cities in *Mistress Branican*, where he cites an account by Désiré Charnay. Closer examination reveals that Verne made extensive and indeed almost exclusive use of Charnay's *Six Semaines en Australie*, but that he adopts a number of significant rhetorical strategies in order to distance himself from his source material. I have discussed this case elsewhere, in my *Textes réfléchissants: réalisme et réflexivité au dix-neuvième siècle*, pp. 148–51, and more extensively in an article entitled 'Plagiarist at Work? Jules Verne and the Australian City', in John West-Sooby (ed.) *Images of the City in Nineteenth-Century France* (Mount Nebo, Qld: Boombana Publications, 1998), pp. 183–99.

tracking them down is an important and ongoing area of Verne scholarship). However, their status as 'foreign bodies' in the narrative is clearly and openly on display. Without naming his sources or quoting the authorities, Verne is able to place such passages into the narrative as pieces that are acknowledged to be in the public domain.

On occasions, as with lists of plants or animals or recitals of historical facts, these interpolations can extend to several pages. This, however, is where they become problematic, for the longer such passages become, the more their narrative function is diluted. At such points the borrowings appear to take over the text and turn it into something apparently non-fictional. While the pedagogical intention always remains clear, it may leave the reader asking questions about how to process the text, as the focus of the writing is displaced from its master narrative to the supporting material. And while such re-alignments might be seen as a modern, experimental feature, doubt may remain about the resulting balance and plausibility of Verne's narratives. The third chapter of *L'Archipel en feu*, for example, is taken up entirely with the history of Greece, from antiquity through to the contemporary wars of independence during which the novel is set (AF, pp. 33–46). It is a digression that starts out almost in the 'Voici comment' ['This is how'] mode of Balzac. Initially it appears recognisable as a narrative technique in which the narrator stands back and recapitulates background details essential to an understanding of the story. Yet as so often happens in the *Voyages extraordinaires*, as the passage proceeds the background information becomes so extensive that it takes over, appearing superfluous in terms of the overall narrative. Even Balzac, famously given to bouts of verbal intoxication, would not go as far as this. It leaves the reader puzzling about how to place and to recuperate Verne's 'digression' in terms of the story as a whole. And although the narrator does make the effort to join up his digression with the main story, we are left feeling that this could have been done with greater precision and brevity. The narrative is in danger of being hijacked and overrun by the historical accounts that are relayed within it, in much the same way that the story of *Vingt mille lieues sous les mers* risks being crowded out by the fabulously detailed descriptions of marine life. The problem is a familiar one to all readers of Verne, and although it is very plausible to argue (as does Compère) that scientific and pedagogical digressions are a sign of the richness of resonance of the Vernian 'voice', this defence will for some seem like special pleading. Perhaps we must simply accept that Verne's method of using and incorporating other texts can produce differing results. While it gives a symphonic and composite quality to much of his writing, it can also contribute to a dilution of the storyline, a loss of momentum, or to a sense of confusion about the narrative conventions being followed. But then, the line of demarcation between 'writing' and 'rewriting' was never likely to be clear or straightforward.

At other moments in the *Voyages extraordinaires*, it might seem that the importation of borrowed texts comes close to plagiarism, and that it represents a real threat to the integrity of Verne's writing. The sources used for *Voyage au centre de la terre* are an especially revealing case, and one 1990s edition of that novel assembled an impressive dossier in which extracts from Verne's text are confronted with the works that he is known to have used. Among these are George Sand's *Laura*, Charles Edmond's *Voyage dans les mers du nord*, Eggert Olafsen's *Voyage en Islande* and Louis Figuier's *La Terre avant le déluge*.[9] The evidence is sometimes overwhelming and, assessing the charge of plagiarism against Verne, the novel's editor concludes that, while we may not know for sure whether he read and deliberately omitted to mention certain texts, there was clearly one author whom Verne plundered to the point of abuse, and that was Louis Figuier: 'Ce qu'il a lu, en revanche, et de très près, c'est l'ouvrage de Louis Figuier, *La Terre avant le déluge*. Si quelqu'un avait pu l'accuser de plagiat, c'est bien cet écrivain et vulgarisateur.'[10] ['On the other hand, one text that he did read very closely was Louis Figuier's *The Earth before the Flood*. If anyone could have accused him of plagiarism, it was this writer and populariser.'] Figuier himself remained unconcerned that his writings should be quarried for other uses, for that was precisely their purpose. But it is a matter of historical fact that there was a lawsuit against Verne resulting from the 1864 publication of *Voyage au centre de la terre*, as documented by Volker Dehs.[11] The accusation was brought by a certain Léon Delmas, who, under the pseudonym René de Pont-Jest, had published a story called 'La Tête de Mimers' in the *Revue contemporaine* in September 1863. Significant similarities can be found between *Voyage au centre de la terre* and this story, in which a German hero finds a document in an old book written in runic characters, and embarks on a journey as a result. Verne did not initially respond to the accusation, but it resurfaced in 1874 and led to a court case

---

9 Jules Verne, *Voyage au centre de la terre*, préface et commentaires de Jean-Pierre Goldenstein (Paris: Presses Pocket, 1991), pp. 403–59. For specific consideration of the connection between George Sand's story and Verne's novel, see also Simone Vierne, 'Deux voyages initiatiques en 1864: *Laura* de George Sand et le *Voyage au centre de la terre* de Jules Verne', in *Hommage à George Sand* (Grenoble: Presses Universitaires de Grenoble, 1969), pp. 101–14.

10 *Voyage au centre de la terre*, ed. Goldenstein, p. 436.

11 Volker Dehs, 'L'Affaire du *Voyage au centre de la terre*', *Bulletin de la Société Jules Verne*, 87 (1988), pp. 19–24.

in January 1877, which Verne won. But this was only one of a number of lawsuits that Verne had to fight during his career, and it confirms the problematic side of his patchwork approach which, exploiting the composite nature of text, can on occasions come perilously close to uncritical copying. When the acknowledged and known sources of *Voyage au centre de la terre* are examined alongside the many texts dealing with underground journeys that Verne may have read, the author's own 'originality' might appear somewhat diminished[12] – except that, as we know, most of the other texts have drifted into oblivion, while Verne's has survived as a classic. This is largely owing to its sheer narrative verve, and no doubt too because of its capacity to pick up on contemporary themes and relay them in expressive and appealing ways. While the famous passage recounting Axel's palaeontological dream in Chapter 32 (VCT, pp. 274–76) is heavily indebted to Darwin – whose theory of evolution it represents in a reverse sequence – few readers would wish to suggest that Verne is guilty of uncreative copying here. On the contrary, he takes ideas and terminology that were in common circulation and gives them a dizzying, hallucinatory, surreal quality that has fascinated readers ever since. This is Verne at his best, notwithstanding the fact that he is writing in echo mode.[13]

Be that as it may, the case brought by Delmas was no doubt one of the factors that subsequently put Verne on his guard against possible accusations of plagiarism. Significantly, as he was writing *Vingt mille lieues* in 1867, Verne moved to quash suggestions that he might have copied his idea from a novel about an underwater voyage being serialised in *Le Petit Journal*, by writing to its editor.[14] Yet his use of source material in that

---

12 In his edition of *Voyage au centre de la terre* (see note 9) Jean-Pierre Goldenstein gives extracts from a number of 'subterranean texts' that Verne may well have known and used. These include Holberg's *Voyage de Nocolas Klimius dans le monde souterrain*, Hoffmann's *Les Mines de Falun*, Sébillot's *La Terre et le monde souterrain*, and Humboldt's *Cosmos: essai d'une description physique du monde*. Again, the evidence suggests that Jules Verne probably used more than he was fully prepared to admit.

13 On other occasions it is clear that Verne indulges in purposefully ironic treatments of Darwinism. Examples are 'Le Humbug', a story in the collection *Hier et demain* which tells of the discovery and commercial exploitation of a fake prehistoric fossil, and *Le Village aérien*, in which a supposedly superior being ruling a colony of ape-men in an African jungle turns out to be the scientist Dr Johausen who has regressed into madness and primitivism.

14 The novel, which appeared from 10 October onwards, was by Pierre-Jules Rengade (pseudonym of Aristide Roger), and was subsequently published in volume form as *Aventures extraordinaires de Trinitus. Voyage sous les flots, rédigé d'après le journal de bord de 'L'Eclair'* (Paris: Brunet, 1868). See Butcher (ed.), *Twenty Thousand Leagues Under the Seas*, p. xiv, and Costello, *Jules Verne: Inventor of Science Fiction*, pp. 101–109.

novel, too, indicates that enduring tendency in his writing to step over the line and to progress from the critical exploitation of source material to the straightforward recopying of it. Since that is arguably the area of greatest originality in Verne's approach, it is also its area of greatest danger. The lists of underwater flora and fauna in *Vingt mille lieues* are themselves 'knowledge' that has been transposed from encylopaedias and manuals, though Verne often gives his lists a poetic resonance through which they clearly transcend their origins. Elsewhere in the novel, as William Butcher has pointed out, we will find echoes of Homer, Plato, Hugo, Michelet, Scott, Poe and Melville. The latter influence is especially important, and is rightly stressed by Butcher, who asserts that '*Moby Dick* presents many affinities in details and in plot' with *Vingt mille lieues*.[15]

But when is an influence more than just an influence? The question will almost certainly attract different answers from different readers, not least according to how sympathetically disposed they are. Successive generations, too, tend to look upon these matters in the light of prevailing critical issues, and since the Barthesian proclamation of the death of the author,[16] and the increased awareness of the intertextuality of all writing,[17] there is perhaps a greater tendency nowadays to take a non-judgmental view of the process. Yet the fact that questions about Verne's source material and his uses of it are so regularly asked is itself significant, for it tells us something fundamental about the nature of his writing. The modern *scripteur* does indeed cross boundaries, making new texts out of a critical, creative act of dialogue with and through other texts. On the other hand, the taboo of 'individuality' has lingered, and the temptation to catch a writer *in flagrante delicto*, plagiarising or copying, remains.[18] Olivier Dumas is one of many critics who point to Verne's sometimes uncomfortably close following of source material, when he draws attention to the uses the author made of a series of articles, published in 1861–62 in *Le*

---

15 Butcher (ed.), *Twenty Thousand Leagues Under the Seas*, pp. ix–xxxi, p. xiii.

16 'La Mort de l'auteur' (1968), reprinted in Roland Barthes, *Le Bruissement de la langue* (Paris: Seuil, 1984), pp. 61–67.

17 On this subject, see Daniel Compère's useful 'Note méthodologique sur l'intertextualité' in *Jules Verne écrivain*, pp. 155–63.

18 The taboo is well illustrated by the more recent case of the prize-winning Camerounian author Calixthe Beyala. Her credibility was severely damaged when on 18 January 1995 the satirical newspaper *Le Canard enchaîné* claimed that certain pages in her 1992 novel, *Le Petit Prince de Belleville*, had been copied from a book by Howard Buten, translated into French as *Quand j'avais cinq ans, je m'ai tué*. On 7 May 1996 the Parisian Tribunal de Grande Instance upheld the charge of plagiarism, against which Beyala made no appeal.

Tour du monde, as he was writing *Le Beau Danube jaune* (originally published as *Le Pilote du Danube*, in a version heavily reworked by Michel
Verne after his father's death).[19] The example is typical, and the observation can be applied to many, if not most, of Verne's novels.

Problems of demarcation and ownership become especially acute in
those cases where Verne works to adapt a text initially written by another
author – as in the cases of *Les Cinq Cents Millions de la Bégum* and *L'Etoile
du sud* (both based on original stories by Paschal Grousset) – or when he
works explicitly in collaboration with another writer. In a culture which
believes it important to establish the nature and extent of the individual
contribution, suspicion is an occupational hazard for any writer who, like
Verne, systematically uses grafting methods in the composition of texts or
who relies on external input. Perhaps the most famous dispute on this
subject in Verne's own lifetime was the 'Affaire Cadol', which arose over
the writing of *Le Tour du monde en quatre-vingts jours* in both its fictional
and dramatic forms. The relay between two authors here is interesting,
not least because it reduplicates the shuttle of the text itself between two
different genres, and the mix becomes especially problematic when a
third author enters the equation. The order of events goes like this.
Edouard Cadol initially wrote a script for the theatre on the basis of a plan
for a novel that Jules Verne himself had composed late in 1871. But as he
was writing his novel early in 1872, Verne quickly moved to distance himself from Cadol, albeit in his private correspondence with Hetzel, to whom
he opined in a letter of 1 April: 'Inutile de vous dire que je laisse de côté
toute préoccupation de pièce, et que pour le livre, je m'écarte souvent du
plan arrêté par Cadol et moi. Je n'ai jamais mieux vu combien un livre dif-
férait d'une pièce.'[20] ['I hardly need tell you that I am leaving behind me
all thoughts about the play, and that for the novel I am frequently moving
away from the plan drawn up by Cadol and myself. I have never seen more

19 The articles, bearing the title 'De Paris à Bucharest', were published by Victor Duruy,
    and are the basis of Verne's descriptions in the novel. See Olivier Dumas, introduction
    to *Le Beau Danube jaune* (Paris: L'Archipel, 2000 [1988]), pp. 7–21.
20 See Dumas, Gondolo della Riva and Dehs (eds.), *Correspondance inédite*, vol. I, pp.
    165–66. The editors of the *Correspondance inédite* suggest that Jules Verne may have
    owed a greater debt to Cadol than he admits. Their view is that the theatre scenario
    itself is a dual venture, and that it is this scenario 'qu'il [Verne] utilise pour faire son
    plus célèbre roman' (p. 166) ['which Verne uses to write his most famous novel']. A
    full account of Verne's collaboration with Cadol and subsequently d'Ennery is given
    by Volker Dehs, 'Un drame ignoré: l'odyssée du *Tour du monde en quatre-vingts jours*',
    forthcoming in *Australian Journal of French Studies*, 'Jules Verne in the Twenty-First
    Century', 42.3 (2005).

clearly how different a novel is from a play.'] After the success of the novel, Cadol then tried to get his scenario accepted, but to no avail, and Verne moved to distance himself from it further by enlisting the services of another playwright, Adolphe d'Ennery, who created the popular stage version on the basis of Verne's novel. But while Verne always remained keen to deny that Cadol's scenario had any part in the novel or its eventual adaptation to the stage,[21] Cadol naturally felt differently and, by late 1873, a public argument had developed which was to spread to the pages of *Le Figaro* and end in the courts.[22] As it turned out, Cadol's unsurprising claim (that his influence on the composition of the novel and on the play was worthy of financial recompense) was upheld by an order that he should receive two and a half per cent of the royalties of the stage version, though he was not named as one of its authors. Whether Verne was right to maintain his own exclusive authorship of the novel is a question that will probably never be answered, and ultimately it is of little importance anyway. What we do know is that on numerous occasions he moved to deny possible collusion with or borrowing from other authors, and even to deny knowledge of certain texts where similarities with his own works might seem uncomfortable. The area of borrowing, collusion and plagiarism is one in which he clearly developed some sensitivity, not least as a result of the accusations that were brought against him. But given his working methods and his uses of other texts, this is almost inevitable, and it illustrates only too well the problems that arise with a writing style that so conspicuously situates itself as a hybrid, at the interface of different textual sources and influences. We do know that Verne occasionally succumbed to the temptation to lift passages uncritically from other writings. On the other hand, we also know that in many cases he successfully adapted other texts to his own style, albeit at the cost of a certain unfinished quality. Let us reconsider, then, the question of how Verne uses scientific and other non-fictional discourses, and examine how these are integrated and narrativised within his own texts.

---

21 See Verne's letter to Hetzel of 24 November 1873 (Dumas, Gondolo della Riva and Dehs (eds.), *Correspondance inédite*, p. 220) in which he sets out precisely what he considers his own and Cadol's roles to have been.

22 For a succinct and useful account of the 'Affaire Cadol', see Daniel Compère, 'Le Jour fantôme' in *Jules Verne 1: 'Le Tour du monde'*, pp. 31–51 (pp. 36–37).

Scientific discourses and their narrativisation

We have seen that the hybrid qualities of Verne's style are themselves a sign that he is creating a new kind of narrative discourse. While its material components may often come from elsewhere, it is their combinations and their remixing which takes the writing onto new territory. Yet, as we have also seen, that process is far from uniformly successful. It is no surprise, then, that critics of Verne should so often have articulated their reading of him in terms of this problem. While at least one critic, Daniel Compère, has produced an emphatic and highly persuasive defence of the author, many remain more sceptical. The role of science, with its terminologies, catalogues and taxonomies, and that of the lists and descriptions of all kinds that figure in the *Voyages extraordinaires*, are particular areas of difficulty. How does the positivistic, apparently 'objective' form of discourse sit with the writing of fiction? How does an imported, scientifically functional language become narrativised, if at all? Let us look at three critical responses to these questions, before suggesting further ways in which we might frame an answer to them.

Michel Foucault, while accepting that the Vernian text is endowed with multiple resonances and sonorities, suggests that scientific discourse is ultimately a voice outside and beyond the text. Rather than becoming integrated into the narrative, science takes it in the direction of something abstract and dehumanised. Thus, says Foucault, 'les voix multiples de la fiction se résorbent dans le murmure sans corps de la science' ['the multiple voices of fiction are absorbed into the disembodied murmur of science'], science being the final, abstract authority in Verne's novels. Though in a sense it acts as the guarantor of unity and coherence, reconciling those other voices 'en contestation les unes avec les autres' ['in conflict with one another'] in the Vernian text, this comes at a cost, for science is like 'une autre voix, plus lointaine, qui conteste le récit ou en accuse la nature fictive, en souligne les invraisemblances' ['another, more distant voice which challenges the story, and brings out its fictional quality by underlining its implausibilities']. Most of all, Foucault claims, science appears as a kind of 'discours immigrant' ['immigrant discourse'] that is 'déposé [...] par grandes plaques' ['dropped in large chunks'] into the body of the text.[23]

23 Foucault, 'L'Arrière-fable', p. 12, p. 6, p. 8. Foucault's argument about the alien quality of scientific discourse in Vernian fiction leads him to a view of the scientist as an abstract, dehumanised creature standing outside of the fiction itself, a pure intermediary who is never at the heart of the adventure: 'Ce n'est pas à lui qu'advient

The view that, for all the symphonic and composite qualities of the Vernian text, science appears as a foreign body within it, is also upheld by Alain Buisine in one of the most illuminating analyses of Vernian description that has ever been carried out. Focusing on the case of *Vingt mille lieues*, Buisine stresses the borrowed, alien character of that novel's descriptive passages, in which 'la pratique descriptive est pratique citationnelle' ['descriptive practice is citational practice'], becoming 'rien d'autre qu'une écriture qui ré-écrit une autre écriture'[24] ['nothing other than writing which rewrites other writing']. This borrowed discourse takes description out of its fictional context, appropriating through its classifications and inventories the world that the novelist represents. It becomes an essentially metonymic process, a matter of accumulation and an archaeology of knowledge, rather than a metaphoric or symbolic approach to description. Thus 'l'écriture glisse du romanesque à l'objectif'[25] ['writing slips from the novelistic to the objective'], often in quite brutal transitions from a poetic, expansive language to a dry, analytical one, where the tense also switches abruptly from the past to the present. There is too, for Buisine, a paradoxical minimalism about Vernian description which, for all its legendary prolixity, reduces representation to a simple nomenclature. While Buisine does suggest that the nomenclature itself takes on poetic resonances, it is for him a poetry of extremes in which all connotations become possible because no word has any privileged connection with any other. And scientific discourses – whilst considered to have certain remote, fascinating qualities in the literary text as 'pure' language – are seen here essentially as a borrowed, foreign element in the literary text. Mimesis fails, because in this recital of names the writer becomes aware that it is impossible to say everything. The language of scientific description is itself a site of narrative collapse.

---

l'aventure, pas lui du moins qui en est le héros principal. Il formule des connaissances, déploie un savoir, énonce les possibilités et les limites, observe les résultats, attend, dans le calme, de constater qu'il a dit vrai et que le savoir ne s'est pas trompé en lui. [...] Le savant ne découvre pas; il est celui en qui le savoir s'est inscrit.' (p. 9) ['He is not the one who undergoes the adventure, or at least he is not its main hero. He formulates knowledge and sets out his learning, states the possibilities and the limits, observes the results, then calmly waits to confirm that he was right and that through him science has not erred. The scientist does not discover things. He is the one in whom science is inscribed.'] Such a view of the Vernian scientist is hard to credit. Over and over again in the *Voyages extraordinaires*, it is the scientist (often also the hero) who dictates the action and links up knowledge and adventure. This is paradigmatically the case in a novel such as *L'Ile mystérieuse*.

24 Alain Buisine, 'Un cas limite de la description', p. 82, p. 91.
25 Buisine, 'Un cas limite de la description', p. 87.

While it makes some concessions to the poeticisation of scientific discourses, Buisine's approach stresses above all that science and the literary text remain opposites, and that Verne's writing does no more than demonstrate their incompatibilities. The borrowed nature of the imported texts always undermines the attempt to integrate them fully into the narrative, and writing is shadowed at every stage by what it rewrites and recycles. As so often in the critical literature about Verne, there is here more than the hint of an accusation of sham on the author's part. But, while recognising that the conflict is a fascinating one, both Foucault and Buisine tend to emphasise Verne's failure to reconcile the warring discourses of science and literature. It is true that for most of the nineteenth century, and for many of its writers, these areas remained polar opposites.

However, another approach to this problem is to place it in the context of a more general progress narrative, in which successive writers are seen to achieve a fuller and more successful integration of science, as they learn how to incorporate it in subtler and more sophisticated ways within the literary text. This is the approach taken by Arthur Evans, notably in two articles which take a broad look at questions of science fiction and 'scientific fiction' in French writing of the nineteenth and twentieth centuries.[26] Evans points out that in France especially, even in the twentieth century, the common view was that scientific and literary discourses were incompatible, but that a closer look at the uses of scientific discourse by a number of writers shows, on the contrary, an increasingly unitary approach to them. In the pre-modern era, he contends, literary texts used science pedagogically (as in Verne's *Voyages extraordinaires*), satirically (as in Flaubert's *Bouvard et Pécuchet*), or narratologically (as in Villiers de l'Isle-Adam's *L'Eve future*). Yet, he claims, even with the sophisticated, highly narrativised uses of scientific discourse that we find in authors such as Villiers, 'the linguistic integrity of "real" scientific discourse in these texts is deliberately sacrificed for the sake of enhanced literary effect'.[27] In the case of Verne's predominantly pedagogical uses of science, science remains a recognisably interpolated discourse, inserted in various ways into the text. Evans identifies three principal modes of insertion: 'en bloc' (where large chunks of external text are dumped into the fiction), 'en passant' (where there is opportunistic inclusion of it as the narrative is progressing), and 'mediated insertion' (in which scientific discourse is

---

26 Arthur B. Evans, 'Science Fiction vs. Scientific Fiction in France: From Jules Verne to J.-H. Rosny Aîné', *Science Fiction Studies*, 15 (1988), pp. 1–11, and 'Functions of Science in French Fiction'.

27 'Functions of Science in French Fiction', p. 99.

relayed by a fictional character).[28] But while Evans effectively makes the argument for looking at how scientific discourse gets narrativised within fiction, his suggestion is that Verne is one of the first in a long line of authors who will gradually learn to reconcile the two more fully. In so far as many of the scientific discourses in Verne are inserted 'en bloc', the pedagogical prerogative takes precedence over full textual integration. Yet Evans does also point to important ways in which, in the Vernian text, science actually becomes part of the fiction, especially through the mode of mediated insertion. Here, science is part of a fictional character's purview, informs his mode of engagement with the world, and impacts directly on the plot. It becomes meaningfully narrativised.

We need to take this further, however, and to look at other ways in which science and its discourses – or the related 'positivistic' languages of taxonomies, lists and descriptions – might be seen as belonging in a deeper sense within the Vernian narrative. What all three critics discussed above seem in the end to suggest (to varying degrees) is that there is something unsatisfactory about Verne's borrowed discourses or descriptions, and that at some level these break an aesthetic law by conspicuously standing out from the text. Our first response, then, must surely be to turn this argument around. It is precisely *because* they stand out from the text that such passages assume a function and a role in the narrative that they could not otherwise have. They deliberately attract attention rather than deflect it, causing us to focus on them and their role within the fiction. They puzzle us, of course, but the sense of bewilderment or curiosity in the reader is no accident, nor should it be overlooked as some undesirable side effect of our processing of the text.

Buisine's recognition of the fact that Verne's lists and taxonomies take on poetic resonance (a point that has been made on many occasions by readers of Verne) is itself an indication that something fundamental happens to these discourses in the process of their transposition or appropriation into a literary text. If they stand out in their starkness and their strangeness, then, it is also because the novelist provides a new context which frames and displays them as 'pure' language. Their very unrelatedness to the momentum of narrative is consequently a significant factor, giving us pause and making us ponder and scrutinise these words in ways we would not do if we saw them in their 'original' context or if they were more fully integrated. In this respect the reader of the Vernian text is placed by the writer in exactly the same position as so many of his characters, who stop short and appear to marvel at the very terms that they are

---

28 'Functions of Science in French Fiction', pp. 83–87.

required to use in order to represent their experience. In *Voyages et aventures du capitaine Hatteras*, Dr Clawbonny (who like so many of the scientists in Verne is an allegorical representation of the writer himself, and an extension of the narrator's persona) stresses from the outset his appetite to delve into the mystery of the words which classify and categorise scientific knowledge:

> On dit que je suis un savant; on se trompe, commandant: je ne sais rien, et si j'ai publié quelques livres qui ne se vendent pas trop mal, j'ai eu tort [...].
> Or, on m'offre de compléter, ou, pour mieux dire, de refaire mes connaissances en médecine, en chirurgie, en histoire, en géographie, en botanique, en minéralogie, en conchyliologie, en géodésie, en chimie, en physique, en mécanique, en hydrographie; eh bien, j'accepte... (CH, p. 24)

> [They say that I am a scientist. That is a mistake, Commander. I know nothing, and if I have published a few books that have sold reasonably well, then I have been wrong to do so. But I now have the chance to complete, or rather to rebuild my knowledge of medicine, surgery, history, geography, botany, mineralogy, conchology, geodesy, chemistry, physics, mechanics, hydrography: well, I accept.]

Language itself is what fascinates Clawbonny here, and like many characters in Verne he gets carried away with the breathless rhythm of his own list, along with the increasingly exotic, almost cabalistic sounds of those words which represent great swathes of learning. Science, here, becomes a profoundly verbal experience, and its focalisation through one of the characters in the story is significant, for the individual's relationship to the quality of words themselves is brought sharply into focus. There is no question here, as Foucault claims, of science being some remote, outside voice that unifies the text in a disembodied, objective, depersonalised space. On the contrary, as Clawbonny points out with Socratic elegance in the same passage, science is ignorance and therefore profoundly human ('Je ne sais rien, vous dis-je, si ce n'est que je suis un ignorant' ['I tell you I know nothing, except that I am ignorant']). The obvious recourse is to focus on the alluring reverberations and sonorities of scientific language itself – recognising that words conceal many a mystery – and to bring science into the domain of writing, just as writing extends to the domain of science.

But if this is what happens with Clawbonny, how much more it is the case with Aronnax, another of those writer-scientists in Verne who, by his role as first-person narrator in the most intensely poetic of all the novels in the *Voyages extraordinaires*, has an exceptional status as a mediator of science. Aronnax's fascination with the strangeness of what he perceives

is paralleled systematically in the strangeness of the words that he uses.
While he may draw attention to the apparent 'dryness' of his scientific
vocabulary, he contrives to give a wondrously exotic aura to his lists.
The scientist, in defiance of all conventions, turns into a poet, and in passages such as the following we become supremely aware of his power to
convey the almost magical qualities of the words that are his professional
language:

> Je termine là cette nomenclature un peu sèche, mais très exacte, par la série
> des poissons osseux que j'observai: passans, appartenant au genre des
> aptéronotes, dont le museau est très obtus et blanc de neige, le corps peint
> d'un beau noir, et qui sont munis d'une lanière charnue très longue et très
> déliée; odontagnathes aiguillonnés, longues sardines de trois décimètres,
> resplendissant d'un vif éclat argenté; scombres-guares, pourvus de deux
> nageoires anales; centronotes-nègres, à teintes noires, qu'on pêche avec des
> brandons, longs poissons de deux mètres, à chair grasse, blanche, ferme, qui,
> frais, ont le goût de l'anguille, et secs le goût du saumon fumé; labres demi-
> rouges, revêtus d'écailles seulement à la base des nageoires dorsales et anales;
> chrysoptères, sur lesquels l'or et l'argent mêlent leur éclat à ceux du rubis et
> de la topaze; spares-queues-d'or, dont la chair est extrêmement délicate, et
> que leurs propriétés phosphorescentes trahissent au milieu des eaux; spares-
> pobs, à langue fine, à teintes orange; sciènes-coro à caudales d'or, acan-
> thures-noirauds, anableps de Surinam, etc. (VML, II, p. 541)

> [I shall conclude this somewhat dry, though completely accurate list, with
> the series of bony fish that I observed: ramblers, belonging to the apteronot
> species, with their very blunt, snow-white snout and handsome black-
> painted body, and their long, slender, fleshy whip; prickly odontagnathae;
> thirty-centimetre sardines, flashing with silver brilliance; scomberesox
> sauri, which have two anal fins; dark-coloured butterfly blennies, two-metre
> long creatures which are fished for with torches, and whose plump, firm,
> white flesh tastes of eel when fresh, and of smoked salmon when dry; semi-
> red labra, with scales only at the base of their dorsal and anal fins;
> chrysopteri, on which gold and silver mingle brilliantly with ruby and
> topaz; golden-tail sparids, the flesh of which is a great delicacy, and whose
> phosphorescent glow betrays them under the water; boop-sparids with their
> slender tongues and orange hues; coro sciaenas with their golden tailfins;
> acanthurus nigricans; Surinam four-eyed fish, etc.]

Whereas, in one sense, the list that Aronnax gives here is purely objective, it is the sheer accumulation of unusual words that gives it such
power. From the reader's point of view, an act of trust is certainly
required, for few of us are likely to be familiar with every species and
every term that Verne's character uses. This means that we are inevitably
brought up against the strangeness of the words themselves, and this

mirrors very precisely the experience of Aronnax himself, who is brought up against the strangeness of nature, in its diversity and richness. That the terms and nomenclatures used by Verne are 'quoted', in the sense that he has clearly transposed them into his text from encyclopaedias and scientific manuals, is obvious. In that sense, his language is borrowed, but it displays itself as such. Yet the open act of borrowing, and the inclusion of this technical discourse in the text as a foreign body, is precisely what enables it to have such a powerful poetic effect. Its alterity – as language from elsewhere, or words not in common circulation – forces us to re-examine it, in ways we would be unlikely to adopt with the reading of an encyclopaedia entry. In so doing, we become more aware of the verbal specificity of the objects in the list, and of the poetic properties of its composition. Bizarre sonorities and rhythms ('odontagnathes aiguillonnés', 'centronotes-nègres, à teintes noires, qu'on pêche avec des brandons') accompany intensely powerful visual associations ('chrysoptères, sur lesquels l'or et l'argent mêlent leur éclat à ceux du rubis et de la topaze') and lively, almost jesting alliterations ('scènes-coro à caudales d'or'). Verne, through his narrator Aronnax, achieves a complete reversal here, as his 'nomenclature un peu sèche' is transformed into warm, intensely evocative language whose incantatory power is typical of so many passages in the text.

It is not only directly through the characters' words that Verne achieves this integration of apparently objective, scientific or descriptive language into the narrative. Often, too, the narrator will step in and articulate a scene or a situation, which nonetheless remains focalised through the characters. Thus we have a joining of the character's and the narrator's perspectives. In *Clovis Dardentor*, the plants of Algeria with their exotic and sensual fragrances are described in a list whose characteristics are not unlike those of the one just quoted from *Vingt mille lieues*, but where clearly the narrator himself is assuming responsibility for verbalising the experience of the travellers:

> Quel bon air on respirait, auquel tant de plantes odoriférantes mêlaient leurs parfums! Partout, en fourrés, des jujubiers, des caroubiers, des arbousiers, des lentisques, des palmiers nains, – en bouquets, des thyms, des myrtes, des lavandes, – en massifs, toute la série des chênes d'une si grande valeur forestière, chênes-lièges, chênes-zéens, chênes à glands doux, chênes-verts, puis des thuyas, des cèdres, des ormes, des frênes, des oliviers sauvages, des pistachiers, des genévriers, des citronniers, des eucalyptus, si prospères en Algérie, des milliers de ces pins d'Alep, sans parler de tant d'autres essences résineuses! (CD, p. 156)

[What fine air one breathed, scented by so many plants whose perfumes mingled with it! Everywhere there were thickets of jujubes, carobs, arbutus, lentiscus, dwarf palms; bouquets of thyme, myrtle and lavender; clumps of the entire range of oaks, so valuable to forests – cork oaks, durmast oaks, oaks with soft acorns, holm oaks; and then thujas, cedars, elms, ash, wild olive, pistachio, juniper, lemon trees, the eucalyptus which grow so well in Algeria, and thousands of Alep pines, not to mention so many other coniferous essences!]

In this case, focalisation of the scene through a group is made clear by an initial use of free indirect discourse, in which an apparent remark or reflection made by a person or a group is transposed into the narrative without the inquit clause – 'they said', 'he reflected', etc. – which is the normal mark of a transition to indirect speech. In free indirect discourse, the imperfect tense (the normal tense both of narrative description and of indirect speech) is the dominant one, as here in the initial verb 'respirait'. This example suggests that the transition from past to present tense, identified by Buisine as one of the signals of Verne's incorporated discourses, is by no means always a feature of such passages. But it is above all the richly sensuous quality of the description, albeit dominated by the dizzying presence of nouns, that takes it out of any purely scientific or geographical context and gives it truly literary credentials. This happens over and over again in Verne, whose long descriptive lists draw heavily on sound, scent, taste, touch and sheer visual richness. Often the sensual perceptions of the so-called 'natural' world mingle together in powerful combinations, suggesting that words themselves are the very locus of experience. For all their self-proclaimed dependency on the language of nineteenth-century science and positivism, there is in the end nothing unliterary about the place of such passages in the fictional text.

However, Verne is also a highly self-conscious, experimental author. His aim is not necessarily to create a seamlessly 'fictional' fiction, in which the reader is able to suspend disbelief comfortably, but also to puncture the very conventions within which he is writing, and to exploit the surprise or the bewilderment that is thereby created. And the juxtaposition of scientific and pedagogical material in his novels is intended, at least in part, to challenge and subvert the traditional characteristics of fiction. By forcing us to reflect on the place of these borrowed discourses, and thereby to consider them more carefully as discourse, Verne is also able to make several points about the nature of literary language and our expectations of it. Not least among these is the fact that we *expect* the literary text to be finished, aesthetically rounded, self-contained, unified. At times, it is none of these things, and in Verne's novels it is subjected to continuous stresses and strains, most obviously in some of those lists and inventories, which can also end up undermining the whole notion of realism through excess of detail.

This being so, another of the areas in which the argument about Verne's so-called inability to integrate science and scientific discourse falls down is surely in its failure to give sufficient weight to irony. Like Flaubert, Verne frequently engages in a debunking of science and its discourses by putting them on open display. Often this happens through the taxonomies that are drawn up, where the mania for classification or precision is shown to be self-destructive. We should certainly not imagine that Verne's relaying of the discourses of positivism, and his recycling of its methods, is always carried out naïvely. Despite a sense of overall respect for nineteenth-century science and positivism that emerges from the *Voyages extraordinaires*, the critique of its follies and delusions is everywhere, and becomes apparent through a process of exaggeration which can in some instances end up as rampant caricature. We will find evidence of a deeply sceptical, ironic attitude in Verne as early as 1851, in a short story entitled 'Les Premiers Navires de la marine mexicaine' (subsequently rewritten and published in 1876 as 'Un drame au Mexique'). Here, one of the characters, starting out with the apparently harmless proposition that Mexico is a rich blend of races, launches into a phantasmagoria of classifications that dizzies and confuses, until finally it undoes itself completely in a sexual innuendo which underlines how much connotation can be extracted from an apparently straightforward metonymic progression:

> Voyez plutôt tous ces croisements de race, que j'ai soigneusement étudiés pour contracter un jour un mariage avantageux! On trouve le mestisa, né d'un Espagnol et d'une Indienne; castisa, d'une femme métis et d'un Espagnol; mulâtre, d'une Espagnole et d'un nègre; monisque, d'une mulâtresse et d'un Espagnol; albino, d'une monisque et d'un Espagnol; tornatras, d'un albino et d'une Espagnole; tintinclaire, d'un tornatras et d'une Espagnole; lovo, d'une Indienne et d'un nègre; caribujo, d'une Indienne et d'un lovo; barsino, d'un coyote et d'une mulâtresse; grifo, d'une négresse et d'un lovo; albarazado, d'un coyote et d'une Indienne; chanisa, d'un métis et d'un Indien; mechino, d'une lova et d'un coyote; sans compter, lieutenant, les belles goélettes blanches que plus d'un flibustier aborde par le travers![29]

> [Just look at all those different mixes of races that I have studied so carefully in order one day to make an advantageous marriage! You will find the

---

29 'Les Premiers Navires de la marine mexicaine', in *Portrait de l'artiste jeune, suivi des quatre premiers textes publiés de Jules Verne*, pp. 53–78 (p. 70).

mestisa, born of a Spaniard and an Indian woman; the castisa, offspring of a half-caste woman and a Spaniard; the mulatto, from a Spanish woman and a Negro; the monisque, from a mulatto woman and a Spaniard; the albino, from a monisque woman and a Spaniard; the tornatras, from an albino and a Spanish woman; the tintinclaire, from a tornatras and a Spanish woman; the lovo, from an Indian woman and a Negro; the caribujo, from an Indian woman and a lovo; the barsino, from a coyote and a mulatto woman; the grifo, from a Negress and a lovo; the albarazado, from a coyote and an Indian woman; the chanisa, from a half-caste and an Indian; the mechino, from a lovo woman and a coyote; not to mention, lieutenant, the fine white schooners that more than one filibuster has taken across the bows!]

So at this point the urge for classification and precision steps over conspicuously into excess and parody. The attempt to apply authoritative and acknowledged terminologies becomes an empty yet absurd imitation of the language of the anthropologist, for who can find meaning in these terms? The humour is underlined (as will so often later be the case in the *Voyages extraordinaires*) by the over-exuberance of a character who wishes to demonstrate his knowledge. Indeed, the impressive knowledge of characters such as Dr Clawbonny, Paganel, Palmyrin Rosette and others is never far from the ridiculousness of pedantry (Aristobulus Ursiclos in *Le Rayon vert*) or the perils of obsession (the astronomer Thomas Black in *Le Pays des fourrures*).

Yet similar risks and failings are often more subtly highlighted by the narrator of the *Voyages extraordinaires* in his own lists and descriptions. On these occasions, Verne does not have the luxury of being able to expose the pomposity or absurdity of a character's attitude and to undermine 'science' as a result. What happens is that the mania for terminological exactitude, by showing itself up as potentially never-ending, gradually descends into self-parody. The process of mimesis, in which the world is represented figuratively, is replaced by that of mathesis, which attempts to use language as a perfect descriptor and in doing so gets caught in futile, endless accumulation.[30] The result is not coherence but proliferation, indeed potential chaos, in which description and representation no

---

30 This process is effectively described by Andrew Martin in *The Knowledge of Ignorance*, pp. 134–35. As Martin explains, the 'reductionist' vision of authors such as Balzac, who try to explain the essence of reality from a coherent vantage point, is surpassed by Verne's project to embrace *all* totalities, and to say everything about everything. It becomes an expansive project in which enumeration is the key to understanding, and the task of description is above all the technique of computation. This, according to Martin, explains the 'numerical intoxication' (p. 135) of Verne's characters.

longer have any clear boundaries or function. Andrew Martin rightly draws attention to the importance of the word 'etc.' in the *Voyages extraordinaires*, denoting the interminability of the writer's own project and the impossibility of totalising knowledge and observations.[31] But the Rabelaisian enthusiasm of Verne's lists, which draw attention to their own repetitive energy, often hints at the ironic intent. The longest list of all in the *Voyages extraordinaires* (I shall not quote it because of its length) comes early in *Cinq semaines en ballon*. In the first chapter of that novel, once Dr Fergusson's project to seek out the sources of the Nile has been announced, a series of toasts are proposed to all past explorers of the African continent. There follows a roll-call of no less than seventy names, in which ritualistic repetition takes the place of narrative representation, and in which the names seem to appear in almost cornucopian profusion. This makes a mockery of 'narrative'. It is just a series of words, completely and deliberately out of proportion to the event being narrated, onto which is imposed a purely conventional order for arbitrary reasons: 'On but à leur santé ou leur mémoire, et par ordre alphabétique, ce qui est très anglais...' (5S, p. 8) ['A toast was drunk to their health or to their memory, and in alphabetical order, which is very English']. The implication is that this alphabetical sequence is merely one possibility among many, and has nothing to do with real meanings or hierarchies. Any order could have been chosen and would have fulfilled much the same effect. Yet, towards the end of the list, among the 'Ws', an invented character makes a fleeting appearance. This is a certain 'Werne'. Is the novelist himself making a ludic entrance on the stage of his own text? If so, it will not be the last time that this happens in the *Voyages extraordinaires*. But, whoever the fictional Werne might be (there appears to be no historically attested explorer by that name), his presence among the last names in the list indicates what by now has become apparent by other means: namely, that fact has been overtaken by fantasy. While most of the names here are real, they end up losing their reality and become mere words on the page, fillers of that blank space, whose function is to cascade vertiginously into, through, and out of the text. Starting out as a historically 'precise' list, the passage concludes by demonstrating its own superfluousness, its own inventedness. Fact is turned into fiction, reality into words that unfurl in repetitive, random sequence. It is astonishing that Verne could have got away with a list of this type so early in his career as a novelist. While *Cinq semaines* was hailed (not least by Hetzel himself) as a new type of literature in which science and exploration were being integrated into the

---

31 *The Knowledge of Ignorance*, p. 170.

novel, nobody seems initially to have realised that this was a send-up of prevailing notions of fiction and of science – a truly textual carnival which was being conducted on the very grounds of scientific exactitude.

The technique of creating a sense of unreality through excess of precision, pioneered by Rabelais with such humorous effects, is one that Verne uses liberally throughout the *Voyages extraordinaires*. But Verne's irony is not always as transparent as in the examples quoted above. At times it can be more difficult to unravel, not least because he lives and writes in an age of scientific optimism, the value of whose methods and language he also upholds and promotes. While he takes the novel quite altruistically in the direction of science and its discourses, he also subjects these to insidious stresses and strains, exposing them as convention and invention, sometimes as downright illusion. Throughout the *Voyages extraordinaires*, as Arthur Evans has noted,[32] we find an obsession with measuring, maps, guides, timepieces or other devices. These instruments of exploration are the objective correlatives of the language of science, and herein, according to Evans, lies the ideological matrix of Verne's work, which is a belief in the comprehensibility of the world and our ability to control and articulate it. The museum and the encyclopaedia are further extensions of this confidence in precision, control, and the power of knowledge, and there is in the *Voyages extraordinaires* an overall conviction that the natural universe, though immensely complex, is ultimately stable. In such circumstances, reading Verne's lists and inventories can be problematic, since it is clear that on many occasions we have to take them as 'genuine' attempts to record, observe and classify phenomena. Yet by pushing these a little beyond what seem reasonable limits, Verne frequently manages to destroy that impression of reality that he has also worked so hard to create. Fergusson's detailed inventory, by weight, of the cargo that his balloon will be carrying (5S, pp. 47–48) is mathematically perfect and technically complete to the last detail, yet by definition it omits the major variable, namely the numerous additions and losses that will occur throughout the journey. Fogg's constantly renewed lists of time spent and distance covered in his itinerary around the world are punctiliously precise, but it is excess of precision that prevents Fogg from seeing the apparently 'irrational' presence of the extra day. The positivist discourses quietly self-destruct within the pages of fiction, and this through their very failure to account fully for the realities that they nonetheless measure so precisely. Verne's words undo themselves, even while they appear to reflect a belief in the absoluteness of scientific language.

32 See 'The Positivist Perspective' in Evans, *Jules Verne Rediscovered*, pp. 37–57.

And so it is too with those inventories throughout the *Voyages extraordinaires*, in which disproportionate accuracy exposes the ultimate absurdity or meaninglessness of language. Such is the case with the description of equipment and rations that the travellers take with them in *Voyage au centre de la terre* (VCT, pp. 100–102), where the redundant nature of the details is highlighted, among other things, by the spurious use of a numbered list suggesting a hierarchy. This turns out not to be a hierarchy at all, but merely a sequence that has been assembled in a speciously meaningful order (like the alphabetical list of names in *Cinq semaines*) and whose elements are interchangeable. And by the inclusion of items such as firearms that the narrator himself admits are unnecessary to the expedition, the list further reinforces the point that it has ventured into irrelevant detail. If the firearms are to play no part in the travellers' adventure, then by definition they are also redundant in the narrative, except in so far as they tell us that this is a narrative of excess. Towards the end of the list, the narrator uses an expression that will turn up in a slightly different form elsewhere in the *Voyages extraordinaires* when he starts a sentence with: 'Pour *compléter* la *nomenclature exacte* de nos articles de voyage, je noterai...' (my italics)[33] ['To complete the exact list of our travel items, I shall note...']. The promise that the list is about to reach completion is immediately undone by its continuation for another two paragraphs, and Axel's insistence on the exactitude of his 'nomenclature' implicitly recognises that the goal of complete accuracy can be achieved only by the amassing of further details. Accumulation takes the place of significance; accuracy comes at the cost of relevance. As the list continues, its words become empty signifiers whose only role is to give an appearance of solidity and precision in a universe which can be continuously, perhaps endlessly atomised.

This impression of the sheer gratuitousness of detail occurs again and again in Verne, undercutting that belief in the value of accuracy on which the entire writing project is nonetheless premised. A spectacular example (among many) comes near the beginning of *Le Pays des fourrures*, where we are treated to an inventory of the different types of pelt, with numbers of each category, that are collected in 1833–34 by the Hudson Bay Fur Company (PF, p. 16). We might immediately be alerted to the randomness of the sample by the fact that the action of the novel itself is set in 1859–60, some 26 years after this snapshot of a season's exports. However,

---

33 Compare this to Aronnax's 'Je *termine* là cette *nomenclature* un peu sèche, mais très *exacte*...' (my italics) ['I shall conclude this somewhat dry, though completely accurate list...'] in the example given earlier, p. 196.

undeterred by the problem of relevance, the narrator lists sixteen different species, the numbers of each varying from 491 through to a dizzying 694,092. The parade of figures recalls the debunking of numerical precision by Rabelais, and suggests the potential absurdity of absolute measurements in a context in which their narrative significance has already been undermined. As for the actual terms in the list, the system of classification is almost immediately put into doubt when the second item, given as 'parchemins et jeunes castors' ['parchments and young beavers'], creates an odd dual category which partially replicates the beavers of the first line. Questions begin to arise. What is the basis of the taxonomy? Can there be an infallible, perfect system in such matters, as this list so clearly suggests? For, while presenting itself as absolute and unchangeable, the list reveals an arbitrariness of classification that belies its initial appearance – the more so when, among the animals with 'fur', we find that feathered creatures (swans) are also included. And, as the paragraph following the list reveals, the actual narrative significance that can be extracted from the facts and statistics that have preceded is simple, banal, brief, remaining in inverse proportion to the list itself. So the gloss that is provided by Verne's narrator comes as a deliberate let-down and an ironic truism: 'Une telle production devait assurer à la Compagnie de la baie d'Hudson des bénéfices très considérables' ['This rate of production would have guaranteed the Hudson Bay Company a very considerable profit']. True, he does go on to say that production has decreased dramatically, but this essential fact of the narrative hardly needed such a complex build-up for its enunciation. But then, it is the contrast between the list itself – so profuse in its detail and its certainty – and its woefully trivial narrative function that is the real point here. We have already seen that Verne is a master at extracting significance from negative information, but now we see an inversion of the technique: here, Verne demonstrates the insignificance of positive information, further undermining the assumptions on which realist narrative is based.

It is certainly the case, as critics such as Foucault and Buisine have stressed, that the discourses of science and positivism invade the Vernian text and appear as foreign bodies within the fiction. Lists, taxonomies and inventories such as the above may on occasions seem spectacularly recalcitrant to narrativisation. Yet part of the point of Verne's lists is to take the language of scientific precision to extremes which display it within the fiction, showing up its folly and its absurdity. In that respect, the 'recycling' of facts, figures and statistics in the body of the narrative becomes an ironic act in which science itself is shown to be one of the great fictions of modernity. Verne works by appearing to confront science and fiction and by revealing their ostensible incompatibilities, yet as fiction becomes invaded by science, science too is overwhelmed by the manifold fictions that lurk within it. The goal of absolute precision and accuracy is exposed as the ultimate fantasy (a point that, to their credit, some of Verne's scientist figures – Paganel and Ardan chief among them – recognise and exploit). To that extent, the borrowed discourses of science that we find throughout the *Voyages extraordinaires* are reframed and, albeit in a sometimes negative manner, assume their full significance within the context of an adventure narrative. By venturing onto the well-trodden terrain of scientific discourse, and by assembling its components in ironically self-destructive patterns, Verne manages to create a new type of fiction.

Old narratives, new itineraries

If by his uses of borrowed scientific and positivistic discourses Verne offers us rich insights into the question of writing itself, many novels in the *Voyages extraordinaires* also turn back and exploit their own fictional antecedents in similar ways. Science by no means has the monopoly as borrowed and recycled material in Verne's work. Since no narrative can exist in a vacuum, the writing of novels is also a journey into familiar fictional terrains and themes. It follows the beaten track and, perhaps, attempts to seek out novelty through this very retracing of the itineraries pursued by earlier writers. But, far from succumbing to the anxiety of influence, on many occasions Verne conspicuously and explicitly navigates in and around the landmarks of known literary works or established genres, in order to rework these from within. This happens in particular with the castaway novels, where the theme of the *robinsonnade* itself is thematised and displayed within the fiction, and with Verne's uses and adaptations of Poe (notably his continuation of *The Narrative of Arthur Gordon Pym* in *Le Sphinx des glaces*). Here, the writing of journeys becomes yet again a journey of writing, wherein a source text or author, or a group of texts, becomes the occasion for overt attentiveness to the processes of fiction itself. The procedure naturally raises questions about originality and novelty. Where a novel grafts itself onto an earlier fiction, or reworks a known stylistic or thematic seam as the basis of its plot, is originality possible? Does the tactic of echoing other works condemn an author to repetition and sameness? Or is it nonetheless possible to discover new horizons through a re-exploration of the old? Once again, we find ourselves at the very heart of the problems of writing that Verne so comprehensively exposes and explores in the *Voyages extraordinaires*. Let

206 Jules Verne: Journeys in Writing

us look more closely at this in two contexts: first, Verne's manipulation in several novels of the *robinsonnade* theme; and second, his reworking of Poe in *Le Sphinx des glaces*.

Many of the stories in the *Voyages extraordinaires* revolve around the castaway theme, and, as commentators have repeatedly pointed out, the image of the island is central in Verne's writing.[34] Pierre Macherey asserts that the destruction of the island at the end of *L'Ile mystérieuse* symbolises the destruction of the very notion of colonisation, and concludes that Verne's novel is written specifically to contest the mythical figure of Robinson that emerges from Defoe's story.[35] For Macherey, Verne's novel comprehensively demonstrates the impossibility of the Robinson myth, since the central paradigm of Robinson literature – that of a return to Edenic origins – is turned around from the outset by the fact that the group of people who find themselves on a remote island invest it with their imperialistic ideologies, education and life skills. It is true that the various *robinsonnade* stories in the *Voyages extraordinaires* subvert and contest the Robinson myth to differing degrees, but the common denominator is that they are all flamboyantly intertextual in their approach. Asserting their status as contributions to an identifiable type of fiction, they also pitch themselves against it. *Seconde patrie*, for example, sets out as a continuation of Wyss's *Swiss Family Robinson*, taking up the plot and the characters of that narrative twelve years after its conclusion.[36] Throughout Verne's novel, the literary origin of his own story is openly

34 On the question of the Vernian reprise of the Robinson theme, see Alain Buisine, 'Repères, marques, gisements: à propos de la robinsonnade vernienne', in François Raymond (ed.), *Jules Verne 2: L'Ecriture vernienne* (Paris: Minard, 1978), pp. 113–39. Buisine comments: 'La fiction vernienne ne va pas cesser de multiplier, déconstruction par l'excès, les références trop explicites, et même ostentatoires, au modèle. Ecriture qui affiche constamment qu'elle est réécriture pour mieux "désécrire".' (p. 130) ['In a gesture of excess designed to deconstruct, Vernian fiction never stops multiplying over-explicit and indeed ostentatious references to the model. Writing constantly underlines its status as re-writing, in order the better to "unwrite".']

35 'L'autre Robinson, celui de Defoe, apparaît entre toutes les lignes du livre de Jules Verne, accablé, contesté' (Macherey, *Pour une théorie de la production littéraire*, p. 225) ['That other Robinson, Defoe's, appears constantly between the lines of Jules Verne's book, where he is challenged and contested'].

36 In his preface, Verne typically emphasises the importance of his early reading and stresses that he is reworking a particular genre. Among other authors he cites Defoe, Wyss, Louis Desnoyers (author of *Aventures de Robert Robert*), James Fenimore Cooper, Mme Mollar de Beaulieu (*Le Robinson de douze ans*) and Mme de Mirval (*Le Robinson des sables du désert*). Wyss's novel, published in 1812, had been translated into French the following year by Mme de Montolieu, who herself wrote a sequel in 1824 (*Le Robinson suisse ou Journal d'un père de famille naufragé avec ses enfants*). A

referred to, and is used to motivate developments in the plot. The island that Wyss's and Verne's characters inhabit in this new novel is emphatically not depicted as a place that 'exists' independently of its literary representations. It is in every respect a fictional construct, displayed as such, and the references to Wyss's story are used to make this point clearer. What is also striking in this story, as in most of the other castaway novels in the *Voyages extraordinaires*, is that the characters themselves explicitly use the tradition of Robinson literature as a kind of 'map' or guidebook with which to confront the uncertainties of their situation (a technique that will, as we shall see, reappear in a different form in *Le Sphinx des glaces*). Their own reading of Robinson texts operates as a *mise en abyme* of the reading strategies we ourselves are engaged in. Texts in hand (or at least in memory), they interpret their situation and cut a path through the literature, by way of constructing their own narrative. What the reader and the characters do is an extension of the process that the author himself is engaged in as he writes the novel. At every level, Verne's narrative repeatedly turns into a negotiation with text itself. It is something of a tour de force to have been able to turn this genre of exploration into the exploration of a genre, and it illustrates once again how closely Verne's central themes mirror his own writing project.

Yet as Verne's castaway characters often discover – again reflecting a problem that is familiar to the author himself – text can be the difficulty, the thing that gets in the way. It dogs their footsteps, closes them to alternative possibilities, and condemns them to think of their situation in terms previously mapped out by other storytellers. However, Verne the author makes light of such a problem and exploits it in humorous ways. In *Deux ans de vacances*, a story about the shipwreck of a group of fifteen children, one of the characters, Service, models himself on Jack in Wyss's *Swiss Family Robinson*. Like Don Quixote or Emma Bovary (though in much less tragic mode than the latter) he tries to act out his life in terms of what has been imagined for him in fiction. In memory of the earlier story, he attempts to tame a wild ostrich to which he gives the borrowed name Brausewind, and throughout the adventure, he uses both Wyss's tale and Defoe's *Robinson Crusoe* to plan out his actions. Often this creates humorous counterpoint between reality and fiction, since the character's

---

new translation by P.-J. Stahl (pseudonym of Verne's editor Hetzel) and E. Muller appeared in 1864 in the *Magasin d'Education et de Récréation*. In a number of other *robinsonnade* novels, Verne's prefaces emphasise the importance of the tradition in which he is writing, and stress the way in which he hopes to make a personal contribution to it.

expectations, moulded by literature, invariably fail to match what happens in his life. A new fiction emerges, and it is a fiction about the failure of fiction. Service's wild ostrich refuses to be tamed, and unlike Jack's, it escapes. Similarly, Service is disappointed, as he contemplates the large number of birds on the island, to discover that there are no parrots as there are in *Robinson Crusoe*. Later, when the group of characters in the novel discover another castaway named Kate, Service suggests that as she has been found on a Friday, she should in honour of Defoe's story be called Vendredine. Kate, though, is having none of it, for she has a name already and quite understandably wants to keep it. This is a minor variation on a situation previously used in *L'Ecole des Robinsons*, where a native turns up on the island on a Wednesday, and it is suggested that he should be called Mercredi, until it is discovered that he too has a name. Thus does Jules Verne ironise upon the conventions of the *robinsonnade*, even as he tells a simple story of characters struggling against and with nature, carrying out their task as colonisers. He always stresses the fictionality, and more generally the literariness, of his own project. And, as we saw earlier, *L'Ecole des Robinsons* further interiorises this process by turning into a parody of Verne's own *L'Ile mystérieuse*,[37] itself a subversion of the Robinson theme. The journey into strange and remote places here becomes an explicit journey into text and an exploration of literary convention, at several significant removes from 'naïve' storytelling.

While Verne makes repeated and extensive use of castaway literature throughout the *Voyages extraordinaires*, there is one author from a somewhat different tradition who has an exceptional place in his writing: Edgar Allan Poe. Verne's lifelong admiration for Poe is well documented and well known, and needs little rehearsing here.[38] Present in Verne's early stories of the extraordinary and the fantastic ('Hans Pfaall' is significantly cited, for example, in the early story 'Un voyage en ballon'), Poe reappears

37 See above.
38 As early as 1941, Kenneth Allot wrote that 'Poe's influence was the most direct of any writer on Verne's work' (*Jules Verne*, p. 81). An excellent recent account of the importance of Poe in Jules Verne's writing is given by Daniel Compère in *Jules Verne, parcours d'une œuvre*, pp. 24–27. For Compère, there is no doubt that 'Edgar Poe constitue le *déclic* qui permet à Jules Verne de trouver son genre personnel' (p. 14) ['Edgar Poe provides the "click" which enables Jules Verne to find his own genre']. Verne's own account of his debt to Poe is fully documented in the long article he wrote for *Le Musée des Familles* in 1864 entitled 'Edgar Poe et ses œuvres'. The article is reprinted in Jules Verne, *Textes oubliés* (Paris: Union Générale d'Editions, Collection '10/18', 1979), pp. 11–53. A copy is also posted on the Jules Verne website at http://jv.gilead.org.il/almasty/aepoe .

at regular intervals throughout the *Voyages extraordinaires*. He is often explicitly used as a literary landmark in the various fictional journeys that Verne's characters undertake, as in the extensive incorporation of 'The Gold-Bug' into *La Jangada* when a cryptogram is being deciphered.[39] Other novels in the corpus draw variously on Poe: the ending of *Le Tour du monde en quatre-vingts jours* owes a considerable debt to 'Three Sundays in a Week', and *Le Château des Carpathes* is among other things heavily reminiscent of 'The Fall of the House of Usher'. However, the most extensive reworking of a Poe story by Verne occurs with the writing of *Le Sphinx des glaces* in 1897. The novel is without doubt the most complex and complete borrowing or re-use of another text in the whole of the *Voyages extraordinaires*.

Verne gives a lengthy account of his source text, *The Narrative of Arthur Gordon Pym*, on two occasions in his work. The first is in the article he writes on Poe for the *Musée des Familles* in 1864. Focusing on the end of Poe's story, he draws attention to the fact that it is an unfinished narrative, and asks: 'Qui le reprendra jamais? Un plus audacieux que moi et plus hardi à s'avancer dans le domaine des choses impossibles.'[40] ['Who will ever take it up again? Someone more audacious than myself, someone bolder at venturing into the domain of the impossible.'] The challenge to complete Poe's story, laid down in the 1864 article, will finally be taken up by Verne himself 33 years later in *Le Sphinx des glaces*, and this provides Verne with his second opportunity to discuss Poe's story at length. In Chapter 5 of *Le Sphinx des glaces*, bearing the specular title 'Le Roman d'Edgar Poe' ['The Novel by Edgar Poe'], Verne gives a long and detailed summary of Poe's text, emphasising that it takes us by degrees from a world that is perfectly real and verifiable into a world that is completely imaginary. The reflection on Poe has to be read as a formulation of Verne's own aims in the novel he is writing. This will become increasingly clear as his story unfolds, for it progressively and systematically blurs the boundaries between fiction and reality (though as we shall see, Verne achieves this effect in a way quite different from Poe). Quoting Baudelaire, whose translation he admires, Verne underlines the power of Poe's imagination. However, even Poe, he claims, was not quite up to the job of finishing this story, and fell back on an old excuse, namely, that the final chapters of the hero's manuscript went missing. Verne thereby suggests that his own task as a novelist is to fill that gap. In so doing, he specifi-

---

39 See above, p. 86.
40 'Edgar Poe et ses œuvres', *Textes oubliés*, p. 151.

cally sets himself up in competition with Poe, taking up the challenge on the point where he believed his predecessor had failed in his task.

If ever there were a revisiting of 'known' narrative territory with the intention of uncovering something new, this is it. Verne's journey as a novelist is precisely the same journey as the one that his characters are to undertake on the traces of a previous text. The journey of writing and the writing of a journey here cease to be mirror images of each other, and become one and the same thing. The characters, too, travel with text in hand, reading and interpreting it as their journey proceeds, with the result that their geographical progression is intimately and indissolubly bound up with an act of reading.

In his discussion of the Poe story, Verne openly draws attention to his own role as a novelist. But, having charged Poe with a rare failure of the imagination, Verne is in danger of being hoist with his own petard. How can he surpass the writer whom he admires above all others, especially since his declared intention is to do no more than emulate him? In the event Verne decides, stylistically at least, to follow a different course. Far from trying to make the reader *forget* that his is a fictional universe – a talent he particularly admires in Poe – he repeatedly draws attention to the fictional parameters of the work that we are reading. Poe's novel is used as a manual or guidebook, both in the narrator's own reflections and in his characters' conversations, around which the story is written. But since the Poe novel is a symbolic mirror of the story being written by Verne and negotiated by his reader, its own status as text and narrative is also highlighted. Questions about the intricacies of fiction and its relationship with reality figure constantly at the forefront of this account of a journey into the remote southern polar regions; but equally, questions about the relationship of fiction with other fictions are central. Verne's story, situated some twelve years after the action of Poe's, piggy-backs on that previous text, though interestingly Verne had asserted to his publisher that it would not be necessary for the reader to be familiar with it.[41] Verne's primary device is that of the sceptical narrator who is, at the outset, firmly convinced that he knows where the frontiers between fiction and reality lie, even if there happen to be geographical frontiers that he has yet to explore. However, as the story progresses, this narrator is

---

41 See Jean Richer, 'Deux lettres à Louis-Jules Hetzel', in *L'Herne: Jules Verne*, 25 (1974), pp. 71–74. Verne writes: 'J'ai pris pour point de départ un des plus étranges romans d'Edgar Poe, les *Aventures de Gordon Pym*, qu'il ne sera pas nécessaire d'avoir lu' (p. 73) ['I took as my starting point one of the strangest novels by Edgar Poe, *The Narrative of Arthur Gordon Pym*, which it will not be necessary to have read'].

confronted with the possibility that Poe's narrative may not have been a fiction after all, but a true account of a journey passed off as the work of one Edgar Allan Poe. The simple certainties that he had set out with are confounded. By the time he encounters characters who appear to be from the earlier narrative, his initial conviction has been shattered.

Now this is an old trick ('some people think this is only a story') but Jules Verne uses it to great effect and with great skill, partly because he applies the argument to two stories standing in a specular relationship to each other. And, by encouraging his own reader to reflect on the artifices of fiction, he enlists a greater – not a lesser – degree of belief in the events of his own story. He does this, too, by showing that there is argument and disagreement about how Poe's – and implicitly, by extension, his own – story should be 'read'. Text is a negotiation, not only with words, but with people. Initially there are conflicting views among Verne's characters about Poe's text. Captain Len Guy, with whom the narrator Jeorling is travelling, is from the outset certain that this is a genuine, 'non-fictional' account, written not by Poe himself but by a real traveller named Arthur Gordon Pym. Since Len Guy claims to be the brother of one of Poe's characters, he obviously has good reason for his convictions. Jeorling, on the other hand, at first dismisses this claim out of hand. However, as he gradually and increasingly has occasion to verify the accuracy of details from the so-called 'story' by Poe, the doubts set in and the boundary between fiction and reality is blurred. He now discovers 'novel frontiers' in two senses – both in his voyage into unknown regions of the globe, and his voyage into the unexpected truth of what appeared to be an imagined story. The journey that Verne's character undertakes is very much a journey of reading and of re-reading, as he returns repeatedly to the details of Poe's text and checks them against his own situation, calculating the progress of events in terms of the earlier narrative. When, finally, the characters in Verne's text discover Pym – killed at the time of the fictional ending of the previous story by the force of a magnetic glacier shaped something like a sphinx – their 'reading' and deciphering of Poe's text is complete, just as their journey reaches its final destination. The completion of the narrative of a journey coincides with the completion of the journey of a narrative. And, by the end, Verne is confident enough to lay down the challenge to others to follow with further sequels, and so perhaps ad infinitum: 'Arthur Pym,' he says in the final line of his novel, 'le héros si magnifiquement célébré par Edgar Poe, a montré la route... A d'autres de la reprendre, à d'autres d'aller arracher au Sphinx des Glaces les derniers secrets de cette mystérieuse Antarctide!' (SG, p. 443) ['Arthur Pym, the hero so magnificently celebrated by Edgar Poe, showed the way… It is now up to others to follow, to go forth and wrest from the ice sphinx the final secrets and mysteries of Antarctica!'] Fiction, it is implied, is itself the route to discovery of the unknown. True journeys are the ones that take place in the imagination and in the texts that we produce or travel through in our quest for discovery. Our physical peregrinations through the natural environment are also journeys in language and narrative, the constant retelling and reworking of prior narratives. That this revisiting of old terrains is a potentially never-ending process of repetitions and re-runs is a notion that has figured throughout Verne's work, and receives its most explicit formulation, as we saw earlier in this study, in the short story 'L'Eternel Adam'.[42]

As a sustained reflection on fiction and on writing, *Le Sphinx des glaces* is a fascinating experiment. Nor is it by any means atypical in the work of Verne, whose uses of fiction within fiction are abundantly in evidence throughout the *Voyages extraordinaires*. But Verne was particularly proud of this story, of which he wrote to Hetzel *fils*: 'J'ai profité de tout ce que Poe a laissé d'inachevé et du mystère qui enveloppe certains de ses personnages. Une idée très lumineuse m'est venue, c'est qu'un de mes héros qui croyait comme tout le monde que ce roman était une fiction se trouvera face à face avec une réalité. Inutile de vous dire que je suis allé *infiniment plus loin* que Poe.'[43] ['I have taken advantage of everything that Poe left unfinished, and exploited the mystery that surrounds certain of his characters. A brilliant idea came to me, namely, that one of my characters, who believed like everyone else that the novel was pure invention, would find himself confronted by its reality. I scarcely need say that I have taken things *much further* than Poe.'] It is clear that Verne believes he has amply met the challenge that he had first identified in 1864 and, specifically, that he has done so by the strategy of focusing on the textual status of that earlier narrative. While he 'borrows' his initial idea from Poe, and engages in a visible rewriting of the already written, he nonetheless manages to strike out beyond the original document and create something new. If all writing is rewriting, then the example of *Le Sphinx des glaces* demonstrates that the rewritten text is capable of profound originality. The novel must surely rank as one of the masterpieces of the *Voyages extraordinaires*, not only in terms of its composition and style, but also, and more importantly, because it both articulates and solves one of the central problems (the re-use of other texts) posed by Jules Verne's writing. It is interesting that, in the letter to Hetzel *fils* quoted above, Verne should

---

42 See above, pp. 46–48.
43 Richer, 'Deux lettres à Louis-Jules Hetzel', p. 73.

himself have phrased his achievement as a 'journey' ('je suis allé *infiniment plus loin* que Poe'). That the novel is a journey back over familiar textual terrains is explicit from the outset. Yet, while it retraces a previous journey and finally reaches precisely the same geographical destination, it succeeds in finding new territories of the imagination. Rewriting here has become a profoundly creative act, accomplished in the very traces of repetition and sameness.

Conclusion

At his death on 24 March 1905, Jules Verne had been a successful author for more than four decades. While the print-runs of his novels naturally waxed and waned – peaking with the sale of 108,000 copies of *Le Tour du monde en quatre-vingts jours* in the 1870s, though suffering something of a decline in the final decade of his life[1] – his commercial value was assured. But his obvious marketability was to increase exponentially in the course of the twentieth century. The *Voyages extraordinaires* would be exploited and adapted (notably in the early stages by Verne's own son Michel, who passed off his rewritten versions of the posthumous texts as 'genuine' Jules Verne novels), then transposed with huge success to other forms and media. With Georges Méliès's two short films *Voyage dans la lune* (1902) and *Voyage à travers l'impossible* (1904), and with Michel Verne's own later ventures into film-making,[2] the enduring tradition of cinematic adaptations of Verne's works was established. Today, Jules Verne is not only a household name, but is recognised as an essential icon of travel, exploration and scientific progress. His place in Western culture is attested among other things by the massive number of events and exhibitions that were organised in France and across the world in 2005 to celebrate the centenary of this enduringly popular author.[3]

However, such obvious appeal comes at a price. A hundred years down the line, Jules Verne is more than ever misrepresented, misread and misunderstood, especially in the popular imagination. Among the so-called 'chattering classes' today, the common image of Verne is of a futuristic author – a cliché which, as we saw earlier in this study, was

1 For a full list of print-runs and sales during Verne's lifetime, see Charles-Noël Martin, *Jules Verne, sa vie et son œuvre* (*Les Œuvres de Jules Verne*, 50; Lausanne: Rencontre, 1971), pp. 301–303, or the same author's *La Vie et l'œuvre de Jules Verne* (Paris: Michel de l'Ormeraie, 1978), pp. 280–81.

2 See Brian Taves, 'Hollywood's Jules Verne', in Taves and Michaluk (eds.), *The Jules Verne Encyclopedia*, pp. 205–48 (p. 206).

3 Central among these events was the Mondial Jules Verne held in Amiens in March 2005 under the auspices of the Centre International Jules Verne.

damagingly reinforced in 1994 with the publication of *Paris au XXe siècle*. Much of what is stated about Verne is based on second-hand information, on recycled and adapted versions of his stories, on inaccurate translations, or on extravagant myths that have become common currency. Even brilliant and respected critics can regularly be found to slip up in their knowledge,[4] and the sheer quantity of works in the corpus means that only the most specialised scholars are likely to have read the entire series of the *Voyages extraordinaires*. True, there are those who might say that an author so cavalier in his plundering of other people's writings deserved no better than to be travestied, reappropriated in alien contexts, misrepresented, and adapted for purposes he did not intend. Yet the case of Verne is a convincing reminder that an author's reputation can sometimes end up being dependent on matters almost entirely peripheral to the writings themselves. This all too easily leads to the belief that re-reading and reinterpretation are not necessary, and that beyond a certain point, an author need only be viewed through the refractions of his or her own cultural legacy. But the legacy can be misleading, or worse still, encourage the accumulation of clichés. Salvador Dali once memorably mimicked the sheer excess and absurdity that can surface in representations of Verne when he wrote mischievously:

> Chaque fois que quelqu'un meurt, c'est la faute de Jules Verne, responsable de l'envie des voyages interplanétaires, juste bons à des boy-scouts ou à des amateurs de pêche sous-marine. Si l'on dépensait à des recherches biologiques les sommes fabuleuses englouties pour ces conquêtes, plus personne ne mourrait sur notre planète. Aussi, je le répète, chaque fois que quelqu'un meurt c'est la faute à Jules Verne.[5]

> [Every time somebody dies, it is Jules Verne's fault. He is responsible for the desire for interplanetary voyages, good only for boy scouts or for underwater fishing enthusiasts. If the fabulous sums wasted on these conquests were spent on biological research, nobody on our planet would die any more. Therefore, I repeat, every time somebody dies, it is Jules Verne's fault.]

The so-called creator of science fiction and the dreamer of interplanetary voyages is, in Dali's supremely ironic take, held responsible for all the negative developments in modern civilisation simply because he is uncritically supposed to have 'foreseen' them. By making us feel uncomfortable

---

4 As was the case with the incomparable Pierre Macherey, who misspelled the name of Lidenbrock as 'Lindenbrock' throughout his chapter on Verne in *Pour une théorie de la production littéraire*.

5 See *Dali par Dali* (Paris: Draeger, 1970), p. 136.

about the sort of discourses that circulate in a form only marginally less absurd than this, Dali too is reminding us that we should take nothing for granted, and most especially that we should not rely on second-hand information.

The goal of this study has in the first instance been to contest and to combat the legacy of misconceptions and clichés about Jules Verne, and to do so by insisting above all else on the primacy of text in the *Voyages extraordinaires*. By this, two things are meant: first and most obviously, that any serious reading of Jules Verne must go back to the original corpus of writings, in the original French language, thus returning him to his roots as a nineteenth-century French novelist; and second, that Verne's own focus on text and on textuality is such a dominant feature of his writing that its role needs to be continuously re-emphasised. As an author, Verne is supremely preoccupied with his own verbal and written medium, which is represented, dramatised, thematised and problematised throughout his work. While cultural appropriations of Jules Verne in other contexts are an important and crucial subject of study in their own right, I have purposefully omitted these from my purview here, highlighting the processes of writing and the literary techniques that are such important features of the *Voyages extraordinaires*. By placing Verne in the context of nineteenth-century realism, alongside other authors of the period struggling with similar themes, it may be that we are in a better position to measure his achievement as a novelist. For if we are to understand Verne as a phenomenon, surely we must first understand him as an author.

As this study has attempted to show, Jules Verne's writing is deeply expressive of contemporary issues and problems, and, by addressing the question of their transposition into fiction, it constantly poses the question of what the novel is, or might be, or could become. Verne's work challenges assumptions about the relationship between science and literature, and echoes the great colonialist and imperialist themes of the nineteenth century through the very style that is adopted. Notions of expansion, conquest and scientific progress are not merely subjects and themes in Verne's novels: they are re-enacted in the writing itself, which is by definition expansive and 'territorial' in its textual pervasiveness. That Verne's world is intensely and abundantly textual, and needs to be read as such, is evident from his own emphasis on texts of all kinds, and on their circulation. Verne stresses the absolute centrality of texts in our representation of the world, and he constantly depicts heroes whose adventures and explorations start with a comprehensive programme of reading, then end up as a newly written text. But, drawing attention to text as commodity and product, Verne also reveals the interdependency of texts, and he tackles the anxiety of influence head-on by revealing rather than concealing his sources. His own works display their debt to the theatre, refer widely to their own literary origins, and stress their artificiality and conventionality as written artefacts in a world that is always textually constructed. Supremely self-conscious, Verne is concerned with the issue of writing itself, addressing through his novels one of the great questions of his own century: how is it possible, when so much has already been written, to produce something new? Part of his originality as an author is to have made this very question one of the central themes of his work.

And, as we have also seen, the preoccupation with text that is such a continuous feature of Verne's work is bound up in myriad and complex ways with the whole question of travel. Barthes famously derided Verne as an armchair traveller, whose books merely appeared to open up vast vistas of travel and exploration while ultimately promoting the comforts and enclosed spaces of the bourgeois domain,[6] but his criticisms seem to have missed the essential point. What Verne proclaims throughout the *Voyages extraordinaires*, indeed throughout his writing, is that travel *is* text, that text *is* travel. Writing is a journey in much more than a simple metaphorical sense (though it is that as well). No journey is possible, either in the imagination or in the natural spaces of remote territories, without some form of textual negotiation. The world is a book that must be read, deciphered, rewritten. It is already text, well before the traveller-explorer produces his own written account, for it is through text that we are able to understand and make sense of the world. Nature must be verbalised and articulated if it is to have any 'meaning' at all, and the conquest of new territories is as much about their writing and recording as about the physical act of being there. Travellers in Verne use written documents as their landmarks, decoding and mapping out unfamiliar territories through the books that are available to them. From *Cinq semaines en ballon* onwards, we find heroes who navigate not only *with* texts, but *through* texts, and who see the production of new texts as a central component of their travels. Text is thus the fundamental precondition of all these fictional journeys. Like Livingstone, Burton, Speke and other African explorers with whose accounts he is familiar, Fergusson sets out from the eastern seabord of the continent and makes his way westwards. Yet, as any real or would-be balloonist knows, a journey into the prevailing headwinds would have been doomed to impossibility from the outset. Fergusson's expedition is in this sense an extravagant fiction, built out of

6 See Barthes's chapter in *Mythologies*, 'Nautilus et bateau ivre'.

text alone. But the author himself, through his specular relationship with Fergusson and his other scientist-explorers, does precisely the same thing that they do. He explores text, works his way through it, covers known textual terrain and rewrites it in order to follow an itinerary through to a new place and break new ground. Narrative, as the example of *Le Sphinx des glaces* demonstrates so well, is both about the exploration of previous narrative, and the plotting of new 'journeys' in terms of an earlier one. Physical space and narrative momentum are conceived along precisely the same lines, and follow the same model.

The evidence of novels such as *Le Sphinx des glaces* shows that Verne is by no means in decline in the final decade of his life. While he may be best remembered for the series of novels written between 1863 (*Cinq semaines en ballon*) and 1875 (*L'Ile mystérieuse*), a number of later works develop and extend themes which are deeply important in his writing and, like *Le Sphinx des glaces*, show him engaging with some of the most fundamental literary questions. Such writings not only develop the complex relationship between literature and travel, investigating the possibilities and paradoxes of the theme, they also link their investigations to a sustained reflection on narrative itself. The sheer energy and inventiveness with which Verne does this, and with which he sustains his momentum over the four decades during which he writes the *Voyages extraordinaires*, is an astonishing achievement. Verne's claim to be treated as a properly literary author must surely be beyond dispute.

Yet for all that, what are we to make of the niggling scepticism about Verne's literary status that has persisted from his own lifetime through to the present day? What of the overall literary quality of the *Voyages extraordinaires*? While many of the novels in the corpus stand out as masterpieces in their own right – *Voyage au centre de la terre* and *L'Ile mystérieuse* as explorations of some of those myths that bind humankind and nature, *Vingt mille lieues* as an intensely evocative hymn to nature, *Le Château des Carpathes* as a tragic reflection on death and loss – it is true that there are also throughout the corpus lapses of taste and of style, moments of excess or of facileness, and instances of poor writing. But, as with Balzac or any other writer – even Proust – who produces a large amount of material, variability of result is an occupational hazard. It would be foolish to claim for Verne some kind of consistency or perfection of style throughout the *Voyages extraordinaires*, and it is beyond all doubt that there are in the pages of his novels many instances of formulaic writing, weak characterisation, repetition, hasty and careless grammar, even lazy and facile plot construction. It would be surprising, however, were this not the case, for it is in the very nature of his writing project that it had to contend with its own imperfections, and indeed to expose them as part of the writing process. Expansion and proliferation are, by definition, rampant and untidy processes. Yet Verne is also supremely conscious that writing must distance itself ironically from its own failures, and his patchworks of different discourses alert us to the sense that text is much more than the sum of its component parts. Unrelentingly modern, Verne shows us the fragmentedness of text, and, for all his ambition to totalise knowledge in the *Voyages extraordinaires*, he forces us to reflect on its unfinished quality. If he provides us with a living example of the occasional excesses and defects of realism when it is pushed to its absolute extreme, or of scientism that becomes bogged down in its very efforts at precision, or of a process of documentation that ends up invading the text, then this is also a consequence of the experiment that he conducts as a writer, and it must be seen as part of his originality. As a novelist, Verne faces head-on the issues of his own century, living out their contradictions and tensions through the pages of his work. To remove him from that context would be to fail to appreciate the extent to which he takes up contemporary issues, articulates and expresses them, and explores their complexities. To look at him in that context, on the other hand, is not to diminish him, still less to overlook his broader cultural importance, but to understand more fully the vital contribution that he made.

Chronology of the Life of Jules Verne

Titles are listed for the year of publication in volume form unless otherwise stated. Year of composition is mentioned in cases where there is significant discrepancy.

1827 27 February: marriage of Pierre Verne and Sophie Allotte de la Fuÿe
1828 8 February: birth of Jules Verne
1829 Birth of Verne's brother Paul
1837 Birth of Verne's sister Anna
1839 Birth of Verne's sister Mathilde. During the summer, Verne attempts one morning to board the *Coralie* sailing for India, but is overtaken by his father at Paimboeuf and returned to Nantes
1840 Verne attends the lycée de Nantes
1842 Birth of Verne's sister Marie
1846 Verne passes his baccalauréat
1847 In Paris, Verne successfully completes his first year of law studies
      Jédédias Jamet, unfinished novel
1848 Birth of Albert Robida (d. 1926), author of *Le Vingtième Siècle* (1883)
1849 Verne's first novel, *Un prêtre en 1839*, is abandoned prior to completion. Verne becomes friends with Dumas *fils*
1850 Performances of Verne's *La Conspiration des poudres* (a five-act tragedy in verse, unpublished) and *Les Pailles rompues* at the Théâtre historique. Also writes *Un drame sous la régence*, and *Abd'allah* (a two-act vaudeville comedy, unpublished)
1851 'Les Premiers Navires de la marine mexicaine'
      'Un voyage en ballon'
      Verne begins *Léonard de Vinci* (retitled *Monna Lisa* in 1855)
1852 *De Charybde en Scylla* (unpublished)
      Les Châteaux en Californie
      'Martin Paz'
      Pierre-Jean

Verne becomes secretary of the Théâtre lyrique (until the death of its owner Seveste in 1854), and lives at 8, boulevard Bonne-Nouvelle with Aristide Hignard

1853 Performances of the opérette *Colin-Maillard* written in collaboration with Michel Carré, with music by Hignard, and of *Un fils adoptif*

1854 *Maître Zacharius*

1855 *Le Mariage de M. Anselme des Tilleuls*
Un hivernage dans les glaces
6 June: first of 24 performances of *Les Compagnons de la Marjolaine* at the Théâtre lyrique
Verne moves to 18, boulevard Poissonnière, Paris
First successful extraction of aluminium

1856 Verne meets Honorine Deviane, whom he marries on 10 January 1857
Monsieur de Chimpanzé, performed in February 1858

1857 10 January: marriage of Jules and Honorine
Verne takes a position at the Bourse as a stockbroker
The first Otis elevator ascends in New York

1858 Launching of the *Great Eastern*

1859 25 July: Verne and Hignard leave Nantes and journey to England and Scotland
Voyage à rebours en Angleterre et en Ecosse (published 1989)
Le Siège de Rome
Darwin publishes *The Origin of Species* (first French translation published in 1862)

1860 Between 1860 and 1861, Verne meets Nadar at the Cercle de la Presse scientifique

1861 *San Carlos*
Onze Jours de siège (with Charles Wallut)
Verne sails to Scandinavia with Hignard
3 August: birth of Verne's son Michel

1862 *Le Comte de Chanteleine. Episode de la Révolution*
23 October: Verne signs the first of his six contracts with Hetzel
First underground railway opens in London

1863 *Cinq semaines en ballon*
Paris au XXe siècle (published 1994)
4 October: Nadar's balloon, *Le Géant*, makes its first flight from the Champ-de-Mars. 18 October: Second flight of *Le Géant*, resulting in an accident on landing in Hanover

1864 20 March: First issue of Hetzel's *Magasin d'Education et de*

Récréation: Encyclopédie de l'enfance et de la jeunesse, including the first section of *Voyages et aventures du capitaine Hatteras*. Verne's 'Edgar Poe et ses œuvres' appears in the *Musée des Familles*
Voyage au centre de la terre

1865   'Le Humbug' (written 1864–65, published 1910), *Les Forceurs de blocus, De la terre à la lune, Les Enfants du capitaine Grant* (1865–67)
The Vernes spend increasing periods of the year at Le Crotoy

1866   *Voyages et aventures du capitaine Hatteras* (written 1863–64)
Verne begins work for Hetzel on the *Géographie illustrée de la France*
Verne buys first sailing craft, the *Saint-Michel*, in Crotoy
Laying of the first transatlantic cable with the *Great Eastern*

1867   18 March: Verne sets out with his brother Paul from Liverpool to New York on the *Great Eastern*, arriving on 9 April
The Great Exhibition takes place in Paris
Marx publishes the first volume of *Das Kapital*

1869   *Autour de la lune*
Opening of the Suez Canal

1870   *Vingt mille lieues sous les mers* (written 1865–69)
May–June: a smallpox epidemic kills Honorine's brother and sister-in-law. Verne sails the *Saint-Michel* to Paris, where he remains for a week moored at the Pont des Arts
July: the Franco-Prussian War is declared
9 August: Verne receives the *Légion d'honneur*
2 September: defeat of Sedan
The siege of Paris lasts from September through to the end of January

1871   *Une ville flottante* (1867–69)
28 March: the Commune is proclaimed in Paris
21 May: peace treaty signed
3 November: death of Verne's father, Pierre

1872   *Une fantaisie du docteur Ox*
Aventures de trois Russes et de trois Anglais
28 June: Verne received as a member of the Amiens Academy

1873   *Le Pays des fourrures*
Le Tour du monde en quatre-vingts jours (written 1871–72)

1874   'Un drame dans les airs' (new version of 'Un voyage en ballon')
The play of *Le Tour du monde en quatre-vingts jours* is performed for the first time at the Theâtre de la Porte-Saint-Martin

1875   *Le Chancellor*
      L'Ile mystérieuse (written 1872–74; an earlier version entitled
      L'Oncle Robinson had been written between 1865 and 1871)
      Une ville idéale
      Constitution of the Third Republic
1876   Invention of the telephone by Bell
      Michel Strogoff
      'Un drame au Mexique' (new version of 'Les Premiers Navires de
      la marine mexicaine')
      Verne has the *Saint-Michel II* built
      Verne meets Aristide Briand
1877   Invention of the phonograph by Cros and Edison
      Hector Servadac
      Les Indes noires
      March: first masked ball at the Vernes' house in Amiens
      Verne buys a new yacht (two masts and steam), called the *Saint-
      Joseph*, which he rebaptises the *Saint-Michel III*
1878   *Un capitaine de quinze ans*
      4 February: Michel Verne, on his father's orders, embarks at
      Bordeaux on a steamer for India
1879   *Les Révoltés de la Bounty*
      Les Cinq Cents Millions de la Begum
      Les Tribulations d'un Chinois en Chine
      October: Michel returns from his travels
1880   *La Maison à vapeur*
      Summer cruise on the *Saint-Michel III* to Norway, Scotland and
      Ireland with Hetzel and Raoul Duval
1881   *Exposition internationale de l'électricité* held in Paris
      La Jangada
1882   *L'Ecole des Robinsons*
      Le Rayon vert
1883   *Kéraban-le-têtu*
      Albert Robida, *Le Vingtième Siècle*
1884   *L'Etoile du sud*
      L'Archipel en feu
      13 May–18 July: Mediterranean cruise in the *Saint-Michel III*
      7 June: Verne has a private audience with Pope Leo XIII
      Michel Verne marries Jeanne Reboul
1885   *L'Epave du Cynthia* (written 1880–84)
      Mathias Sandorf (written 1882–84)
      Frritt-Flacc (written 1883)

8 March: second masked ball at the Vernes' house in Amiens

1886 *Robur-le-conquérant*
      Un billet de loterie
      15 February: Verne sells the *Saint-Michel III*
      9 March: Verne shot in the foot by his nephew Gaston
      17 March: death of Hetzel

1887 *Nord contre sud*
      Le Chemin de la France
      Gil Braltar
      15 February: death of Verne's mother, Sophie

1888 *Deux ans de vacances*
      Un Express de l'avenir
      13 May: Verne is elected on a Republican ticket to the Conseil
      Municipal in Amiens

1889 *Famille-sans-nom*
      Sans dessus dessous
      'La Journée d'un journaliste américain en 2889'
      Construction of the Eiffel Tower

1890 *César Cascabel*

1891 *Aventures de la famille Raton* (written 1886), *Mistress Branican*

1892 *Le Château des Carpathes* (written 1888), *Claudius Bombarnac*

1893 *P'tit-bonhomme*
      M. Ré-Dièze et Mlle Mi-Bémol

1894 *Les Mirifiques Aventures de maître Antifer*

1895 *L'Ile à hélice*
      Verne joins the Board of Directors of the Caisse d'épargne
      d'Amiens

1896 *Clovis Dardentor*
      Face au drapeau
      The engineer Turpin, seeing a portrait of himself in the mad
      scientist of *Face au drapeau*, sues Verne for libel

1897 *Le Sphinx des glaces*
      27 August: death of Verne's brother, Paul

1898 *Le Superbe Orénoque* (written 1893–94)

1899 *Le Testament d'un excentrique* (written 1896–97)

1900 *Seconde patrie* (written 1894)

1901 *Les Histoires de Jean-Marie Cabidoulin* (written 1898)
      Le Village aérien

1902 *Les Frères Kip* (written 1897)

1903 *Bourses de voyage*

1904 *Un drame en Livonie* (written 1894-1902)

Maître du monde (written 1894-1903)

1905   *L'Invasion de la mer* (written 1886-1905)
       Le Phare du bout du monde (written 1901)
       24 March: death of Jules Verne

1906   *Le Volcan d'or* (written 1899)

1907   *L'Agence Thompson et Co.* (written 1891–92)

1908   *La Chasse au météore* (written 1901)
       Le Pilote du Danube (written 1901, republished in 1988 as *Le Beau Danube jaune*)

1909   *Les Naufragés du Jonathan* (written 1897–98, republished in 1987 as *En Magellanie*)

1910   'L'Eternel Adam' (first version probably mid-1870s)
       Le Secret de Wilhelm Storitz (written 1901–1905, republished in the original version 1985)
       29 January: death of Verne's widow, Honorine

1914   *L'Etonnante Aventure de la mission Barsac* (written 1902–1905)

Bibliography

Reference edition for the *Voyages extraordinaires*

Les Œuvres de Jules Verne, 50 vols. (Lausanne: Rencontre, 1966–71):

1   *Cinq semaines en ballon*
2   *Voyage au centre de la terre*
3   *De la terre à la lune. Autour de la lune*
4   *Voyages et aventures du capitaine Hatteras*
5   *Vingt mille lieues sous les mers* (I)
6   *Vingt mille lieues sous les mers* (II). *Une ville flottante*
7   *Les Enfants du capitaine Grant* (I)
8   *Les Enfants du capitaine Grant* (II)
9   *L'Ile mystérieuse* (I)
10 *L'Ile mystérieuse* (II)
11 *Le Tour du monde en quatre-vingts jours*
12 *Le Docteur Ox. Les Forceurs de blocus*
13 *Michel Strogoff*
14 *Hector Servadac*
15 *Les Cinq Cents Millions de la Begum. Les Tribulations d'un Chinois en Chine*
16 *Robur-le-conquérant. Maître du monde*
17 *Les Indes Noires. Le Rayon vert*
18 *Nord contre sud*
19 *Le Pays des fourrures*
20 *Un capitaine de quinze ans*
21 *La Jangada*
22 *Kéraban-le-têtu*
23 *Mathias Sandorf* (I)
24 *Mathias Sandorf* (II)
25 *Le Secret de Wilhelm Storitz. Hier et demain*
26 *L'Ecole des Robinsons*
27 *Deux ans de vacances*
28 *Le Chancellor. Martin Paz. Un billet de loterie*
29 *La Maison à vapeur*
30 *César Cascabel*
31 *L'Archipel en feu. Sans dessus dessous*
32 *Mistress Branican*

33 *Le Sphinx des glaces. Edgar Poe et ses œuvres*
34 *Aventures de trois Russes et de trois Anglais. L'Invasion de la mer*
35 *Les Naufragés du Jonathan*
36 *Le Château des Carpathes. Le Volcan d'or*
37 *Claudius Bombarnac. Le Pilote du Danube*
38 *L'Etoile du sud. L'Epave du Cynthia*
39 *L'Agence Thompson and Co. Frritt-Flacc. Gil Braltar. Dix Heures en chasse.
    Les Révoltés de la Bounty*
40 *Clovis Dardentor. Les Frères Kip*
41 *P'tit-Bonhomme. Les Histoires de Jean-Marie Cabidoulin*
42 *Seconde patrie. Un drame en Livonie*
43 *Bourses de voyage. La Chasse au météore*
44 *Le Testament d'un excentrique. Un drame au Mexique*
45 *Mirifiques aventures de maître Antifer. Le Phare du bout du monde*
46 *L'Ile à hélice. Le Village aérien*
47 *Face au drapeau. Le Superbe Orénoque*
48 *Le Chemin de France. Famille-sans-nom*
49 *L'Etonnante Aventure de la mission Barsac. Le Comte de Chanteleine*
50 Charles-Noël Martin, *Jules Verne, sa vie et son œuvre*

Critical editions, re-edited manuscripts

Soriano, Marc, *Portrait de l'artiste jeune, suivi des quatre premiers textes publiés de Jules Verne* (Paris: Gallimard, 1978)

Verne, Jules, *Contes et nouvelles de Jules Verne*, introduction de Volker Dehs, postface d'Olivier Dumas (Rennes: Editions Ouest-France; Paris: Le Grand Livre du Mois, 2000)

—— *En Magellanie*, préface et notes d'Olivier Dumas (Paris: Gallimard, 1999 [1987])

—— *Le Beau Danube jaune*, préface et notes d'Olivier Dumas (Paris: L'Archipel, 2000)

—— *L'Oncle Robinson*, édition établie par Christian Robin (Paris: Le Cherche Midi, 1991)

—— *Le Secret de Wilhelm Storitz*, version d'origine présentée et annotée par Olivier Dumas (Paris: Folio, 1999 [1985])

—— *Le Volcan d'or*, version d'origine présentée et annotée par Olivier Dumas (Paris: Folio, 1999 [1989])

—— *Paris au XXe siècle*, édition établie par Piero Gondolo della Riva (Paris: Le Cherche Midi, 1994)

—— *Poésies inédites*, manuscrit inédit appartenant à la ville de Nantes, édition établie par Christian Robin (Paris: Le Cherche Midi, 1989)

—— *San Carlos, et autres récits inédits*, édition établie par Jacques Davy, Régis Miannay, Christian Robin, Claudine Sainlot (Paris: Le Cherche Midi, 1993)

—— *Textes oubliés* (Paris: Union Générale d'Editions, Collection '10/18', 1979)

—— *Un prêtre en 1839*, édition établie par Christian Robin (Paris: Le Cherche Midi, 1992)

—— *Voyage à reculons en Angleterre et en Ecosse*, édition établie par Christian Robin (Paris: Le Cherche Midi, 1989)

Critical editions in translation

Verne, Jules, *Around the World in Eighty Days*, translated by William Butcher (Oxford: Oxford University Press, World's Classics, 1995)

—— *Around the World in Eighty Days* and *Five Weeks in a Balloon*, introduction and notes by Roger Cardinal (Ware: Wordsworth Editions, Wordsworth Classics, 2002)

—— *Invasion of the Sea*, translated by Edward Baxter, introduction and notes by Arthur B. Evans (Middletown, CT: Wesleyan University Press, 2001)

—— *Journey to the Centre of the Earth*, translated by William Butcher (Oxford: Oxford University Press, World's Classics, 1992)

—— *Paris in the Twentieth Century*, translated by Richard Howard, with an introduction by Eugen Weber (New York: Random House, 1996)

—— *The Adventures of Captain Hatteras*, translated by William Butcher (Oxford: Oxford University Press, World's Classics, 2005)

—— *The Begum's Millions*, translated by Stanford Luce, edited by Arthur B. Evans, introduction and notes by Peter Schulman (Middletown, CT: Wesleyan University Press, 2005)

—— *The Lighthouse at the End of the World*, translated and edited by William Butcher (Lincoln: University of Nebraska Press, 2005)

—— *The Mighty Orinoco*, translated by Stanford Luce, edited by Arthur B. Evans, introduction and notes by Walter James Miller (Middletown, CT: Wesleyan University Press, 2002)

—— *The Mysterious Island*, translated by Sidney Kravitz, edited by Arthur B. Evans, introduction and notes by William Butcher (Middletown, CT: Wesleyan University Press, 2001)

—— *The Underground City*, translated by Sarah Crozier with a foreword by Ian Thompson (Edinburgh: Luath Press, 2005)

—— *Twenty Thousand Leagues Under the Seas*, translated and annotated by Walter James Miller and Frederick Paul Walter (Annapolis: Naval Institute Press, 1991)

—— *Twenty Thousand Leagues Under the Seas*, translated by William Butcher (Oxford: Oxford University Press, World's Classics, 1998)

Correspondence

Parménie, A., 'Huit lettres de Jules Verne à son éditeur P.J. Hetzel', *Arts et Lettres*, 15 (1949) (special issue on Jules Verne), pp. 102–107

Dumas, Olivier, Piero Gondolo della Riva and Volker Dehs (eds.), *Correspondance inédite de Jules Verne et de Pierre-Jules Hetzel (1863–1886)*, vol. I (1863–1874), vol. II (1875–1878), vol. III (1879–1886) (Geneva: Slatkine, 1999, 2001 and 2002)

Gondolo della Riva, Piero, 'Jules Verne: Une correspondance inédite', *Europe*, 613 (1980), 103-51

Verne, Jules, 'La Correspondance familiale de Jules Verne', in Olivier Dumas, *Jules Verne* (Lyon: La Manufacture, 1988), pp. 235–493

—— 'Trente-six lettres inédites', *Bulletin de la Société Jules Verne*, nouvelle série, 65–66 (1983), pp. 4–50

—— 'Vingt-deux lettres de Jules Verne à son frère Paul', *Bulletin de la Société Jules Verne*, nouvelle série, 69 (1984), pp. 3–25

—— Letter to Nadar, 22 August 1903, Letter to Alexandre Dumas fils (2 September 89?), *L'Arc*, 29 (1966), Documents, pp. 83–85

—— 'Sept lettres à sa famille et à divers correspondants: 1851 à 1895', *L'Herne: Jules Verne*, 25 (1974), pp. 63–70

—— 'Deux lettres à Louis-Jules Hetzel', *L'Herne: Jules Verne*, 25 (1974), pp. 71–74

—— 'Lettres à Nadar', *L'Herne: Jules Verne*, 25 (1974), pp. 75–80

—— 'A propos de Turpin (lettre de Verne à son frère Paul)', *L'Herne: Jules Verne*, 25 (1974), pp. 81–82

Theatre (excluding adaptations of the *Voyages extraordinaires*)

Carré, Michel and Jules Verne, *Le Colin-Maillard* (Paris: Michel Lévy, 1853), reprinted in *Bulletin de la Société Jules Verne*, 120 (1996), pp. 18–45

—— *L'Auberge des Ardennes* (Paris: Michel Lévy, 1860)

—— *Les Compagnons de la Marjolaine* (Paris: Michel Lévy, 1855)

—— *Monna Lisa* suivi de *Souvenirs d'enfance et de jeunesse* (Paris: L'Herne, 1995)

Verne, Jules, *Les Châteaux en Californie* (1852), in Marc Soriano, *Portrait de l'artiste jeune, suivi des quatre premiers textes publiés de Jules Verne* (Paris: Gallimard, 1978), pp. 101–39

—— *Les Pailles rompues* (Paris: Beck, 1850), reprinted in *Revue Jules Verne*, 11 (2001), pp. 31–94

—— *Un fils adoptif* (1853), published in *Bulletin de la Société Jules Verne*, 140 (2002)

—— *Un neveu d'Amérique, ou les deux Frontignac* (Paris: J. Claye, 1873)

—— *Voyage à travers l'impossible*, ed. François Raymond and Robert Pourvoyeur (Paris: J.-J. Pauvert, 1981). *Journey Through the Impossible*, translated by Edward Baxter, introduction by Jean-Michel Margot (Amherst: Prometheus Books, 2003)

Verne, Jules and Charles Wallut, *Onze jours de siège* (Paris: Michel Lévy, 1861)

Interviews, witness accounts

Belloc,Marie A., 'Jules Verne at Home', *Strand Magazine* (February 1895), online at http://www.gilead.org.il/belloc

Compère, Daniel and Jean-Michel Margot (eds.), *Entretiens avec Jules Verne 1873–1905* (Geneva: Slatkine, 1998)

Dehs, Volker, 'Une interview ignorée de Jules Verne', forthcoming in *Australian Journal of French Studies*, 42.3 (2005)

Jones, Gordon, 'Jules Verne at Home', *Temple Bar*, 129 (June 1904), pp. 664–71, online at http://jv.gilead.org.il/evans/Gordon_Jones_interview_of_JV.html

Roussel, Raymond, *Comment j'ai écrit certains de mes livres* (Paris: Pauvert, 1963)

Sherard, R. H., 'Jules Verne at Home: His Own Account of his Life and Work', *McClure's Magazine* (January 1894), online at http://jv.gilead.org.il/sherard. html

—— 'Jules Verne Revisited', *T.P.'s Weekly* (9 October 1903), online at http:// jv.gilead.org.il/sherard2.html

Critical and biographical works

Allott, Kenneth, *Jules Verne* (London: The Cresset Press; New York: Macmillan, 1941)

Allotte de la Fuÿe, Marguerite, *Jules Verne, sa vie, son œuvre* (Paris: Hachette, 1953 [1928])

Avrane, Patrick, *Un divan pour Phileas Fogg* (Paris: Aubier, 1988)

—— *Jules Verne* (Paris: Stock, 1997)

Barnes, Julian, 'Back to the Future' (review of *Paris in the Twentieth Century*), *The New York Times* (26 January 1997), p. 4

Barthes, Roland, 'Nautilus et bateau ivre', in *Mythologies* (Paris: Seuil, 1957), pp. 90–92

—— 'Par où commencer?', *Poétique*, 1 (1970), pp. 3–9

Becker, Beril, *Jules Verne* (New York: Putnam, 1966)

Borgeaud, Georges, 'Jules Verne et ses illustrateurs', *L'Arc*, 29 (1966), pp. 46–48

Brion, Marcel, 'Le Voyage initiatique', *L'Arc*, 29 (1966), pp. 26–32

Buisine, Alain, 'Un cas limite de la description: l'énumération. L'exemple de *Vingt mille lieues sous les mers*', in *La Description: Nodier, Sue, Flaubert, Hugo, Verne, Zola, Alexis, Fénéon*, textes réunis par Philippe Bonnefis et Pierre Reboul (Lille: Presses Universitaires de Lille, 1981), pp. 81–102

Butcher, William, *Verne's Journey to the Centre of the Self: Space and Time in the 'Voyages extraordinaires'* (New York: St Martin's Press, 1990)

——'Long Lost Manuscript: The True Antecedents of Professor Lidenbrock, his Nephew Axel and their Glorious Adventure Underground', *The Modern Language Review*, 93 (1998), pp. 961–71

Butor, Michel, 'Le Point suprême et l'âge d'or à travers quelques œuvres de Jules Verne', in *Répertoire I* (Paris: Minuit, 1960 [1949]), pp. 130–62

—— 'Lectures de l'enfance', *L'Arc*, 29 (1966), pp. 43–45

Carrouges, Marcel, 'Le Mythe de Vulcain chez Jules Verne', *Arts et Lettres*, 15 (1949), pp. 32–58

Chelebourg, Christian, *Jules Verne: L'Œil et le ventre, une poétique du sujet* (Paris: Minard, 1999)

Chesneaux, Jean, *Une lecture politique de Jules Verne* (Paris: Maspero, 1982 [1971])

—— *Jules Verne, un regard sur le monde* (Paris: Bayard, 2001)

Compère, Daniel, *Approche de l'île chez Jules Verne* (Paris: Minard, 1977)

—— *Un voyage imaginaire de Jules Verne: Voyage au centre de la terre* (Paris: Minard, 1977)

—— *Jules Verne écrivain* (Geneva: Droz, 1991)

—— *Jules Verne, parcours d'une œuvre* (Amiens: Encrage, 1996)

—— 'Jules Verne and the Limitations of Literature', in Smyth (ed.), *Jules Verne: Narratives of Modernity*, pp. 40–45

Costello, Peter, *Jules Verne: Inventor of Science Fiction* (London: Hodder and Stoughton, 1978)

Crosland, Maurice, 'Popular Science and the Arts: Challenges to Cultural Authority in France under the Second Empire', *British Journal of the History of Science*, 34 (2001), pp. 301–22

Dehs, Volker, 'L'affaire du *Voyage au centre de la terre*', *Bulletin de la Société Jules Verne*, 87 (1988), pp. 19–24

—— 'Un drame ignoré: l'odyssée du *Tour du monde en quatre-vingts jours*', forthcoming in *Australian Journal of French Studies*, 'Jules Verne in the Twenty-First Century', 42.3 (2005)

Dekiss, Jean-Paul, *Jules Verne, le rêve du progrès* (Paris: Gallimard, 1991)

—— *Jules Verne l'enchanteur* (Paris: Editions du Felin, 1999)

Diesbach, Ghislain de, *Le Tour de Jules Verne en quatre-vingts livres* (Paris: Perrin, 2000 [1969])

Dumas, Olivier, *Jules Verne* (Lyon: La Manufacture, 1988)

—— *Voyage à travers Jules Verne* (Paris: Stanké, 2000)

Dupuy, Lionel, *Espace et temps dans l'œuvre de Jules Verne* (Dole: La Clé d'argent, 2000)

Evans, Arthur B., *Jules Verne Rediscovered: Didacticism and the Scientific Novel* (Westport, CT: Greenwood Press, 1988)

—— 'Science Fiction vs. Scientific Fiction in France: From Jules Verne to J.-H. Rosny Aîné', *Science Fiction Studies*, 15 (1988), pp. 1–11

—— 'Functions of Science in French Fiction', *Studies in the Literary Imagination*, 22 (1989), pp. 79–100

——'Literary Intertexts in Jules Verne's *Voyages extraordinaires*', *Science Fiction Studies*, 23 (1996), pp. 171–87

——'Jules Verne's English Translations', *Science Fiction Studies*, 32 (2005), pp. 80–104

Evans, Arthur B. and Ron Miller, 'Jules Verne, Misunderstood Visionary', *Scientific American*, April 1997, pp. 92–97

Evans, I. O., *Jules Verne and his Work* (London: Arco, 1965)

Foucault, Michel, 'L'Arrière-fable', *L'Arc*, 29 (1966), pp. 5–12

Froidefond, Alain, *Voyages au centre de l'horloge: essai sur un texte-genèse 'Maître Zacharius'* (Paris: Minard, 1988)

Gautier, Théophile, 'Les Voyages imaginaires de M. Jules Verne', *Le Moniteur Universel*, 16 July 1866, reprinted in *L'Herne: Jules Verne*, 25 (1974), pp. 85–87

Gilli, Yves, Florent Montaclair and Sylvie Petit, *Le Naufrage dans l'œuvre de Jules Verne* (Paris: L'Harmattan, 1998)

Gondolo della Riva, Piero, 'A propos des œuvres posthumes de Jules Verne', *Europe*, 595–96 (1978), pp. 73–78

Haining, Peter (ed.), *The Jules Verne Companion* (London: Souvenir Press, 1978)

Helling, Cornélis, 'Le roman le plus poe-esque de Jules Verne', *Bulletin de la Société Jules Verne*, 1 (1967), p. 8

Huet, Marie-Hélène, *L'Histoire des Voyages Extraordinaires: Essai sur l'œuvre de Jules Verne* (Paris: Minard, 1973)

Jules-Verne, Jean, *Jules Verne* (Paris: Hachette, 1973)

Lacroix, M., 'Présence et influence de *Vingt mille lieues sous les mers* dans l'œuvre poétique de Rimbaud', *Bulletin de la Société Jules Verne*, 148 (2003), pp. 2–51

Lengrand, Claude, *Dictionnaire des 'Voyages extraordinaires' de Jules Verne* (Amiens: Encrage, 1998)

Lottman, Herbert R., *Jules Verne: An Exploratory Biography* (New York: St Martin's Press, 1996)

Macherey, Pierre, 'Jules Verne, ou le récit en défaut', in *Pour une théorie de la production littéraire* (Paris: Maspero, 1966), pp. 183–275

Marcucci, Edmondo, *Les Illustrations des Voyages extraordinaires de Jules Verne* (Paris: Editions de la Société Jules Verne, 1956)

Margot, Jean-Michel, 'Jules Verne, Playwright', *Science Fiction Studies*, 32 (2005), pp. 150–62

Martin, Andrew, *The Knowledge of Ignorance: From Genesis to Jules Verne* (Cambridge: Cambridge University Press, 1985)

—— *The Mask of the Prophet: The Extraordinary Fictions of Jules Verne* (Oxford: Clarendon Press, 1990)

Martin, Charles-Noël, *La Vie et l'œuvre de Jules Verne* (Paris: Michel de l'Ormeraie, 1978)

Micha, René, 'Les légendes sous les images', *L'Arc*, 29 (1966), pp. 50–55

Mikkonen, Kai, 'The Electric Narrative in Jules Verne's *Le Château des Carpathes* and *Paris au XXe siècle*', in *The Plot Machine: The French Novel and the Bachelor Machines in the Electric Years (1880–1914)* (Amsterdam: Rodopi, 2001), pp. 69–107

Minerva, Nadia, *Jules Verne aux confins de l'utopie* (Paris: L'Harmattan, 2001)

Moré, Marcel, *Le Très Curieux Jules Verne: Le Problème du père dans les Voyages extraordinaires* (Paris: Gallimard, 1960)

—— *Nouvelles Explorations de Jules Verne: musique, misogamie, machine* (Paris: Gallimard, 1963)

Picard, Michel, *La Lecture comme jeu* (Paris: Editions de Minuit, 1986)

Pourvoyeur, Robert, 'Jules Verne, écrivain de théatre ou romancier dramatique?', *Bulletin de la Société Jules Verne*, 70 (1984), pp. 54–57

—— 'Les trois opéras-comiques de Verne', *Bulletin de la Société Jules Verne*, 70 (1984), pp. 71–78

—— 'Jules Verne et le théâtre', preface to Jules Verne, *Clovis Dardentor* (Paris: Union Générale d'Editions, 1979), pp. 5–30

Rivière, François, *Jules Verne: images d'un mythe* (Paris: H. Veyrier, 1978)

Robien, Gilles de, *Jules Verne: Le Rêveur incompris* (Paris: Michel Lafon, 2000)

Robin, Christian, 'Le Récit sauvé des eaux: du *Voyage au centre de la terre* au *Sphinx des glaces* – réflexions sur le narrateur vernien', *Revue des Lettres Modernes*, Jules Verne 2 (1978), pp. 33–55

Roudaut, Jean, 'L'*Eternel Adam* et l'image des cycles', *L'Herne: Jules Verne*, 25 (1974), pp. 180–212

Serres, Michel, *Jouvences sur Jules Verne* (Paris: Editions de Minuit, 1974)

Smyth, E. J. (ed.), *Jules Verne: Narratives of Modernity* (Liverpool: Liverpool University Press, 2000)

Soriano, Marc, *Jules Verne: le cas Verne* (Paris: Julliard, 1978)

—— *Portrait de l'artiste jeune, suivi des quatre premiers textes publiés de Jules Verne* (Paris: Gallimard, 1978)

Stewart, Doug, 'Prescient and Accounted For', *The Smithsonian Magazine* (March 2005), pp. 103–107

Tadié, Jean-Yves, 'Jules Verne', in *Le Roman d'aventures* (Paris: PUF, 1982), pp. 69–112

—— *Regarde de tous tes yeux, regarde!* (Paris: Gallimard, 2005)

Taves, Brian and Stephen Michaluk (eds.), *The Jules Verne Encyclopedia* (Lanham: The Scarecrow Press, 1996)

Terrasse, Pierre, 'Jules Verne et les chemins de fer', *L'Herne: Jules Verne*, 25 (1974), pp. 311–16

Tournier, Michel, *Les Météores* (Paris: Gallimard, 1975), pp. 347–49

Unwin, Timothy, *Verne: 'Le Tour du monde en quatre-vingts jours'* (Glasgow: University of Glasgow, Glasgow Introductory Guides to French Literature, 23, 1992)

—— 'Plagiarist at Work? Jules Verne and the Australian City', in John West-Sooby (ed.), *Images of the City in Nineteenth-Century France* (Mount Nebo, Qld: Boombana Publications, 1998), pp. 183–99

—— 'Langage pédagogique et langage poétique chez Jules Verne', in *Langues du XIXe siècle*, textes réunis par Graham Falconer, Andrew Oliver, Dorothy Speirs (Toronto: Centre d'Etudes Romantiques Joseph Sablé, 1998), pp. 155–64

—— 'The Fictions of Science, the Science of Fiction', in Smyth (ed.), *Jules Verne: Narratives of Modernity*, pp. 46–59

—— 'Verne et les limites du réalisme', in *Textes réfléchissants: réalisme et réflexivité au dix-neuvième siècle* (Oxford and Bern: Peter Lang, 2000), pp. 113–52

—— 'Technology and Progress in Jules Verne, or Anticipation in Reverse', *AUMLA* (*Journal of the Australasian Universities Language and Literature Association*), 93 (2000), pp. 17–35

—— 'Eat My Words: Verne and Flaubert, or the Anxiety of the Culinary', in John West-Sooby (ed.), *Consuming Culture: The Arts of the French Table* (Melbourne and Newark: University of Delaware Press, Monash Romance Studies, 2004), pp. 118–29

—— 'Jules Verne: Negotiating Change in the Nineteenth Century', *Science Fiction Studies*, 32 (2005), pp. 5–17

Vierne, Simone, 'Deux voyages initiatiques en 1864: *Laura* de Georges Sand et le *Voyage au centre de la terre* de Jules Verne', in *Hommage à Georges Sand* (Grenoble: Presses Universitaires de Grenoble, 1969), pp. 101–14

—— *Rite, roman, initiation* (Grenoble: Presses Universitaires Grenobloises, 1971)

—— *Jules Verne* (Paris: Balland, 1986)

—— *Jules Verne: Mythe et modernité* (Paris: Presses Universitaires de France, 1989)

Winandy, Andre, 'The Twilight Zone: Imagination and Reality in Jules Verne's *Strange Journeys*', *Yale French Studies*, 43 (1969), pp. 97–110

Zola, Emile, 'Jules Verne', in *Les Romanciers naturalistes* (Paris: Charpentier, 1881), pp. 356–57

Conferences, special numbers, series, collections, press items

L'Arc, 29 (1966), special issue on Jules Verne

Arts et Lettres, 15 (1949), special issue on Jules Verne

Australian Journal of French Studies, 42.3 (2005), 'Jules Verne in the Twenty-First Century'

Bulletin de la Société Jules Verne, première série, 13 issues (1935–38)

Bulletin de la Société Jules Verne, nouvelle série (1967-)

Europe, 595–96 (1978), special issue on Jules Verne

Europe, 909–10 (2005), special issue on Jules Verne

Géo, hors série, Jules Verne (2003)

Le Figaro, hors série, 'Jules Verne 1905–2005: l'incroyable voyage' (2005)

Le Monde des livres, spécial Jules Verne, 18 March 2005

L'Herne: Jules Verne, 25 (1974)

Jules Verne et les sciences humaines (Colloque de Cerisy, 11–21 juillet 1978), sous la direction de François Raymond et Simone Vierne (Paris: Union Générale d'Editions, 1979)

Jules Verne, écrivain du XIXe siècle (Colloque d'Amiens, 11–13 novembre 1977), I: *Nouvelles recherches sur Jules Verne et le voyage* (Paris: Minard, 1978)

Jules Verne, écrivain du XIXe siècle (Colloque d'Amiens, 11–13 novembre 1977), II: *Jules Verne. Filiations – rencontres – influences* (Paris: Minard, 1980)

Jules Verne 1: 'Le Tour du monde', ed. François Raymond (Paris: Minard, 1976)

Jules Verne 2: L'Ecriture vernienne, ed. François Raymond (Paris: Minard, 1978)

Jules Verne 3: Machines et imaginaire, ed. François Raymond (Paris: Minard, 1980)

Jules Verne 4: Texte, image, spectacle, ed. François Raymond (Paris: Minard, 1984)

Jules Verne 5: Emergences du fantastique, ed. François Raymond (Paris: Minard, 1987)

Jules Verne 6: La Science en question, ed. François Raymond (Paris: Minard, 1992)

Jules Verne 7: Voir du feu, ed. Christian Chelebourg (Paris: Minard, 1994)

Jules Verne 8: Humour, ironie, fantaisie, ed. Christian Chelebourg (Paris: Minard, 2003)

Livres de France, 5 (1955), special issue on Jules Verne

Modernités de Jules Verne, études réunies par Jean Bessière (Paris: Presses Universitaires de France, 1988)

Revue Jules Verne

'Géants des mers', 1 (1996)

'Jules Verne et l'argent', 2 (1996)

'Un écrivain célèbre et méconnu', 3 (1997)

'Voyageur ou sédentaire', 4 (1997)

'L'Or', 5 (1998)

'L'énigmatique Orénoque', 6 (1998)

'Jules Verne et la cité', 7 (1999)

'Un vingtième siècle d'images', 8 (1999)

'Jules Verne au féminin', 9 (2000)

'Entretien inédit: Julien Gracq', 10 (2000)

'Le théâtre de jeunesse, avec *Les Pailles rompues* (pièce non éditée depuis 1850)', 11 (2001)

'Un voyage en ballon', 12 (2001)

'Entretien avec Michel Serres', 13/14 (2002)

'Jules Verne et les Etats-Unis', 15 (2003)

'Les Territoires de l'espace', 16 (2003)

'Jules Verne et les pôles', 17 (2003)

'Conversation avec Michel Butor et Peter Esterhazy', 18 (2005)

Science Fiction Studies, 32 (2005), 'A Jules Verne Centenary'

Bibliographical sources

Dehs, Volker, *Bibliographischer Führer durch die Jules-Verne-Forschung. Guide bibliographique à travers la critique vernienne. 1872–2001* (Wetzlar: Phantastische Bibliotek, 2002)

Dehs, Volker, Jean-Michel Margot and Zvi Har'El, *The Complete Jules Verne Bibliography* (work in progress), online at http://jv.gilead.org.il/biblio

Gallagher, Edward J., Judith A. Mistichelli and John A. Van Eerde, *Jules Verne: A Primary and Secondary Bibliography* (Boston: G.K. Hall, 1980)

Gondolo della Riva, Piero, *Bibliographie analytique de toutes les œuvres de Jules Verne. I: Œuvres romanesques publiées. II: Œuvres non romanesques publiées et œuvres inédites* (Paris: Société Jules Verne, 1977 and 1985)

Margot, Jean-Michel, *Bibliographie documentaire sur Jules Verne* (Amiens: Centre de Documentation Jules Verne, 1989)

Index